Studies in Russian and Slavic Literatures, Cultures and History

Series Editor: *Lazar Fleishman*

Ivan Konevskoi,
"Wise Child" of Russian Symbolism

Joan Delaney Grossman

Boston
2010

Library of Congress Cataloging-in-Publication Data

Grossman, Joan Delaney.
 Ivan Konevskoi, wise child of Russian Symbolism / Joan Delaney Grossman.
   p. cm. — (Studies in Russian and Slavic literatures, cultures and history)
 Includes bibliographical references and index.
 ISBN 978-1-61811-827-1
 1. Konevskoi, Ivan, 1877-1901. 2. Poets, Russian—19th century—Biography. 3. Symbolism (Literary movement)—Russia. I. Title.
   PG3467.O6Z67 2010
   891.71'3--dc22
                                  2009054032

Book design by Ivan Grave
On the cover: Akseli Gallen-Kallela. Lemminkäinen's Mother. Tempera, 1897
The painting illustrates the episode from the Kalevala which is also the subject of Konevskoi's poem "The Exile's Return," treated in Ch. 6.

Published by Academic Studies Press in 2009
28 Montfern Avenue
Brighton, MA 02135, USA
press@academicstudiespress.com
www. academicstudiespress.com

Contents

Key to frequently used abbreviations 7
Acknowledgements. 8
Introduction 9
Chapter 1
The Drive for Life 21
Chapter 2
Chronicle of My Travels 53
Chapter 3
A Love Affair with the World's Waters 81
Chapter 4
Two Meetings 101
Chapter 5
"Dreams and Meditations". 127
Chapter 6
The Power of the Word. 149
Chapter 7
Abolishing Death (1) 169
Chapter 8
Finland, Novgorod, St. Petersburg 193
Chapter 9
Abolishing Death (2) 211
Afterword. 225
Index. 229
Appendix
Selected Poems in Russian 244
Illustrations 270

Key to frequently used abbreviations

AVL — Aleksandr Lavrov. *Pisateli simvolistskogo kruga. Novye materialy. (Writers of the Symbolist Circle. New Materials).* St. Petersburg: Dmitrii Bulanin, 2003.

Br./Vengerov — Valerii Briusov, "Ivan Konevskoi." *Russkaia literatura XX veka 1890-1910.* Ed. S. A. Vengerov. 2 vols. Moscow: "XXI Vek — Soglasie," 2000. Vol. 2: 280-293.

Br.-Efr. — *Entsiklopedicheskii slovar' (Encyclopedic Dictionary).* 82 vols. Leipzig-St. Petersburg: Brokgauz-Efron, 1890-1904.

LN 85 — *Valerii Briusov. Literaturnoe nasledstvo. Vol. 85. (Literary Heritage.)* Moscow: "Nauka," 1976.

LN 92 — *Aleksandr Blok. Novye materialy i issledovaniia. (New Materials and Research.) Literaturnoe nasledstvo. Vol.92.* (5 bks.) Moscow: "Nauka," 1980-1993.

LN 98 — *Valerii Briusov i ego korrespondenty. (Valerii Briusov and His Correspondents.) Literaturnoe nasledstvo. Vol.98.* (2 bks.). Moscow: "Nauka," 1991-1994.

MD — Ivan Konevskoi. *Mechty i dumy (Dreams and Meditations).* St. Petersburg, 1900.

RGALI — *Russkii gosudarstvennyi arkhiv literatury i iskusstva (Russian State Archive of Literature and Art).* Moscow.

SP 1904 — Iv. Konevskoi. *Stikhi i proza. Posmertnoe sobranie sochinenii (1894-1901).* Moscow: "Skorpio," 1904.

SP 2008 — Ivan Konevskoi. *Stikhotvoreniia i poèmy (Poetry and Poems).* Introduction, commentary, A. V. Lavrov. St. Petersburg, Moscow: Progress-Pleiada, 2008.

Acknowledgments

My serious interest in Ivan Konevskoi and his poetry began in 1986, during a research visit to Moscow sponsored, like several others since, by the International Research and Exchanges Board (IREX). Over this extended period of time I have accumulated many debts of gratitude to numerous Russian colleagues and scholars, most particularly, A. V. Lavrov, N. A. Bogomolov, and Margarita Pavlova. The University of California at Berkeley, along with making possible a 1989 research trip (through an exchange with Leningrad University), has been a steady source of support for research assistance over these years. My warm appreciation goes to Berkeley colleagues Irina Paperno, Hugh McLean, and Jonathan Stone, and especially to Irene Masing-Delic of the Ohio State University. Special appreciation goes to Lazar Fleishman, who has guided this work to satisfying completion. In addition, I thank Marco Di Costanzo for offering his professional skill and judgment in preparing the cover and other illustrations. And, finally my warm gratitude for every kind of aid and encouragement goes, as always, to Gregory Grossman.

Introduction

"Ivan Konevskoi is dead, he on whom I placed my hopes, more than all the other poets together."¹ The symbolist poet Valerii Briusov wrote this to a close friend upon learning of Konevskoi's accidental drowning in July 1901. Soon afterward, he wrote an obituary, "Wise Child *(Mudroe ditia)*," to appear in the journal *World of Art (Mir iskusstva)*.² Briusov revised and enlarged "Wise Child" several times thereafter, by this means fixing Ivan Konevskoi's image in the poetic tradition for decades to come. The oxymoronic nature of the phrase seemed to capture the young poet's essence. Naïve, inexperienced in life, Konevskoi yet wrote poetry that was "saturated with thought, reflection." Briusov's masterful simile expressed it perfectly: "[H]is poems are illuminated with these, as blades of grass with their life's juices" (*World of Art*, 38).

However, if in 1901 Konevskoi appeared to Briusov the talent above all others capable of leading Russian poetry into a new era, the situation by 1904 had altered radically, with new poets and new ideas giving distinctive shape to the symbolist movement. When "Scorpio," the symbolist publishing house co-founded by Briusov, published Konevskoi's posthumous collection, *Poems and Prose (Stikhi i proza, 1904)*, the critical response was modest.³ Over the next few years, no other major poet joined Briusov in his crusade to make Konevskoi's poetry better known and understood.

Yet there were interesting individual responses. Aleksandr Blok's case is a striking one. (See Ch. 8.) Despite his expressed desire to write an extended study of Konevskoi's poetry, he achieved only a brief lyrical sketch embedded in another review.⁴ Nevertheless, he left ample evidence in his own writings of Konevskoi's importance to his inspiration. Another notable instance was Viacheslav Ivanov's response when Briusov sent him a copy of *Poems and Prose,* suggesting that he write a review. Ivanov showed immediate interest in Konevskoi: "C'est une révélation, that little book." However, in effect, he declined Briusov's suggestion: "It attracts me — but the difficulty of such a delicate task frightens me."[5]

The general refusal, in 1904 and after, of the symbolists — even the Moscow group around "Scorpio" — to recognize Konevskoi as "one of them" was doubtless linked in some degree to the rapidly changing literary scene. But it had even more to do with the fact that, truly, he was *not* one of them. By 1901 Briusov recognized that Konevskoi stood apart from his comrades in the new art. Later he acknowledged that, despite their common allegiances, "Konevskoi was, in a much greater degree than the entire Moscow circle, mystically inclined."[6]

Nonetheless, Briusov continued to plead the case for Konevskoi's poetry. When he included an enlarged version of "Wise Child" in a 1910 collection of critical writings, he added a "P.S.", explaining why, in his opinion, Konevskoi's poetry "has not had the influence on Russian literature that it deserves." He rejected the romantic notion that Konevskoi was a fated visitor passing fleetingly at a crucial moment in time. Instead, as the didactic critic he often was, Briusov offered a forthright explanation: "[A]cquaintance with the creative work of Iv. Konevskoi is hindered for many by the originality of his language and his prosody."[7] There followed three paragraphs of instruction and helpful hints about deciphering Konevskoi's syntax and linguistic and metric practices, concluding with strong assurances that the poetry is worth the effort. One remark of Konevskoi's, quoted in the "postscript," became a favorite of certain later literary historians and poets: "I like it when the poetic line is a bit rough" (6:248). Osip Mandel'stam wrote of his lines that they were sometimes "like the rustling of a forest down to its roots."[8]

However, as years passed, *Poems and Prose* became a bibliographical rarity, while its author assumed the role of "forgotten genius."[9] A. V. Lavrov well observed, "[H]is influence on poetry at the start of the twentieth century was not definitive, but, in its way, peripheral, sporadically emerging with authors belonging to various generations."[10] In 1920, in a short article on "The Symbolists" for *The London Mercury,*

INTRODUCTION

D. S. Mirsky identified Ivan Konevskoi for his foreign readership as the young poet who drowned in 1901 at age twenty-three, leaving a small collection of poetry that contained "moments of revelation, majestic and intense, that few poets have dreamed of." Mirsky capped his sketch by declaring: "[Ivan Konevskoi] is one of the esoteric classics of Russian poetry."[11] Cautiously he predicted that Konevskoi "will often turn up again as a poet's vademecum." Konevskoi seemed destined to be regarded as a "poet's poet," of whom little was known except the fact of his genius.

Who, then, was Ivan Konevskoi? His biography, printed anonymously in *Poems and Prose*, is easily summarized. Born Ivan Oreus in 1877 into a cultivated family of military gentry, Konevskoi was reared and educated in St. Petersburg. After his mother died in 1891, he lived a relatively isolated life with his father as chief companion. He read voraciously in literature and philosophy in several languages and began to write poetry in 1895. Two trips to Germany and Austria in the summers of 1897 and 1898 broadened his experience significantly and expanded his knowledge of Western art. In autumn 1898 he fell in love with Anna Nikolaevna Gippius. The relationship, brief as it was, left a significant mark. In December 1898, his poetry caught the attention of Valerii Briusov at a gathering of poets. That meeting led to a close friendship that worked greatly to the advantage of both. At the end of 1899 he published at his own expense the collection of poetry and prose he called *Dreams and Meditations (Mechty i dumy)*. It circulated among a small number of associates, attracting little attention elsewhere. After completing requirements for a degree in the historical-philological division of St. Petersburg University, he left for a brief trip in the Baltic region and Finland. He drowned accidentally on 8 July 1901, in a river near the Livonian town of Segevold (Sigulda, Latvia, today).

If *Poems and Prose* became a bibliographical rarity, Konevskoi's own publication, *Dreams and Meditations* (1900), was that from the beginning. Nonetheless, the latter has undergone a remarkable resurrection in this century. At the time when Konevskoi was preparing *Dreams and Meditations* for publication, he knew that he had reached some sort of turning point in his life. Therefore he devised a form that, idiosyncratic as it was, sought to impose a coherent pattern on his thoughts, experiences, and discoveries of the previous three years. The form itself could be called a meditation. Arrangement was broadly chronological, though dates of individual works were largely omitted, and actual chronology was altered at will. The real organizing principle was thematic; it included varying approaches to the subject matter — observational, emotional, and meditative. Poetry and prose alternated by sections or were intermingled. There was no actual table of contents, only indications of sections, printed on the cover. Readers were left to accept the text this way or not at all: *Dreams and Meditations* was meant for the few, not the many. Its contemporary readers were indeed very few.

Unwavering in his view that Konevskoi's poetry was a treasure worthy of being meticulously exhibited and preserved, Briusov nonetheless considered *Dreams and Meditations* poorly presented.[12] When his turn came just a few years later to edit the writings for publication, he turned for permission to Konevskoi's father. General Ivan Ivanovich Oreus gave him complete freedom in editorial matters.[13] Next Briusov solicited the help of Konevskoi's close friends in gathering relevant materials, including letters and memoirs. These friends apparently envisioned this as a substantial memorial volume, with biographical sketches and testimonial letters by those close to the poet, and with *Dreams and Meditations* as its centerpiece. However, one intimate, Nikolai Mikhailovich Sokolov, wrote judiciously to Briusov: "Oreus's personality was so full and many-sided that it is impossible to omit a single aspect; it would be better to select the *typical*" (*LN* 98:1:544).

In the end, the final decision was made by Briusov, the designated editor and the only professional among the group. He abandoned the subjective, confessional format of *Dreams and Meditations* and adopted a neutral chronological form, with appropriate scholarly apparatus, variants, and bibliographical information.[14] Poetry, then prose, appeared in that order, with dates and places of composition given when available; notes followed the text. The short biographical account, anonymous and scrupulously factual, written by General Oreus, together with Briusov's "Wise Child," provided an introduction.

INTRODUCTION

No doubt, Briusov wished to pay his debt to this astounding talent that he had been privileged to know and value. Yet — and here Briusov differed markedly from Konevskoi's Petersburg friends — he undertook this project not only, and probably not chiefly, as a tribute to a young genius who died early. Rather, he believed that publication of *Poems and Prose* by "Scorpio" distinguished it as an important contribution to the "new art" and to the future of Russian poetry. At the same time, it ensured for Konevskoi's work a niche in the growing annals of symbolism. This edition, then, was a necessary step in preserving a remarkable body of poetry for potential readers and scholars. Briusov accomplished these goals faithfully and well.

However, Konevskoi's guiding ideas, along with significant features of the poet's personal image, were erased, or nearly so, by the format chosen by Briusov. The question posed for the next editor was: what to do, if anything, to restore these elements. After an ambitious two-volume edition undertaken in the 1930s was aborted, a long interval of neglect ensued.[15] Then in the 1980s and 1990s signs of interest in this remote but intriguing figure began to emerge. A few important publications appeared.[16] Finally, at the beginning of this twenty-first century, two editions of his work undertook in different ways to restore some of the features sacrificed in the "Scorpio" edition. In 2000, a century after its first publication, *Dreams and Meditations* was republished under the editorship of E. I. Necheporuk. Included also were Konevskoi's later poetry and the prose that had appeared first in *Poems and Prose*.[17] Likewise included were some letters and a section entitled "Ivan Konevskoi in Poetry, Critical Writings, Reminiscences by Contemporaries," all previously published. By gathering these items together, this edition offered a foundation for the editor's belief that Ivan Konevskoi's reputation was now beyond all doubt. Indeed, he wrote: "It is impossible to understand the poetic culture of Russian symbolism without Ivan Konevskoi.[...] He was broader than symbolism and other streams in the channel of the literary process at the turn of the century" (3-4). This and other claims made in the introductory essay raised important questions that surely must be examined further. Meanwhile, possibly the greatest service to a readership largely unacquainted with Konevskoi is the publication itself, which led one scholar to exclaim: "It is time for his word to be heard."[18]

Eight years later, in 2008, a long-delayed promise was fulfilled: Konevskoi's collected poetry finally appeared in the distinguished series *Novaia biblioteka poèta (New Library of Poets),* under the title *Stikhotvoreniia i poèmy (Poetry and Poems).*[19] Its editor was A. V. Lavrov, who, by his carefully researched introductions and notes to archival publications from the 1980's onward, has done more than any other scholar since Briusov to lay a foundation for Konevskoi studies. Lavrov's introductory essay to this new volume is clearly the result of two decades and more of study. Publication in the series *New Library of Poets* presumably called for exclusion of the large sections of prose in the original. Inclusion of certain prose fragments is explained as completing the "artistic integrity" of *Dreams and Meditations* (219). The overall aim is clear: undivided attention is focused on Ivan Konevskoi the *poet* and the place he merits in the history of nineteenth- and twentieth-century Russian poetry.

The two editions of Konevskoi's poetry in the first decade of this century form a major beginning to the rediscovery of the man and his work. Yet, unquestionably, much remains to be done. However valuable these and earlier publications may be, they go only so far toward unraveling the mystery of the individual whom his friends remembered as "full and many-sided." Likewise, the closest reading of Konevskoi's poems can reveal only so much of that person and his inner self. New insights in that area should, in turn, further illuminate the poetry. It seems time, therefore, to offer another approach.

The present study is in no way intended as a full biography. Rather, the author hopes, by attentive examination of the complex puzzle that was Konevskoi's inner life, to come closer to rendering the excitement and energy of that life as he experienced it. During the six- or seven-year period to which his notebooks, writings, and letters allow access, his mind, his will, his imaginative and creative powers seemed in a state of almost continuous dynamic — even kaleidoscopic — activity. While the creative powers seemed at times to ebb and surge as he coped with challenges inner and outer, the drive toward new and wider horizons was unflagging. Uneventful as his outer existence was, for the main part, there was nothing static about his inner life, as his conception of the universe and his relation to it unfolded, sometimes dramatically.

From very early days, Konevskoi's passionate drive for life and its obverse, terror of death and determination to overcome it, powered virtually all of his activity. His goals were grandiose, but genuine. Of these the primary one was to discover ways of penetrating to the core of the universe, so as to share actively in its boundless life. His early belief in himself as poet led him to rely on poetry as chief tool for achieving those goals. For him, the notion of "poet" was an open-ended one, its scope and limits unknown. Poets were the inventors of language, who knew and commanded the power of words: they were magicians. The extent to which he chose to take these notions literally and to develop and apply them in his pursuits is a puzzle left unsolved by his death.

However, the conviction ripened in him early in his career that a genuine poet must be, first of all, a mystic. Though initially not quite sure what the term implied, Konevskoi grew more and more aware of something called the "new mysticism" that hovered in the atmosphere like a bird unseen. One watches him in those days, trying to deduce from a few outstanding examples — Shelley, Maeterlinck, Tiutchev — what it was in its essence. When, in summer 1897, the mystical moment actually arrived — followed by many others, if we accept his witness, — he redoubled his efforts to understand the mystical state itself: what could it mean for one whose thirst for spiritual knowledge was unlimited? The "new mysticism," it appeared, embraced a spiritual arena broader than the mysticism commonly known in earlier eras. At the end of his detailed historical article on the subject that appeared in the Brokgauz-Efron *Encyclopedic Dictionary* in 1896, Vladimir Solov'ev cautiously noted that some scholars were ready to class as mysticism even the new field of psychic research. (37:455).[20]

Already in the mid-1890s Konevskoi was reading widely in the new poetry and criticism in French, German, and English.[21] For the next few years, as new artistic trends made their way into Russia, he became expert in these areas. One trend called "decadence," fashionable since the mid-1980s in France and Belgium, advertised itself as also a new set of moral and philosophical attitudes and behavior. Briusov, who in his first years deliberately painted himself as a "decadent," in "Wise Child" was able, shrewdly and with penetration, to place Konevskoi exactly where he belonged in all this:

> Konevskoi sought two things: freedom and power. But at the time when others sought them in overstepping boundaries, in permitting themselves all that for any reason was considered forbidden, whether in the area of morals or simply in versification, Konevskoi took the matter deeper. He saw man's enslavement and impotence, not in the conditions of common life, but in those relations to the external world imposed on us from the beginning, with which we come into existence: in the force of heredity, in the laws of perception and thought, in the dependence of the spirit on the body (*SP 1904*, xiii).

Briusov's insights and understanding of both decadence and of Konevskoi are worth remembering when reflecting on pronouncements such as this.

Another movement, loosely called occultism and also closely allied to current artistic and literary trends, had already reached its peak in Europe in the 1890s. Konevskoi was knowledgeable about many topics that fell under that rubric, from mediumism to gnosticism. Unfailingly interested as Konevskoi was in whatever offered to extend power to penetrate hidden secrets, it might seem almost obligatory to link him in some way to occultism. Yet Konevskoi was no occultist. N. A. Bogomolov has shown in his book *Russian Literature at the Beginning of the XX Century and Occultism*, the pervasive presence of occultism in Russian symbolism came in that movement's high period (mid-1900s) and in post-symbolism.[22] Konevskoi, who died in 1901, did not truly witness this phenomenon. Nor can he be considered a factor in its spread, since he had no significant readership during the time when Russian interest in the occult was at its height.

However, awkward timing is not the primary argument against treating Konevskoi as an occultist. At no time was he interested in espousing a specific doctrine or movement to serve as his guide. Rather, total freedom of mind and spirit was his ideal. His goals, taken together, amounted to broadening and deepening the life of the *persona*, extending it beyond any conceivable limits: *life* and *persona* were the key words. Properly used, they were keys to the universe. Other key words that figured importantly in his quest were: first, as has been seen, "poet." Others, in close relation, were "mystic" and "pantheist," and, latterly, "prophet." It is essential to note that Konevskoi by no means confined himself to the commonly understood definitions of these and similar terms. Rather, his habit was to seize on concepts and terms drawn from the culture, then to adapt their content to meet his individual needs and purposes. This practice, needless to say, requires anyone trying to follow his thought to be extremely attentive to his words and their meanings.

It appears, then, that, splendid as many of his poems are, and diligently as he attended to their perfection, his fundamental project was not primarily aesthetic, but *profoundly epistemological*.[23] Yet, in his mind the two were, for all purposes, inseparable. He might speak about "penetrating by direct sense to the secret essence of things," but he was also engaged in a highly poetic love affair with the universe.[24] One of those few who, in 1904, favorably reviewed *Poems and Prose* was S. Krymski, who wrote: "In that chaste love for the cosmos is hidden, it seems to me, all the beauty and charm of his poetry."[25]

Thinker, mythmaker, visionary, mystic: to Konevskoi, the sum of all these was contained for him in the word "poet." By the time of his death, he seemed to be on the way to a tentative "structure" that eventually might accommodate his grand designs. But he was only at the beginning. Of his poetry, of course, the same must be said. What we have represents, perhaps, as Briusov wrote, merely the foundation of a grand monument. But, as he also said, "O! on what a splendid plan!"[26]

Notes

1 *Literaturnoe nasledstvo 85.* (Moscow: "Nauka," 1976), pp. 646-647. Letter to A. A. Shesterkina, 15 Aug. 1901.
2 "Mudroe ditia," *Mir Iskusstva 1901*, No 8-9, 136-139. Briusov used the phrase first in an early, incomplete draft of an article. It replaced another variant: "mudryi iunosha *(wise youth)*". ("O Oreuse". Publ. and commentary S. I. Gindin. *LN* 98:1:550.)
3 One notably positive review was entitled "Neizvestnyi poet (*Unknown Poet*)." It appeared in the journal *Sem'ia* (1904. No. 6, pp. 10-11). It was signed "S. Krymskii," pen-name of "Sergei Georgievich Kara-Murza." Reprinted in: *Ivan Konevskoi (Oreus). Mechty i dumy*. Tomsk: "Vodolei", 2000, pp. 487-489.
4 Review of A. L. Miropol'skii. *Ved'ma. Lestnitsa*. Aleksandr Blok. *Sobranie sochinenii v 8-kh tomakh*. Moscow-Leningrad: GIKhL, 1962. 5:598-600.
5 *LN* 85: 446-447. Briusov mentioned, possibly as an inducement, that a recent critical article had found similarities between the two, Konevskoi and Ivanov. (The critic was S. Krymskii). However, Ivanov may have found this a hindrance, rather than an encouragement.
6 Valerii Briusov, "Ivan Konevskoi (1877-1901 gg.)." *Russkaia literatura 1890-1910*. Ed. S. A. Vengerov. 2 vols. Moscow: "Soglasie", 2000. Vol. 2, p. 281.
7 Valerii Briusov, *Sobranie sochinenii*, 7 vols. Moscow: Khudozhestvennaia literatura, 1973-1975. 6:248-249.
8 Osip Mandel'stam. "Shum vremeni", *Sobranie sochinenii v 2 tt*. New York: Inter-Language Literary Associates, 1966. 2:126.
9 Meanwhile, two reprints, one in Germany, another in the United States, kept Konevskoi's poetry alive among Western students of Russian literature. *Stikhi i proza (Poems and Prose)* was reprinted by Wilhelm Fink Verlag, Munich, in 1971 as: Ivan Konevskoi, *Sobranie sochinenii (Collected Works)*, introduction by Dmitrij Tschiżewskij. *Mechty i dumy (Dreams and Mediations)* was reprinted by Berkeley Slavic Specialties, 1989 (from a photocopy in the collection of Prof. Oleg A. Maslennikov, University of California, Berkeley).
10 A. V. Lavrov, "'Chaiu i chuiu'. Lichnost i poeziia Ivana Konevskogo." Ivan Konevskoi. *Stikhotvoreniia i poemy*. Novaia Biblioteka Poeta. St. Petersburg, Moscow: DNK, Progress-Pleiada, 2008. P. 60.

[11] D. S. Mirsky, *Uncollected Writings on Russian Literature*. Ed., introduction, and bibliography by G. S. Smith. Berkeley: Berkeley Slavic Specialties, 1989. P. 53.

[12] Valerii Briusov, *Dnevniki 1891-1900*. Moscow, 1927. (Hereafter: *Dn.*) Reprinted: Letchworth Herts. England: Bradda Books Ltd. 1972, p. 78.

[13] *LN* 98:1:546-547. After several years' work with the historical journal *Russkii arkhiv* and with the publishing house "Scorpio," which he co-founded in 1900, Briusov had proved his capabilities as editor.

[14] Nikolai Mikhailovich Sokolov, close friend of Konevskoi and willing collaborator with Briusov in the task of publication, raised the question of publishing all variant texts and other relevant material. However, he drew back quickly upon realizing the bulk of material in question. (*LN* 98:1:543-544.)

[15] An account of the scholarly edition undertaken by N. L. Stepanov, with strong encouragement from the noted Formalist critic Yu. N. Tynianov, and its destruction by fire during the war years was provided by A. E. Parnis, in his introduction to selections from Stepanov's "Ivan Konevskoi. Poet mysli", *LN* 92:4:179.

[16] In the same *LN* volume (Vol. 92, part 4, printed in 1987), together with Parnis's publication of the Stepanov selection, there appeared a substantial article by V. Ia. Morderer: "Blok i Ivan Konevskoi" (92:4:151-178). Following this, in 1991, another *LN* volume (Vol. 98, part 1-2), *Valerii Briusov i ego korrespondenty*, was published. Part 1 included "Perepiska s Iv. Konevskim," notes and commentary by A. V. Lavrov, Morderer and Parnis, and extensive scholarly introduction by Lavrov.

[17] *Ivan Konevskoi (Oreus), Mechty i dumy*. Tomsk: "Vodolei", 2000.

[18] S. I. Gindin, "Ego slovu pora byt' uslyshannym. Ivan Konevskoi." *Russkii iazyk*, No. 26 (2001).

[19] The previous edition, which never reached print, was that N. L. Stepanov. (See n.16.)

[20] Vladimir Solov'ev's article "Mistika, — tsizm," attempting to clarify in the public mind the notion of mysticism, offered an exhaustive survey of the history and types of mysticism. It appeared in the Brokgauz-Efron encyclopedic dictionary in 1896. (Br-Efr. 37: 454-456.)

[21] Briusov wrote in the first, 1901, version of "Mudroe ditia" that Konevskoi "was probably Russia's sole expert on the newest poetry in the West" (*Mir*

19

iskusstva, No. 6, 1901. P.136). In his final, expanded version, Briusov related a story, at once diverting and revealing. In 1896 or 1897 young Ivan Oreus wrote to several of his favorite French and Belgian poets — Verhaeren, Henri de Régnier, Francis Viélé-Griffin, — requesting information about their biographies, representing himself as a Russian writer who intended, through translations, to acquaint the Russian public with writings of French symbolists. Having seen the answering letters, Briusov could attest to the truth of this story, and also to Konevskoi's conviction at a young age that he was a major poet. (Br./Vengerov 2:285) This stance of Konevskoi's obviously irked Briusov, yet he repeatedly asserted his own belief in the same claim.

22 N. A. Bogomolov, *Russkaia literatura nachala XX veka i okkul'tizm* (Moscow: Novoe literaturnoe obozenie, 1999). See in particular Ch. 1.

23 Briusov summed up his own view many years later: "In the final analysis, for Konevskoi poetry was, nonetheless, only a means, not an end in itself. In whatever sense it was used, the formula 'art for art's sake' was unacceptable, even intolerable" (Br./Vengerov, 2: 281), see n. 21.

24 Quoted from an archival source by N. L. Stepanov, *LN* 92:4:182. See Ch. 1.

25 S. Krymskii, 623. (See n.3.)

26 Under the impact of news of Konevskoi's death, Briusov wrote of the designs never to be realized: "He merely began, marked out the path, laid the foundation (O! on what a splendid plan!) but the temple will never exist — only stones, only drawings, a dead wasteland and the sky above it" (*LN* 85:647).

Chapter 1

The Drive for Life

1. Setting the Goals

At the end of 1894, just after he turned seventeen, Ivan Konevskoi wrote a short exuberant lyric that, for him, said it all. "Fragment" unfurled a vision of the world newly discovered, a dazzling vision that filled him with boyish longing to embrace everything in one sweeping gaze. Though not one of his more artistically polished efforts, "Fragment" nonetheless projected the central themes that drove Ivan Konevskoi's spiritual and intellectual explorations from that day forward. His was to be a fiercely energetic, single-minded quest, leavened by bursts of youthful excitement, creative flights, and sudden, stunning insights.

In the brief biographical account published anonymously in the 1904 posthumous edition of Konevskoi's poetry, General Ivan Ivanovich Oreus, the poet's father, described the passionate temperament that, from childhood on, infused his son's every undertaking: "Having learned to read at age seven, he threw himself avidly on books. From that time on, reading was his favorite occupation".[1] The atmosphere of the Oreus home as Ivan was growing up was scholarly, literary, in touch with Petersburg cultural life of the 'eighties and 'nineties. The entry under General Oreus's name in the *Brokgauz-Efron Encyclopedic Dictionary* described him first as a writer, and only then as "lieutenant-general, member of the General Staff Commission on Military Education..."[2] Military historian, director of the Military-Historical and Topographical Archive, he was also a contributor to the *Encyclopedic Dictionary*.[3] Though Ivan's interests differed from his father's, he perused every volume of the *Dictionary* as it appeared, marking articles of particular interest. For example, from Vol. 29 (1895) he noted: "Kierkegard," "Keats," "C[K]lassicism," and from Vol. 38 (1896): "world soul [*mirovaia dusha*]," "Mikhailovskii," "Maupassant," and so forward, alphabetically.[4]

The ambitious enterprise sketched in "Fragment" resounded in a different key a year later. A notebook entry for 1 November 1895 recounted a solemn discussion between Konevskoi and a classmate and close friend, Aleksei Veselov. Veselov, on this occasion morose and gloomy, asked himself if life was worth living. "And what about you, Ivan?" Konevskoi recorded his stalwart response:

> My instinct says yes. Furthermore, I'm not yet sated with the joys of life. These joys are: creative work, comprehending the World Soul and the meaning of our existence, penetrating by direct sense to the secret essence of things so as to receive luminous revelations about the structure and meaning of our nature.

Veselov's reply was pardonably ironic: "And what if that doesn't happen?" Konevskoi answered crisply: "Go out of my mind or die as I approach the limits of human knowledge. Anyway, that's better than killing myself straight away...."[5] Scarcely unique for the time and circumstances of its participants, this exchange is worth noting chiefly in light of later events. N. L. Stepanov put the incident in context:

> "These juvenile conversations about the goal of life, the 'meaning of our nature,' so typical for the intelligentsia in the 1890s, point at the same time to Konevskoi's basically optimistic outlook and at that striving to 'approach the limits of human knowledge' that defined his activity for the rest of his short life" (*LN* 92:4:182). Remembering his son's intense nature, his father ruefully reported how those close to the boy often urged him to give himself a rest from mental work — but to no effect. His answer was always the same: "I cannot! This is my whole life! How is it possible not to think!" (*SP 1904*, viii)

2. "Resurrection"

In summer 1899, when preparing *Dreams and Meditations* for print, Konevskoi bypassed "Fragment" and chose another early poem to launch the poetic record of his journey thus far. "Resurrection," too, opens on an exuberant note: the love of life that henceforth was a constant feature of his worldview. However, hints emerge of a blight that marred the poet's inner life during his early adolescence. The first stanza ends jubilantly: "I have wakened from a deep numbing sleep." While subsequent stanzas exult in his poetic powers so recently discovered (or recovered), he fears that the recovery may not be permanent. However, the expanded final stanza triumphantly affirms his new life in a sweeping image of the sea — an image frequently invoked in Konevskoi's later poetry.

What was that mysterious "sleep"? No one knew better than Valerii Briusov how intensely personal his friend's writing usually was. Moreover, he knew Konevskoi's tendency to share his moods and ailments with his intimates. Therefore, a few months after Konevskoi's drowning in July 1901, Briusov pursued the matter with General Oreus. Citing the poem "Resurrection (*Voskresenie*)," he raised the question of his friend's health, physical or emotional, during his early teens. Apparently puzzled, General Oreus replied that his son's physical health, on the whole, was excellent. However, he offered a possible explanation: if Ivan spoke to Briusov of some kind of illness, he probably referred to a sickly state of mind that came on between fourteen and sixteen, connected with puberty and affecting his nerves.[6]

Plausible as this hypothesis is, another factor asks to be considered. Ivan (Oreus) Konevskoi was the youngest of four siblings, the other three of whom died in childhood. His mother, Elizaveta Ivanovna Anichkova, died on 28 February 1891, when Ivan was thirteen.[7] He had entered the *gimnaziia* only months before.[8] Curiously, no allusion to her death appears in his published poetry, nor is it mentioned in his other extant writings, including correspondence. Nor — incredibly — does it appear in his father's biographical account of his son or in the elder Oreus's correspondence with Briusov during the preparation of *Poems and Prose*. Nonetheless, that early and close encounter with death, whatever other effect it may have had, arguably played a central role in making the conquest of death the driving force in his spiritual and intellectual development.

Sometime before 16 February 1897, Konevskoi composed a third-person narrative that very likely refers to this early experience. He inserted it in a paper entitled "Lyric Poetry in Contemporary Russia (*Stikhotvornaia lyrika v sovremennoi Rossii*)," which he read before a group of his fellow university students. (More will be said later about this essay, as well as about the student circle before which it was delivered.) The existing manuscript, missing its opening pages, begins in mid-narrative. It describes how a certain child gradually learned from parents and others, by word and example, that Sacred Scripture is irrelevant to real life, and that no one has real answers to questions about life and death:

> It happened that, several times during his childhood, that boy witnessed the death of persons close to him. On those occasions he heard around him only muted words about the irreplaceable loss, about the deceased's excellent qualities, about his or her great services to society, and, oh, yes, about the fact that he now rests in "eternal sleep". But in the Gospels and the catechism one read that after death begins "eternal life."
>
> Soon, of course, the circumstances of death disappeared from the boy's surrounding world, and with them faded the agitation that had troubled his consciousness. When he again heard of someone's death, he already knew that, yes, there had existed a man, but nothing now remained of him — and that thought, it seemed, glided over his soul without trace. But then, when he was already in one of the lower classes at *gimnaziia*, he began to suffer strange nighttime attacks. Lying in bed, he began to doze off, his limbs became limp — and suddenly, shaking off his drowsiness, he leaped out of bed in frozen terror.
>
> In that instant, when consciousness fades, when one part of the body, then another, loses awareness, and one gently, silently slides into the abyss, he seemed to glimpse another swoon — a fatal swoon, with no return to life, a dark wave taking possession of him forever, forever.... and his every vein stretched feverishly, all his being cried out: *I want life — more brilliant, more*

*resounding, more burning! And he began to rush about the room with eyes wide open...(ital. mine).*⁹

Here the account breaks off: what happens next? If this account is autobiographical, Konevskoi shows narrative skill in hiding the fact. He suddenly distances himself from his tortured young subject, subtly suggesting to the reader or listener that, of course, this has nothing really to do with him: "I'll never forget how I heard this confession from the lips of one of my comrades, on a street somewhere, under a street lantern, one evening in deep winter.[...] It is painful to think of" (*AVL*, 92).

How are we to understand this? Is it, as the author represents it, a story related to him by another schoolboy in a Dostoevskian or Blokian Petersburg setting? Or is this indeed his personal history thinly disguised? In favor of the latter supposition is the vividly detailed description of the boy's inner experience; it seems hardly conceivable that such a vivid account of nighttime psychic trauma came to him secondhand. In any case, the final dramatic lines starkly set out the dynamic that was to inform Konevskoi's entire life enterprise. The boy, gradually dozing off, suddenly leaps from his bed, roused by fear that any surrender to drowsiness will betray him into that irreversible "fatal swoon." From this horror of death springs a fierce desire to live: "Life — more brilliant, more resounding, more burning!" (*AVL*, 91-92).

Where will he find what he seeks? And what is he actually looking for? That quest would lead Ivan Konevskoi to fascinating, unforeseen places, as a thinker and as a poet. Yet, one thing is certain: maintaining hold on his essential self, his *persona*, was a passionately held prerequisite for any further life and growth.

3. "*Every small leaf so sure of itself...*"

Initially, young Konevskoi's interest in the world outside himself appeared to be focused on human history and experience, rather than on nature. Nearly everything in his environment and upbringing urged him to learn about human affairs, past and present. "The Oreus family belonged to the military service milieu, in which the ancient noble traditions and moral foundations were strong, and were linked to the intellectual refinement and culture of the intelligentsia" (*LN* 92:4:181). His mother's family, the Anichkovs, likewise belonged to the military nobility. Ivan's urban childhood was punctuated by summer visits to relatives' country homes and dachas. However, the Oreuses, with their Swedish/Finnish ancestry, had no roots in the Russian landholding gentry or any strong ties to the countryside.

No strong expressions of interest in nature *per se* emerge in Konevskoi's early notebooks. Yet two poems written three months after "Resurrection" show his reactions when confronting it, so to speak, face-to-face. The first of these, entitled, again, "Fragment *(Otryvok)*" and dated 15 May 1895, is the first evidence in his poetry of the strong effect that the end of winter and late coming of a Petersburg spring always produced on him. It opens with a brilliant burst of feeling and delicate sensory perceptions: "The primal freshness and keenness of spring, the strong odor of spring's elements!" (*SP 2008*, 79)

The lyric "Nature (*Priroda*)," written five days later, is a more thoughtful, indeed puzzled, piece. (*SP 2008, 176-177*) The boy's failure to respond emotionally to nature's charms is conveyed by the metaphor of a sailor just back from his voyage, who stands unsteadily on dry ground. Lamenting his insensibility, he yet apprehends nature's orderly rhythm and, above all, its authority over all of life. Sadly, he feels himself an alien amid this beauty, where "every small leaf is so sure of itself," while he stands distraught, alone.

This poignant confession was omitted from *Dreams and Meditations*, doubtless because, long before summer 1899, nature's mysteries had ceased to be for him a sealed book. An important early factor in this development certainly was his immersion in the poetry of Tiutchev and Fet in the fall of 1895.[10] Moreover, Konevskoi's voracious reading had familiarized him with movements in thought and art, primarily Western European, which assisted him to an entirely new way of looking at exterior and interior reality. Finally, in 1897 his momentous first summer journey in Western Europe solidified his identity as a mystical pantheist. Before that, however, there were significant markers to be passed.

4. "Son of the Sun": Mikhailovskoe

After completing the *gimnaziia* course in mid-April 1896, Konevskoi began a well-earned holiday. As often before, he spent the time from June till late August at Mikhailovskoe, the estate of Ippolit Aleksandrovich Panaev. (*LN* 92:4:182) Mme Panaeva, Konevskoi's godmother, died in 1892. However, he continued his frequent visits to Mikhailovskoe, attracted no doubt by the conversation and inspiration of his host. Like his more famous cousin I. I. Panaev, I. A. Panaev was a writer of fiction and, in his later years, of numerous philosophical and moralistic works of a popular-publicistic nature. A. V. Lavrov wrote:

> Konevskoi's early awakened interests in the area of abstract thought were strongly encouraged by his contacts with Panaev and influenced notably by this mentor's opinions and judgments. [...] Conversations with him and, possibly, the reading of his books may be reflected in the convinced and logical apology for Christianity that Konevskoi elaborated during his *gimnaziia* years.[11]

Panaev's numerous books, beginning with *Seekers of Truth* (1878), a two-volume collection of studies of German philosophy starting from Kant, reaching to *The Light of Life* (1893), his attack on irreligious scientific trends in contemporary society, were full of ideas and sentiments that find echoes in Konevskoi's early writings.[12] For example, in a rambling, unfinished composition begun in 1893 Konevskoi attempted to summarize and draw conclusions (from ideas not well digested) about philosophy's role in a spiritually ailing Russian society.[13] Under the tutelage of Panaev, Konevskoi became convinced that only genuine philosophy was capable of healing the "sick thought" of that generation. Its leading exemplar, of course, was Kant. Panaev's views may have led him to the fascination with Kant that played both a positive and a negative role in his development hereafter.

A fellow guest that summer at Mikhailovskoe was the philosophy student Sergei Petrovich Semenov, who subsequently became one of Konevskoi's close friends. The Panaev estate thus provided the ideal milieu for pursuing the ambitious program he had outlined to Veselov a few months earlier. Along with all its other advantages, Mikhailovskoe possessed the ambience that offered freedom — physical and spiritual — and closeness to nature. The first poem Konevskoi wrote there, "In Flight (*Na letu*)" (*SP 2008*, 79), not only shows him in a new relationship with the natural surroundings, to some degree it looks toward the mystical experiences of a year later. The four stanzas describe a horseback ride in wide-open country with great attention to detail — clothes flying loose, eyes wide, wider, trying to take in the whole horizon, impressions of light, wind, space that take his breath away. The impact of the experience is both sensual and spiritual. Each stanza begins with a plea to be possessed by the elements, by wind, by rays of light. "Gasping for breath, I trembled, felt ecstasy and pain." Here, it seems, the barrier between his psyche and nature has finally fallen.

Beginning early in August, Konevskoi channeled his creative energy into the writing of sonnets. The most memorable result of that effort was the series that later became the sonnet cycle "Son of the Sun (*Syn solntsa*)."[14] Though only two of the five sonnets were written at Mikhailovskoe, these two set out important directional indicators for his whole exploratory enterprise. In the course of this summer, as his relationship with nature deepened, he found himself pulled in what at first seemed opposite directions. On the one hand there was his passionate attraction to the external world's opulent variety, coupled with the desire to penetrate its essence. On the other was the imperative to protect his *persona* from dissolution in the all-embracing life in nature. Preservation of that *persona* intact and free from outside intrusion, he believed, was the essential guarantee of personal immortality. Written over the period from August to November 1896, the cycle "Son of the Sun" sets forth in brilliant images Konevskoi's fierce conviction that no opposition exists, or can exist, between the two imperatives. His prolonged struggle to establish philosophical proof for this argument lay just ahead.

The first Mikhailovskoe sonnet, "Growth and Delight (*Rost i otrada*)," is a celebration of a life fully and joyfully immersed in nature. The second (in time of composition), "Starres Ich," shows the speaker fiercely defending his *persona* before the forces and seductions of chaos and even death. The other three sonnets are linked to one or another of these, creating a tension that is released with the last sestet of the final sonnet. The cycle itself, not ordered chronologically, was assembled sometime after 20 November, when the last poem was completed.

The first sonnet introduces the *lyrical subject,* the individual to whom the entire sequence was subsequently dedicated: Konevskoi's closest friend Aleksandr Bilibin, whom he later sometimes called "Son of the Sun". "Growth and Delight" presents a youth who has grown up in full harmony with nature, and whose considered philosophy is that of the grasshopper in Krylov's fable "The Grasshopper and the Ant."[15] From all we know of the two, Aleksandr Bilibin seems to have been in many ways Ivan Konevskoi's total opposite. And yet, despite — or because of — this, Konevskoi shows him ideally, a golden, sun-bathed figure possessing a joyful completeness. Nonetheless, unable to accept his friend's carefree thinking, he shaped the sonnet sequence as his response.

The second sonnet, "Amid the Waves (*Sred' voln*)" adds brilliance to the initial picture. Here the young hero appears in constant movement, fully alive and fully at home in his watery milieu. "Water is my element!" he exclaims, as he dives and splashes. Full of affectionate admiration for this vital being, the poet now perceives in his comrade hitherto unsuspected depths. He cannot accept that such wholeness should co-exist with the frivolous philosophy professed. In the final sonnet, "From Sun to Sun (*Ot solntsa k solntsu*)," the theme of surging life is reaffirmed. With an authority deriving from his own passion for life, the poet totally rejects the possibility that this vivid life could be extinguished in "eternal sleep."

A visit to the mechanical section of the Nizhnii Novgorod exhibition at the end of August inspired Konevskoi to write the sonnet "Machines."[16] Awed by the "mysteries" he saw, he yet reminded himself that the mechanical monster before him was inferior to man's spirit. However, the theme of indomitable spirit received a far more powerful statement in "Starres Ich," where the young speaker wakes at night, as if roused by the massive, smothering darkness that surrounds him. Leaping from bed he roams through rooms he cannot see, willing himself to face down the chaos that threatens to swallow his existence. Dated 16-17 August and dedicated to Semenov, this sonnet presumably is related to their summertime discussions. In any case it is a prime statement of a fundamental conviction rooted in Konevskoi's nature: survival of the independent *persona* is essential, and it is firmly linked to the will.

When, in December 1896, Konevskoi began composing "Lyric Poetry in Contemporary Russia", four of these five sonnets found their place in the text, as did the account of the boy's encounter with death. Moreover, in that essay's structure, the sonnet sequence serves as a companion piece to that other account. This is especially striking in the case of "Starres Ich," where the speaker's defiance of the encroaching dark and his assertion of his personal existence form an obvious sequel to the boy's frantic appeal for "Life!"

Thus, in the sonnet sequence "Son of the Sun," Konevskoi's thirst for life melded with powerful attraction to the natural world, which he suspected of harboring mysteries still beyond his reach.

5. The New Mysticism

At what point did pantheism present itself to Konevskoi as a fruitful approach to the essence of the world structure? This is not certain, although the notion was certainly widely available in the literature he was reading.[17] As Vladimir Solov'ev wrote a year or two later, "A multitude of people have passed through and are passing through the religious experience of pantheism — through the inner perception or sense of their identity with the all-unifying substance of the world."[18] In fact, for Konevskoi, Solov'ev himself may have provided the crucial nudge. Konevskoi's notes dated "Autumn and winter 1895/96" indicate intensive reading of the poetry of Tiutchev and Fet. (*LN* 92:4:185) This fact, of course, does not preclude earlier reading of either poet. However, Solov'ev's article "The Poetry of F. I. Tiutchev," which appeared first in the April 1895 number of *Messenger of Europe (Vestnik Evropy)* stands out as a major event in Tiutchev's emergence as the veritable forefather of Russian Symbolism. It was reprinted in March 1896 in the volume *Philosophical Currents in Russian Poetry (Filosofskie techeniia russkoi poezii)*, edited by P. P. Pertsov, with a selection of Tiutchev's poetry. Both of these sources presumably were accessible to Konevskoi.[19]

In any case, Solov'ev's article certainly was at the center of his attention the day after his return from Mikhailovskoe. That day he borrowed overnight from the Semennikov Library the last two numbers of *Northern Messenger (Severnyi vestnik)*. "In the evening I read aloud to my father A. L. Volynskii's 'Literary Comments' about *Philosophical Currents in Russian Poetry* and about Tiutchev."[20] His excitement is palpable. Returning from two months in the countryside, when his efforts to bond with nature were to some extent successful, he was doubtless especially sensitive to Tiutchev's deep relationship with the natural world as interpreted by Solov'ev. Moreover, Volynskii's retelling had its own agenda. While freely but closely paraphrasing, he omitted Solov'ev's more abstract explanatory passages, concentrating instead on the heart of the message:

> Tiutchev not only felt, but also thought like a poet. He was convinced of the objective truth of the poetic view of nature. [...] He knew and felt that nature has a soul, and that unshakable conviction laid out for his inspiration the path to the most secret sources of the world's life (Volynskii, *NM* 230).[21]

Should there be any doubt about Solov'ev's meaning, Volynskii rephrased the thought: "He who is able to understand the life of nature, to hear its secret language, he who feels the movement of the world soul — from a blade of grass to a man — in the entire universal system, he is a poet" (231). Here, indeed, was what Konevskoi wanted to hear. The image of Tiutchev projected in Vladimir Solov'ev's essay, reinforced by Volynskii, as a poet-mystic who found a way to the universe's secrets, utterly captivated him.

It also left him with numerous unanswered questions. Like many of his contemporaries, Konevskoi was convinced early on, quite apart from formal religious doctrine, of the existence of a reality accessible only to faculties other than ordinary human reason. He was possessed by an urgent need to penetrate its secrets. In this endeavor, as he was discovering, he had a great deal of company.

This quest, the object of mystics from time immemorial, had developed new dimensions in the current era. By opening fresh perspectives on the universe, contemporary science raised challenges not to be ignored, even by those who rejected science's authority over any but the physical facts of existence. Moreover, in the current questioning atmosphere, topics ranging from the occult to scientific studies of consciousness, extrasensory perception, and other psychic phenomena were being discussed and debated in widely differing venues, often under the heading of "mysticism."

For many like Konevskoi it was an article of faith that art and mysticism were by definition intertwined.[22] Among the newest French and Belgian poets were some in whose writings over the next few years Konevskoi found guidance and encouragement. Summer at Mikhailovskoe found him working on a project linked to this pursuit. His archive holds drafts of an article on the Belgian poet Maurice Maeterlinck dated "May-June 1896. Petrograd-Mikhailovskoe," along with the plan of a larger work, of which the Maeterlinck piece was to form a leading part. The first draft opens with the following outline:[23]

Memento: Contemporary heralds of artistic mystikism [sic]:

I. Maurice Maeterlinck: his poetry and philosophy.

II. The worldview of the English "Pre-Raphaelites" in painting and poetry (Rossetti, Morris, Swinburne, Burne-Jones, Millet). IV. Joyous mystic (several new words on the worldview of Aleksei Tolstoi). V. The lightsome wise man (Robert Browning). III. Mysteries of the moral world (Henrik Ibsen) (259.1.15.4ob).

Of all those poets now writing in French, Konevskoi describes Maeterlinck as "the noblest herald of true symbolism, infused with philosophical and psychological conceptions." In his earlier work *Serres chaudes*, Maeterlinck was hampered by the "dull soullessness (dominant around and in himself) of self-satisfied vulgarity and coarseness," which "cuts him off from contemplation of the unknown eternal essence of the world." But now, with *Le Tresor des Humbles*, Konevskoi sees him entering a new philosophical phase: "This is a stunning elevating exemplar of inner rebirth and transformation of the contemporary spirit, into the joyous mystical worldview, out of the darkness of stinking, exhausted decadence." These critical remarks were doubtless heavily indebted to Konevskoi's assiduous reading in a number of Russian and foreign periodicals. However, the notion that the "new mysticism" is informed by "philosophical and psychological conceptions" was destined to become a central point in his thinking.

Yet, at this stage of discussing the topic of mysticism, Konevskoi clearly was still a novice, though a well-read one. Nor was he assisted by the general terminological confusion existing at the time, not only in Russia. Indeed, as Vladimir Solov'ev wrote in an early essay, "for the majority, the very name [mysticism] has become a synonym for all that is unclear and incomprehensible" (1:264). However, while Konevskoi readily accepted the belief that art, in at least some of its manifestations, was closely allied with the mystical worldview, his notion of the "new artist-mystic" was still a rather hazy one.

Vladimir Solov'ev's article "Mysticism," which appeared in the Brokgauz-Efron *Encyclopedic Dictionary* in 1896, attempted to clarify both concept and usage of this term.[24] Solov'ev began by defining mysticism as "the combination of appearances and actions linking man in a special way to the world's secret essence and forces, independent of conditions of space, time, and physical causality." He then set forth an exhaustive taxonomy, as well as a historical survey, from ancient times to the present (*Br-Efr.* 37:454). In the latter connection, he cautiously referred to the new field of psychic research: "At the present time observations and experiments dealing with the facts of artificial hypnosis and imposition of will on the subject require some scholars to concede in that area, along with deceit and superstition, some basis in fact" (37:455). Interestingly, as one of four bibliographical items appended, he included Baron Karl Du Prel's *Die Philosophie der Mystik* and its Russian translation. (Of this work and its author much more will be said below.) However, one fact was becoming clear to many: with new discoveries about the nature of human psyche, the long history of mysticism was about to open a new chapter.

Konevskoi's notebook entries "from September 1894 through 15 November 1896" show him reading, along with Shakespeare (in German), Darwin (in Russian), Maeterlinck (in French), Edgar Allan Poe (in Bal'mont's Russian translation), many articles in a variety of periodicals. One of these periodicals was *Problems of Philosophy and Psychology (Voprosy filosofii i psykhologii)*, established in 1889 and issued five times a year as journal of the Moscow Psychological Society. This journal promised broad up-to-date coverage of developments in "experimental and physiological psychology," as well as "general surveys of the literature" and "reviews of studies and works by Western-European philosophers and psychologists" (*PPP*, from the prospectus for 1893). It was a menu of predictable appeal to a reader hungry to learn from authoritative sources more about the human personality's potential for expansion.

Another journal Konevskoi perused at about the same time, no doubt with similar questions in mind, was *Rebus*, founded in 1881 as the weekly journal of Russian mediumism or spiritualism (*spiritizm* in Russian usage).[25] The spiritualist movement began in New York state in 1848, and soon spread widely in Western Europe and then to Russia.[26] Its claim of putting its followers in touch with those who had "passed over" appealed to a wide spectrum of the public. At the same time it aroused controversy and opposition in religious and intellectual circles. In Russia, the debate led in 1875 to formation of an investigative committee headed by the eminent scientist Dmitrii Mendeleev. Established explicitly to "work against the spread of mysticism," the committee reached resoundingly negative conclusions.[27]

The Mendeleev report probably had little impact on the wider public's interest in spiritualism. In contrast, the program of *Rebus* was aimed at a broad audience. Its announcement for the year 1895 promised that articles to be published concerning "*hypnotism, magnetism, clairvoyance, and mediumism* (spiritualism) will give a full picture of the contemporary view of these mysterious phenomena."[28] Its pages carried every kind of content from reports of séances in provincial towns to articles on hypnotism, telepathy, somnambulism, and other psychic phenomena, sometimes written by researchers whose names were well known outside the spiritualist following.

A name that occurred frequently in *Rebus* was that of the German scientist, philosopher, and spiritualist Baron Karl Du Prel. Du Prel's writings had a substantial readership in Russia during the 1880s and 1890s among those interested in spiritualism, mysticism and the occult. *Die Philosophie der Mystik* appeared in M. S. Aksenov's Russian translation in 1895. The index to the first twenty years of *Rebus* (March 1901) lists twenty contributions under his name, some continued over several issues. Three of these later appeared as a volume entitled *Der Spiritismus* (Leipzig, 1893; *Spiritizm*, Moscow, 1904).

Konevskoi probably encountered Du Prel's work first on the pages of *Rebus*. By September 1896 his name figured prominently in Konevskoi's reading notebooks.[29] Other notebooks, designated as "supplementary," contained extensive excerpts copied from works of various authors, including Du Prel.[30] Gathered together in one section are quotations from many sources on consciousness, the nervous system's structure and the brain, as well as much on sleep, dream, and somnambulism. It becomes obvious that, in this first year of his university studies, along with other serious interests, Konevskoi was determined to understand as thoroughly as possible the human psychic equipment that could allow an extension of the rational daytime mind.

6. "The Literary-Intellectual Circle"

Of all Konevskoi's new experiences that first year at university, possibly the most stimulating was participation in the "Literary-Intellectual Circle."[31] He was introduced to this group by Sergei Semenov, who probably saw him as a reinforcement of his own position in the group, where members' interests lay primarily in the social sciences.[32] Indeed, according to one member, both the style and substance of Konevskoi's contributions caused him to be perceived initially as an alien presence: "Special language, excessively clever expressions, the philosophical-poetic tradition in his circle of conceptions (Dostoevskii)." Nonetheless, he became one of the most active participants, acting that year as the group's secretary. (*LN* 92:4:183)

Konevskoi's presentations in the circle during the next few months tell much about the direction and development of his thinking. His interest in contemporary research findings on topics like somnambulism and the true extent of psychic powers continued unabated. One of his presentations was a report on Du Prel's *Der Spiritismus*, available in book form in German, chapters of which had appeared in Russian in *Rebus*.[33] Early in that work Du Prel proposed a theory about somnambulism with obvious relevance to Konevskoi's concerns:

> Among the abilities of somnambulists are some that unquestionably do not admit of physiological explanation: for example, seeing and acting at a distance. It is impossible, for instance, to ascribe somanbulists' clairvoyance in time to the activity of cells of the brain. Anyone who, even once, has witnessed clairvoyance must, by force of logic, suppose the existence of a carrier of somnabulistic capacities that is distinct from and independent of the human body. But we do not know of such an entity.

Du Prel then came to a conclusion that must have electrified Konevskoi:

> From this it follows that our self-consciousness does not embrace the totality of our being. Hidden in us and eluding our earthly awareness of self is the core of our being, which manifests an adaptation to the external world completely different from our earthly adaptation. *This core is the carrier of our occult capabilities. Therefore man is a twofold being [...] and our earthly body together with our consciousness mediated by our body is only one part of our total being.* (*Spiritizm*, 13-14. Ital. mine).

Though later Konevskoi sometimes spoke dismissively of Du Prel as a derivative source, the impression of this particular insight remained with him and indeed became a central element of his thinking. Two years later he wrote to his friend Veselov: "I think and sometimes believe that the essence of nature and of man [...] is penetrated by that other consciousness that appears with special fullness in the sleep of a somnambulist, [...] that inner life of our *persona* about which Du Prel speaks" (*AVL*, 173).

Meanwhile, Konevskoi's main goal remained unchanged: unlimited knowledge about the nature and meaning of the universe. This goal was by now inseparably linked to intense concern for the *persona's* survival and the desire to comprehend and expand its powers to the fullest. If those powers allowed it to overcome the limitations of time, space, and causality, then some transformed version of the "self" conceivably might escape the ultimate limitation, death. Yet, without an understanding of the yet larger context, even this consideration was meaningless.

Konevskoi's formal debut in the circle occurred on 14 October 1896 with a paper entitled "Beauty in Motion" (later renamed: "Beauty in Action"). In it, as he explained to Aleksei Veselov a year later, he attempted to formulate "my thoughts about the features of the all-embracing, all-uniting Essence of the world" (*AVL,* 167). This presentation was an ambitious beginning of a project that he continued to work on in the months following. It also marked a major new intellectual departure.

While still a *gimnazist* Konevskoi had impressed his instructors by his broad reading and his thirst for knowledge.[34] Among the authors named in his earliest notebooks, philosophers were not prominent, though he consistently read articles on philosophers and philosophical topics in the Brockgauz-Efron encyclopedia. However, with his entrance into the university, the situation changed. St. Petersburg University was the stronghold of Russian neo-Kantianism; its main exponent, Aleksandr Vvedenskii, was chairman of the philosophy department and a popular and influential lecturer on modern European philosophy.[35] One of the first lectures Konevskoi attended was Vvedenskii's on Descartes's *Discours de la méthode.*[36] A month later the topic was Spinoza. Konevskoi's intensive reading of philosophy apparently began in the second half of 1897, with Schopenhauer, Kant, and others.[37] All of this fueled his intellectual endeavors in the immediate future.

For some time to come, Konevskoi's main effort was directed at finding a philosophically supportable conception of the *world structure* that would free the individual *persona* from the inexorable threat of absorption into the All-One. Without the text of "Beauty in Motion" it is, of course, impossible to assess his progress in this task in autumn 1896. However, by November

1897, his assiduous study of philosophers had moved his thinking forward appreciably.

Of particular relevance here were certain ideas of Vladimir Solov'ev's that led Konevskoi to form a set of tentative conclusions about the *world structure* and its relation to the individual. The universe, he explained to his friend Veselov, exists in a constant state of inner tension between warring forces, "[t]he two root forces — the force of inertia, which drags everything toward motionlessness, stagnation, dissolution into one indistinguishable mass, and the force of separation, distinction, individuation." As long as that state of affairs continues, separate entities do not merge into one. The obvious difficulty, from Konevskoi's point of view, lay in finding firm assurance that the force of inertia will not overcome its opposite, thus causing the active forces tending toward separation and variety to collapse into one featureless mass. The very existence of this state of universal tension is, he confesses, "a very great mystery." Nonetheless, it is logically necessary. And finally (by a leap of reasoning) he concludes, this state of tension must be supposed to be without foreseeable terminus. (*AVL*, 170).[38] The November 1897 letter to Veselov evidently represented at least a temporary respite in Konevskoi's efforts to find a tenable philosophical basis for his convictions. Nonetheless, that challenge would drive his thinking and searching as long as he was alive.

7. *"Lyric Poetry in Contemporary Russia"*

Konevskoi's second major presentation in the circle ostensibly dealt with a different, less abstract topic. From 25 December 1896 to 16 February 1897 he worked on an extended composition entitled "Lyric Poetry in Contemporary Russia," which he delivered in two installments on 17 and 25 February.[39] Specific and timely as that title might seem, the work's actual subject turned out also to be very close to his on-going philosophical concerns. It in fact reveals him at a crucial moment in his development. Near the midpoint of his first year at university, he still, in many ways, stood firm on the moral and intellectual values prevailing in home and family, as well as in his *gimnaziia*, where his favorite teacher and mentor,

Fedor Aleksandrovich Luter, exercised considerable influence on him.[40] At the same time he was exploring ideas that would soon lead to a radical questioning of and shift in certain of those values.

Prepared as it was for oral presentation before a group of peers, "Lyric Poetry ..." is a problematic, not to say highly idiosyncratic, document. Written by a novice with limited experience of public speaking, it bristles with strong opinions and a wealth of thoughts and feelings that he seemed determined to expound to his hearers. As tone shifted abruptly from apparently objective critical judgments to intensely private reflections and accounts of personal experience, the effect surely was disconcerting. This was especially so to some listeners who, at least initially, found Konevskoi's style "repulsive (mechanically)" and burdened with esoteric language and ideas. (*LN* 92:4:183.)

An initial problem is posed by the text itself, since, according to authorial pagination, the extant autograph lacks the first sixteen pages (*AVL*, 93). However, a short article "At Daybreak (*Na rassvete*)," printed in the 1904 volume edited by Briusov (*SP 1904*, 125-136) and identified by Briusov as "introductory pages in an article about the contemporary Russian lyric," presumably defines the general topic (*SP 1904*, 245). That article's opening paragraph reveals the author's idealist orientation: "During the last ten, fifteen years our entire literary and, generally, our intellectual life has undergone dark and senselessly stormy days." The "inner unrest" of the 1880s found its best interpreter, we are told, in "the most visionary man of that time," Dostoevskii, and its fullest expression in the drama of the Karamazovs (125). However, neither Dostoevskii nor his great peer Lev Tolstoi was able to offer a sure path out of that murk. (Tolstoi, it is implied, because of his total rejection of any mystical dimension, has become in fact a false prophet.) Nor have any of the lesser figures, like Nadson and Garshin, done more than dramatize by their sad fates in Russia's pre-dawn spiritual darkness.

Pursuing this theme in the main text, Konevskoi attempts an ambitious, if brief and impressionistic, survey of the entire nineteenth century, ending with a guardedly hopeful glance into the future, where a few timid lights gleam. For his central discussion, Konevskoi selected six poets whose recent work, in his view, gave greater or lesser hope of imminent change of direction. These were Nikolai Minskii, Konstantin Fofanov, Fedor Sologub, Aleksandr Dobroliubov, Dmitri Merezhkovskii, and Vladimir Solov'ev, all of whose poetry appeared in collected volumes in 1895 or 1896.[41] While in no way disregarding esthetic values, the critique focused chiefly on each poet's degree of success in overcoming the influence of nineteenth-century positivism and the malaise of the '80's, and in searching out new spiritual paths. The integrity and clear-sightedness of each one's worldview were scrutinized, and ultimately all were found wanting. The standard against which each was measured was, of course, Konevskoi's own worldview.

So far, the essay's plan seems a cogent, if not an outstandingly original, one. Surveys of current literature, anxiously probing for signs of revival of Russian national values (however defined), had been appearing in the more forward-looking periodical press and elsewhere for some time. However, if actual inspiration for Konevskoi's undertaking is to be sought, doubtless the most likely source was Dmitrii Merezhkovskii's landmark essay "On the Causes of Decline and of New Currents in Contemporary Literature."[42]

In his introductory and summary chapters, Konevskoi describes the century's literary-spiritual malaise in terms that do not seriously contradict Merezhkovskii's. For him, too, the villain is materialistic science. However, his diagnosis of the ailment is far more profound, and his prescription for renewal makes more rigorous demands on the patient than does Merezhkovskii's. Writing several years after Merezhkovskii, he detects a more hopeful trend in poetry than did Merezhkovskii — one that is moving toward "elimination of the soulless curse laid by science on the area of our speculation about eternal universal principles and about the purpose of our being" (*AVL*, 125). This very assessment already suggests a major difference between the two critics. For Konevskoi, a return to idealism is not enough; any artistic renewal worthy of the name must arise, not from mere recognition of the spiritual dimension of human life called for by Merezhkovskii, but from a true philosophical understanding of the universe's structure. Translated into concrete terms, this requirement resolves inevitably into the artist's capacity and willingness to address the central problems of death and the survival of the individual *persona*. This essay, then, actually continues the topic of Konevskoi's previous presentation. The tension between All-Oneness and multiplicity in the world structure, with its fateful implications for the ultimate survival of the *persona*, remains Konevskoi's chief preoccupation.

"Lyric Poetry in Contemporary Russia" is at bottom a very personal meditation. The extant text begins in mid-description of a boy's early encounter with death (related above) and his vivid reactions to it. This arresting and relatively lengthy narrative is then integrated into the critical text, ostensibly to illuminate the inner sufferings of poets like Fofanov, who are stifled by the scientific worldview so destructive of the earlier, healthier, more mystical outlook. The presumed missing pages (were they actually written?) might or might not have tightened the link to the central discussion.

Turning to his selected poets, Konevskoi proceeds with a clear set of criteria. Minskii is the forerunner, "the first to strain toward reunion with the world unity after the dull alienation of Russian life held captive by positivism" (*AVL*, 94). Sadly, he concludes, Minskii has nothing to offer but his peculiar philosophy of "meonism"[43]: union with the great "non-being." In the final analysis, he is a "failed mystic."(98) Fofanov, Sologub, and Dobroliubov, each in his own way, come closer to the ideal, united as they are by "the force of life's disorderly energy, inseparable in them from a thirst to participate in the divine principle of the universe." Yet they are "people who are, at one and the same time, sick and impotent," unable thus far to achieve the vision Konevskoi holds up to them (101).

Of the six poets discussed, it is Fofanov who receives Konevskoi's most sympathetic attention. This "visionary 'holy fool,' who [...] sings like a bird" finds poetry in the most unlikely surroundings. (101) Yet his inspiration does not function solely on the level of intimate experience. Indeed, for Konevskoi, the poetry and worldview of this sufferer take on metaphysical significance. Fofanov's personal struggle between transgression and repentance becomes, in Konevskoi's eyes, the struggle between two world forces, angelic and demonic, and, inevitably, the tension between unity and multiplicity:

> Rarely does anyone experience as profoundly as does this poet the eternal drama of the universe — the clash between the principle of stability, harmony, measure, general restraint, and peacefulness and the principle of rebelliousness, the principle of disorder, straining now toward self-annihilation, now toward self-isolation (*AVL*, 103).

Yet, whatever his shortcomings, Fofanov's attitude toward life is "far more penetrating than Mr. Minskii's worldview" (111).

Konevskoi's attempt to demonstrate Fofanov's metaphysical reach ends by becoming a vehicle for his own intimate concerns. Nor does he confine himself to the poetry of Fofanov in elaborating his own position. For example, stanzas by the English Pre-Raphaelite Dante Gabriel Rossetti, which are recalled "as I sat on the bank of the great Finnish waterfall," lead directly to his personal meditation on the fatal, irreversible ravages of time:

> It is torture to consider the nothingness of the *persona* in the torrent of time and the march of world events, and also its nothingness in the ocean of the one impersonal spirit of the world. [...] Our "I" is merely a formless, undefined cloudlet, eternally changing, eternally streaming, lost in the chaos of time (109-110).

The terror of extinction expressed so poignantly here and earlier, in the boy's comprehension of death, finds its echo, not only in Fofanov and Rossetti, but also in their entire poetic generation, in which Konevskoi includes himself. "All the poet-sufferers of our time are engulfed by this horror of the waterfall" (110).

This treatment of Fofanov signals the early appearance of a method that Konevskoi employed regularly in later studies of writers and artists with whom he felt kinship of sympathies and ideas. Textual or other evidence was not necessarily at issue when he endowed those individuals with artistic values and worldview close to his own. One commentator acutely observed, "The characteristics that Konevskoi bestowed upon his favorite authors, for all their keenness of perception and power of broad generalization, were often ahistorical and abstract; inevitably projected on these portraits was the *persona* of Konevskoi himself" *(LN* 98:1:431).

An interesting variant of this approach appears toward the end of the Fofanov passage in this essay. At this time, as has been seen, Konevskoi was much occupied with probing the nature of the "self." Among those then writing on the subject, perhaps Karl Du Prel came as close as any to pointing the direction that Konevskoi's own explorations would take in the near future. As central to the phenomenon of somnambulism Du Prel identified a "second self": "the kernel of our being, manifesting a totally different adaptation to the external world than our earthly adaptation to it" *(Spiritizm,* 13). Against this background, apparently, Konevskoi easily interpreted Fofanov's relatively uncomplicated verses as the prophetic introspections of a poet-mystic,

> which he brought forth from the consciousness of his own nature when he heard how in his soul there stirred a second, unconscious "I", inseparable from himself, irremovable, "often giving him answers to questions," and manifesting "wisdom and love, alpha and omega." By means of direct poetic penetration he has come close to that truth that many psychologist-metaphysicians of our day attempt to base on science (*AVL,* 111).

Another source of relevant information and ideas in this area was the American psychologist William James, whose *Psychology* was translated and published in St. Petersburg in 1896.[44] References to it appear in Konevskoi's notebooks and writings that fall and later, and it is possible to see James's chapter "The Self" (translated in Russian as "Persona"), reflected in his reading of Fofanov, where Konevskoi implicitly credits him with anticipating modern thinking on the stability and permanence of the *persona.* (*AVL,* 110)

Of the six poets under discussion, the only one who engaged Konevskoi to a comparable degree was Dmitrii Merezhkovskii. However, Konevskoi's response to Merezhkovskii was, to say the least, ambivalent. He finds much to praise in one whose best lyrics exhibit immense love for the world's rich variety. Yet, in his view, the earlier poetry is marred by a grave flaw that seems to cancel this virtue: "the ecstatic heralding of the cult of World Unity, which is expressed first of all in *renunciation of one's unitary persona*"(*AVL*, 130; ital. mine). Yet Konevskoi hopes to find that Merezhkovskii's true self lies elsewhere. In this he is greatly aided by the poet's spiritual kinship with Homeric Greece. From this base "there remains to him but one step to heralding the broadest rights of multiplicity, of the unitary *persona*." But he goes further, sharing with Merezhkovskii his own fervent hope: "He sensed clearly that, besides this, somewhere here, already among us, there exists the perfect state of two-in-one harmony, but that, while we are simply people, full understanding of that harmony is unattainable" (131).

For Konevskoi, Merezhkovskii at times comes close to resolving the inner contradictions that tormented Fofanov. But never close enough. In order to dramatize the fatal weakness he finds in this poet's worldview, Konevskoi again employs an interpolated narrative — in this instance, the sonnet sequence "Son of the Sun." The first two sonnets, it may be recalled, portray a brilliant, vital explorer of life's elements — sun, air, water, light — who finds in this his fulfillment. The parallel with Merezhkovskii, while not perfect, serves to underline the latter's intense love of life. Konevskoi's appreciation of him rises to its highest as he discusses the poem "Leda." Then abruptly the tone changes as he espies a fatal weakness: "He speaks a great deal about reconciliation with death, about the joyfulness of death, but almost nowhere in his poetry or critical sketches can one discern what his views are on the position of personal existence in relation to death" (135). All credibility is lost when Merezhkovskii's attitude toward death and survival of the *persona* is fully exposed to view. For all the "wisdom" that his poetry offers, he undercuts himself with a single line in the lyric "Noise of the Waves (*Shum voln*)": "Pointless to live, pointless to die" (135).

Konevskoi's sense of betrayal is intense: if this is so, then all Merezhkovskii's wise words "lose charm and meaning" (136). Konevskoi's tone resembles that of a disillusioned disciple, as he scornfully compares Merezhkovskii's frivolous utterances to the old Latin student song and celebration of careless youth, "Gaudeamus igitur (*Let us therefore rejoice*)...." Finally, as an exhortation to his fallen hero, he quotes the last two sonnets of his sequence. "Starres ich" dramatizes the poet's defense of his *persona* against the forces of oblivion and nothingness; "From Sun to Sun" follows with its pledge of endless life. Only by such lines as these, he insists, could the positive element of Merezhkovskii's message be restored. Alas, they are not to be found in his *oeuvre*.

One poet remains for consideration. Like Merezhkovskii, in Konevskoi's opinion, Vladimir Solov'ev brings something new to Russian lyric poetry. Moreover, he is not open to the same reproaches as Merezhkovskii, whose feeble stance before death negates the wide visions of which he showed himself capable. While as a poet Solov'ev has not yet fulfilled his promise, Konevskoi's critique displays an expectation of something to come in Solov'ev that neither he nor his readers can as yet imagine.[45]

8. Mystical Pantheism and the Expanded Persona

With Solov'ev, the circle closed, as it were, on Konevskoi's study of the spiritual state of contemporary Russian lyric poetry. His analysis ends with the optimistic declaration: "And so, at last, after every sort of weakness and grieving, mad bliss and insane self-immolation, all these motives that dominate our contemporary poetry, now, with the arrival of Vladimir Solov'ev, there breathes on us the spirit of the *bogatyr* heroes" (141).[46]

Still, after all this, Konevskoi had only begun to work out in his own mind a full and satisfying definition of "the poet." His early poetic experiments gave some indication. The overflowing delight and curiosity before the world's rich variety in "Fragment" was his starting point. "Resurrection" shows him already exulting in his power as wielder of words. The second "Fragment" and "Nature" (May 1895) show him still an outside observer, chafing at his inability to read nature's language. Soon, however, helped by reading the poems of Tiutchev and Fet, he grasps a central fact: the poet must truly know — things, objects, but above all, nature — from inside out. The notion of mystical pantheism now assumed major importance: in a word, the true poet, he believed, must be the poet-mystic.

The pantheism of Tiutchev and others, offering access into the secrets of being, had great appeal to many in Konevskoi's generation. But common belief, holding that total union with the All-One, or world soul, was the ultimate goal, was for him fatally flawed. As we have seen, in "Beauty in Movement," Konevskoi attempted to envision a situation that would secure the permanent, independent place of the individual *persona* in the universe.

Karl Du Prel's *Spiritizm* contributed importantly to Konevskoi's inquiry into the hidden potential of that *persona*. This quest, in turn, was linked to his developing ideas of mystical pantheism and of the poet-mystic. It was Du Prel, apparently, who introduced Konevskoi to the notion that beyond the "daytime" conscious self, representing possibly only a small part of the human psyche, there lie powers that enable access to the entire realm called mystical. The notion of a second, amplified self remained a central feature in Konevskoi's thinking, though it underwent various transformations. But the basic idea was set: if through the agency of that expanded self, the limitations placed upon the conscious self might be negated, then insights into ever deeper levels of the life of the universe were possible, even probable.

Konevskoi had already come some way since leaving the *gimnaziia*. Now, as his first year at the university drew to a close, he prepared for a journey that would allow his mind and spirit to be enhanced, his powers to be tested. It was a journey that would take him across more borders than he knew.

Notes

[1] "Ivan Konevskoi. Svedeniia o ego zhizni". Ivan Konevskoi. *Stikhi i proza*. Moscow: "Skorpio", 1904. P. vii. (Reprinted by: Wilhelm Fink Verlag, Munich, 1971. Hereafter: *SP* 1904).

[2] "Oreus. (Ivan Ivanovich)". *Entsiklopedicheskii slovar'*. 43:138. St.-Peterburg: F. A. Brokgauz, P. A. Efron, 1897. (Hereafter: Br.-Efr.)

[3] A notebook dated 1893, when Konevskoi was fifteen or sixteen, contains an extended imaginative work bearing the title: "Brief Reports about the Great People of Rosamuntii of XIXc. In dictionary form". For more details, see: A. V. Lavrov, "'Chaiu i chuiu'. Persona i poeziia Ivana Konevskogo," foreword to *Ivan Konevskoi. Stikhtvoreniia i poemy*. St. Petersburg, Moscow, 2008 (hereafter *SP 2008*). Pp. 9-10. Allusion — perhaps humorously ironic — to some Brokgauz-Efron articles, including his father's, can be surmised. It may also be seen as a kind of inner rehearsal for his opening outward to the whole world that was soon to come.

[4] *Rossiiskii gosudarstvennyi arkhiv literatury i iskusstva (RGALI)*. Fond 259. Opis' 1, ed. khr. 6. "Tetrad' so spiskami prochitannikh knig i statei 1894-1901". 119 pp. His notes begin in 1894 and continue for several years.

[5] N.L. Stepanov, "Ivan Konevskoi. Poet mysli". Foreword, comm. A. E. Parnis. *Aleksandr Blok. Novye materialy i issledovaniia. Literaturnoe nasledstvo (LN)* 92: 4:182.

[6] *Valerii Briusov i ego korrespondenty. Literaturnoe nasledstvo (LN)* 98, 1:541-2.

[7] A letter from his father to the director of the *gimnaziia* asked that Ivan's entrance examination be delayed until the end of August (1890), because the boy "is with his mother, whose serious illness prevents her from returning from the south of Russia earlier than the end of August". Cited from archival sources by A. V. Lavrov, "Chaiu i chuiu". p. 13, n. 1.

[8] The *gimnaziia* in Russia and in several other European countries was a school roughly equivalent in period of study to American middle school and high school combined. Graduates of the *gimnaziia* might enter higher educational institutions or the civil service. Konevskoi entered the third *gimnaziia* class at age 13, after earlier home preparation, and completed the course in 1896.

⁹ "Iz arkhiva Ivana Konevskogo". Foreword, comm. A. V. Lavrov. Pp. 91-92. *Pisateli simvolisticheskogo kruga*. St. Petersburg: "Dmitrii Bulanin", 2003. Pp. 89-149.

¹⁰ Konevskoi's immense desire to penetrate to the heart of nature was an essential feature of his worldview, and somewhat akin to Tiutchev's romantic lament over man's "disharmony" with nature. Konevskoi's attitude, however, rather than lament, was one of determination to overcome. N. K. Gudzii used "Nature (*Priroda*)" and several other lyrics written between 1895 and 1897 to support his belief that "of early Russian symbolists the most organically linked with Tiutchev was I. Konevskoi." Yet his generally insightful analysis concerning Konevskoi seems flawed by his parallel drawn between Konevskoi's vexation expressed in "Nature" and Tiutchev's "There is melody in the sea's waves." ("Tiutchev v poeticheskoi kul'ture russkogo simvolizma", *Izvestiia otdeleniia russkogo iazyka i slovesnosti AN SSSR*, 2 (1930): 465-549). P. 485.

¹¹ "Chaiu i chuiu", p.12. See this essay for further details about I. A. Panaev's influence on Konevskoi's early formation.

¹² For fuller information about I. A. Panaev's career, see L. F. Guchkova's entry in: *Russkie pisateli. 1800-1917. Bibliograficheskii slovar'*. Vol. 4. Moscow, 1999. Pp. 519-120.

¹³ RGALI 259.1.2.1-30 followed by rougher drafts on loose sheets. (259.1.2.7-7ob)

¹⁴ "Syn solntsa". (*SP 2008*, 86-88).

¹⁵ "The Grasshopper and the Ant (*Strekoza i muravei*)," I. A. Krylov. *Basni*. Ed. A. P. Mogilianskii. Moscow-Leningrad: Izd. Akademii nauk SSSR: 1956. Pp. 52-53. The fable tells the story of the grasshopper, who, having sung all summer, finds herself without food for the winter. Turning to the industrious ant for assistance, she receives the scornful reply: "You sang all summer, now go, dance!" The basic story plot traces back through LaFontaine to Aesop's fables.

¹⁶ This was Konevskoi's first published poem and the only one published under his family name: I. Oreus, "Snariady." *Knizhki nedeli*, 1896, November, p. 96.

¹⁷ Konevskoi was also reading a great deal of the English romantic Percy Bysshe Shelley, who for him continued to rank with the very highest exemplars of mystical pantheism among European poets.

[18] *"Poniatie o Boge."* Vladimir Sergeevich Solov'ev. *Sobranie sochinenii.* 2nd ed. St. Petersburg: Prosviashchenie, 1911. Vol. 9, p.16.

[19] In a notebook entry for May 1896 Konevskoi listed readings from *Philosophical Currents in Russian Poetry*: "articles on Fet, Polonskii [...] Lermontov, Ogarev, Baratynskii." He did not mention the Solov'ev article on Tiutchev, which may suggest that he had already read it. (259.1.6.15)

[20] *RGALI* 259.1.16.23.

[21] "Literaturnye zametki, III. [Vladimir Solov'ev o Tiutcheve]", *Severnyi vestnik*, July, № 7, 1896 (230-241).

[22] His wide reading over the next several years reflects his desire to acquaint himself with the latest and best in modern European literature, with special attention to this subject. See: "Tetrad' so spiskami prochitannykh knig i statei... (*Notebook with lists of books and articles read...*)". (259.1.6.4ob).

[23] *RGALI* 259.1.15.4ob-10.

[24] Br.-Efr., vol. 37, pp. 454-456, 1896.

[25] How and when Konevskoi was introduced to mediumism is not certain. In any case, he read *Rebus* while still in the *gimnaziia*. (*RGALI* 259.1.6.7ob.) Concerning active interest — attendance at séances, etc. — , there is no available information. Later, in Moscow, he apparently became close to Valerii Briusov's boyhood friend Lang-Miropol'skii, who dedicated his mediumistic poem *Lestvitsa* to him posthumously.

[26] See: Joan Delaney Grossman "Alternative Beliefs. Spiritualism and Pantheism among the Early Modernists," *Christianity and the Eastern Slavs, III. Russian Literature in Modern Times.* Eds. Boris Gasparov, Robert P. Hughes, Olga Raevsky Hughes, Irina Paperno. Berkeley-Los Angeles: University of California Press, 1995 (113-133).

[27] More details about Dmitrii Mendeleev's views and his activities in this matter appear in Grossman, 120-121, and 129 nn. 16, 17.

[28] *Rebus*, 1894, No. 52, p.12.

[29] "NB read: Du Prel, Vl. Solov'ev, Renan, Hoeffding, Wundt..." (*RGALI* 259.1.16.46). I.e., French philologist and historian Ernest Renan; Harald Hoeffding, Danish philosopher; Wilhelm Wundt, German physiologist and psychologist.

30 One sampling includes, along with Du Prel, the German physicist, anatomist, and physiologist H. L. F. Helmholtz, American philosopher and psychologist William James, fellow student and poet Vladimir Gippius, modern Norwegian author Knut Hamsun (whose novel *Mysteries* was cited), and poet-mystic Aleksandr Dobroliubov (of whom more below). (*RGALI* 259.1.11.14).

31 The schedule for presentations in the Literary-Intellectual Circle [*Literaturno-myslitel'nyi kruzhok*] that year appears in Konevskoi's notebook as a double-page spread. *RGALI* 259.1.17.63ob-64.

32 The topic of consciousness was central to Sergei Semenov's presentations that year and very likely figured in his and Konevskoi's discussions the previous summer. The titles of Semenov's papers were: "About consciousness"; "About art (its meaning for consciousness)"; "Analysis and synthesis of the two-in-one principle of unconsciousness" (*RGALI* 259.1.17.63ob-64).

33 *LN* 92:4:183. Konevskoi read *Der Spiritismus* in German between mid-November and the end of December, 1896. (259.1.6.25)

34 A note on his *attestat* (30 May 1896) particularly noted his zeal "in the study of philology, in which he acquired, by work that was to a significant degree independent, a body of knowledge remarkable for his years" (*LN* 92:4:182).

35 Catherine Evtuhov, "An Unexpected Source of Russian Neo-Kantianism: Alexander Vvedensky and Lobachevsky's Geometry." *Studies in East European Thought*, Dec. 1995, 248-251.

36 *RGALI* 259.1.17.3.

37 *RGALI* 259.1.6. 42-43.

38 For authoritative support Konevskoi turned to Vladimir Solov'ev's *Criticism of Abstract Principles (Kritika otvlechennykh nachal)*, and specifically chapter forty-four, which bears the highly relevant title "Absolute being and absolute becoming. Man as second absolute…" (Vladimir Sergeevich Solov'ev, *Sobranie sochinenii*, 2nd. ed. 10 vols. St. Petersburg: Prosveshchenie, 1911. 2:323).

39 *RGALI* 259.1.17.63ob-64. The text appears in: *AVL*, 89-149.

40 F. A. Luter, who taught ancient languages in the No.1 St. Petersburg *gimnaziia*, influenced students especially through a circle he organized to discuss literary

and philosophical topics. Konevskoi of course was a member of this group. He later regarded Luter as his friend and dedicated several poems to him. (*LN* 98:1: 503.)

41 The table of contents originally listed Konstantin Bal'mont with two recent titles: *Pod severnym nebom* (1894) and *V bezbrezhnosti* (1895). However, both name and titles were crossed out. (*RGALI* 259.3.5.)

42 Merezhkovskii's "O prichinakh upadka i o novykh techeniiakh sovremennoi russkoi literatury" was published in January 1893. Though possibly aware of it earlier, Konevskoi gave this work serious attention only during his final year in the *gimnaziia*. (259.1.6.7ob)

43 From the Greek me on, "nothing."

44 For William James's links to Russian thought in the late nineteenth and early twentieth centuries, see *William James in Russian Culture*, eds. Joan Delaney Grossman and Ruth Rischin, Lanham, Boulder, New York, Oxford: Lexington Books, 2003. Interest in James's writings among Konevskoi's peers is discussed in: Joan Delaney Grossman, "Philosophers, Decadents, and Mystics: James's Russian Readers in the 1890s" (pp. 93-111).

45 See Chapter 8 for further discussion.

46 The term *"bogatyr"* refers to the mythological warrior heroes of ancient Rus'. The *"bogatyrs"* and the *bogatyr* spirit will play an increasingly important role in Konevskoi's own mythology, as will be seen.

Chapter 2

Chronicle of My Travels

1. "It smells, literally smells, of Europe". Warsaw, June 1897

Waiting on the railway platform in St. Petersburg for the train to Warsaw, Ivan Konevskoi could hardly have been in higher spirits. A brand-new notebook, headed "Chronicle of Travels I," soon held several pages of light-hearted observations of everything from his fellow train-passengers to the amount spent at various stops for refreshments (Luga — dinner, soup 25 kopecks. 2 veal sandwiches 10k. — 35k. Pskov — glass of tea with roll 15k.).[1] His delight in detail, always wide-ranging, was now enhanced by an eagerness for new sights and experiences of every description. The overriding goal of the venture on which he was now embarked was shared by many Russian travelers before and after: to experience a new world and to make his own discoveries there. For him the first major moment of realization came when he reached Warsaw: "It smells, literally smells, of Europe."[2]

But Warsaw was merely a signpost on the journey. Konevskoi's planned route lay through Vienna and on to Salzburg for a dutiful visit to his father's relative whom he called his "Austrian aunt." Even before reaching Salzburg, he marvelled at a landscape totally new to him: "Mountains, entirely covered by thick forest, like green curls or fleece."[3] In a burst of boyish ecstasy on 10 June he wrote: "One wants to climb trees, leap about under the heavens, run about, howl madly. The heart frolics in the breast."[4]

Writing from Munich on 28 June to his friend the art student Ivan Bilibin, Konevskoi described his ten days in Salzburg as "the happiest time of my life" (*AVL*, 152).⁵ However, he cut short his raptures, recalling that the Bilibins, summering in the Savoy Alps, were viewing scenes possibly even more majestic than those around Salzburg. Still, he enclosed two recent lyrics (his first since the previous December). Nor could he resist sharing his impressions of the road from Salzburg to Berchtesgaden, along which he felt at each step the approach of "ever greater and greater majesty" (*AVL*, 152). The excursion to Berchtesgaden on 14 June included the nearby Königsee, described in Baedeker as "clear, dark-green [...] enclosed by grand mountains rising above it to a height of 5000 to 6500 feet. It is the gem of this region and vies with the finest of Alpine lakes."⁶ Konevskoi's impressions, saturated with color, sound, and feeling, hint also at the mystical mood that wafted over him in these splendid surroundings.

A diary entry the following day suggests that these impressions did not fade overnight but deepened. Enchanted by beauty seen and felt, he nonetheless sensed that beneath all this there lay much more. Speculating on the mysteries concealed by surface phenomena, he employed an image suggested by Dante Gabriel Rossetti's sonnet "Memorial Thresholds." Such outward appearances were likened to an ancient structure where a seemingly firm plank may give way, and "it was suddenly as if before us there opened unknown caverns and secret passages."⁷ His expectation of — and readiness for — admission into a deeper reality clearly had reached a high point. The stunning scenes among which he had spent the last weeks, profoundly as they moved him, derived their greatest appeal from the intimations of mystical power that emanated from them.

2. Munich: the art pilgrim's shrine

Following ten memorable days in Salzburg and environs, Konevskoi's itinerary took him to Munich. In St. Petersburg (and elsewhere when the opportunity arose), at least for the past year, he had been an assiduous viewer of art exhibits. Now, like so many other Russian visitors to

Munich, he reveled in the city's galleries, exhibits, and museums. The international exhibition at the "Glaspalast" offered a huge array of attractions, including the rich Dutch and Belgian sections.[8] But best of all were the English Pre-Raphaelites. Of Burne-Jones's sequence of paintings portraying the legend of St. George and the Dragon he wrote to Ivan Bilibin: "These seven pictures with imperceptible force carry you away into the soft magical air of a half-medieval, half-oriental dense, mysterious forest, full of quiet, light, and open revelations " (*AVL*, 154).

While Konevskoi was far from insensitive to the aesthetic qualities of the paintings he saw, their interest and value for him were ultimately determined by what he termed their "mystical feeling." Among those he singled out for this quality were certain works of the Dutch artist Jan Toorop. True, some of Toorop's drawings he found repellent. However, others "reveal startling mystical feeling" (*AVL*, 154). To both Ivan Bilibin and Sergei Semenov he wrote that these drawings recalled an article he had read about a Parisian exhibit of "Art Mystique." There the French writer Henri Antoine Jules-Bois noted that some of the drawings resembled the automatic writing produced by mediums in trance. The drawings by Toorop, Konevskoi continued, appear to be "direct efforts toward embodiment by the wandering forces of the world soul that have not yet found the means to achieve this state" (162).

Several short prose pieces composed during the earlier part of his journey were devoted to descriptions of art seen in Munich, for which parts of letters to friends obviously served as drafts.[9] However, one important piece that, despite its title, fell outside this category was "Before the Paintings of Schwind (*Pered zhivopis'iu Schwinda*)" (*SP 1904*, 137-142.) The works of the early German romantic Moritz von Schwind that Konevskoi saw in Munich's Schack-Galerie provided a useful point of reference in his continuing effort to define mystical trends in contemporary art. Schwind's illustrations of legends and fairy tales, which earned fame during his lifetime, struck Konevskoi as pardonably naïve, given the time they were created. "Romanticism of the beginning of the [nineteenth] century," he exclaimed, "how childlike, how uncomplicated it seems, compared with the profound ambiguity and questioning of present day mystical art." Both generations attempt to resurrect the mystical feeling of the middle ages, but what a difference! Earlier romanticism shared the simple Christian faith of those times, almost inseparable from belief in fantastic beings. In contrast, "[c]ontemporary mysticism attempts to look more deeply into the unconscious depths of the medieval worldview." And in so doing, interestingly, it draws closer to "the most penetrating researches of contemporary science" (*SP 1904*, 137).

A year earlier, in his draft article on Maeterlinck, Konevskoi had struggled to identify the features that differentiated the "new mysticism" from its predecessors. At that time he concluded that the newer version was marked by "philosophical and psychological generalizations." Now he could distinguish other, highly significant features as well. In the article on Schwind he wrote: "A deep and dark shadow of incomprehensibility, or, at very least, doubt about the comprehensibility of being, has engulfed contemporary mysticism. In connection with the sense of incomprehensibility in contemporary mysticism there entered the leaven of pantheism" (137-138). The link made here between "pantheism" and "incomprehensibility of being" is intriguing. Its significance would become clearer as his own understanding of contemporary mysticism, the topic that so exercised him, was enriched by new experiences.

Meanwhile, passing over German and French romantics, Konevskoi turned his attention to England's five great romantic poets, and most of all to Shelley, whom he ranked as "one of the greatest and most consistent pantheists of all time" (139). Taken together, in his scheme these five form the bridge between early German romanticism and the English Pre-Raphaelites and, most recently, the new French poets. The line between the innocent, and, in some instances, shallow and self-dramatizing earlier generation and the new mystic-artists was now sharply evident. Returning to the place where his meditation began, in a gently patronizing tone he summed up his thoughts and feelings. But most importantly, he established his own position: "*We mystics of the end of the century, early grown old,* gazing at the pictures of Schwind with, as it were, painful affection, recall our childhood dreams" (*142; ital. mine*).

One more artist who figured importantly in his journey remains to be accounted for: the Swiss painter Arnold Böcklin, whose seventieth birthday occasioned a wide display of his works in Munich, the city where his career had flourished. Böcklin's acclaim came relatively late. However, Russian artists and art enthusiasts, especially modernists, had joined an international company who paid homage to Böcklin. Konevskoi's pilgrimages to Böcklin, in summer 1897 and the following year, were of major importance in his developing worldview and will be treated more fully at a later point.

Konevskoi had left Russia with a tentative plan of traveling on from Germany to join the Bilibins in Savoy. But after the exhilarating time in and around Salzburg, he began to wonder how many new impressions he could comfortably accommodate. Adding the Savoy Alps to his store now seemed a dubious undertaking. Moreover, he wrote to Sergei Semenov from Thuringia, the artistic experiences of Munich "have decisively overturned my original plan" (*AVL*, 159). Finally, an opportunity to obtain a ticket to a performance of Wagner's *Parsifal* in Bayreuth settled the matter entirely, "owing to purely economic considerations" (160).

Meanwhile, writing to Ivan Bilibin from Munich in late June, Konevskoi excitedly laid out his plans to explore the Thuringian forest. "I'll try to seek out some remote spot (insofar as that is possible in Germany) in the area of Coburg or Meiningen." His "Austrian aunt," whom he had once characterized as an eccentric individual of markedly "mystical" outlook, presumably during his stay with her, had encouraged him in this idea. His expectations drew also on his reading of German fairytales and fantastic literature. Looking ahead, he told Ivan Bilibin,

> "The whole countryside is awash with ancient German tales: here are all the elemental spirits of German nature — gnomes, elves, nixies, mixed with Christian notions of gods of the ancient world" (*AVL*, 153).

Whimsical as all this might seem, Konevskoi was deeply serious about his objective and the conditions for attaining it. Now was the time, he felt, and this was the place to establish, once and for all, the identity he believed was destined to be his: *poet-mystic-pantheist*.

3. Mystical encounters

Soon after dispatching the letter to Ivan Bilibin, Konevskoi set off by way of Nuremberg for his Thuringian destination. A letter to Semenov traced his progress, often on foot, through a region superbly suited to his mood. The environs of Schwartzburg, a village nestled in a deep, wooded ravine, at the bottom of which "gurgled the stream Schwartza," fully satisfied his designs. Writing from the spa town Ilmenau on 8 and 9 July, Konevskoi reported his latest experiences. After a day or two spent exploring the mountains and forests surrounding the Schwartza, he set out early the evening of 7 July along the road from Schwartzburg to Blankenburg. "I'm entirely in the fairytale world of medieval forests. The air is full of terrors and visions." Night had fallen when the desired moment arrived:

> I began to recite loudly some of the most prophetic poems of Tiutchev and Fet: they were like incantations that called forth from my soul inner spirits that answered to the air of night. And I sensed how I released from my soul some sort of invisible waters from behind high weirs. Can you believe that I felt terror and delight at the sounds of my own voice that issued from my breast, completely unknown, unexpected. I understood clearly that it was not I who spoke, but someone else spoke through me. This of course was something very close to a "mediumistic" condition. But at the same time I felt myself in no way the powerless slave of the being that had taken possession of me; no, that being instantly in some way merged, formed one closed circle with the whole of my conscious self. More than ever, I felt myself powerful and deliberate in my movements. Yes, never before have I experienced such an ecstatic condition (*AVL*, 163).

Perhaps the first striking feature of this account is his self-induced state of readiness. As he presumably knew quite well, such preparation is part of the mystical tradition; in fact, it is of the essence. Obviously for him this process began early in his travels — indeed, as soon as he encountered the Austrian mountains. His choice of locale was, of course, highly calculated. Similarly, he selected dusk as the most propitious time for his expedition. It was no accident that he found himself chanting "the most prophetic poems of Tiutchev and Fet." The results were much as he hoped.

At the heart of the experience lay two important discoveries. First was the awareness of a hitherto unknown entity within him, called forth by carefully selected "incantations." He was at some pains to characterize this newly-emergent "unknown," describing it as "inner spirits" that respond to "air of night" — i.e., to nature. Then, sensing this entity's force, he compared it to waters rushing from behind high weirs — waters that *he himself released*. And finally, he heard his *own voice,* as if used by someone else, speaking through him. The second discovery is foreshadowed in the first. It may equally be called a confirmation, for it gave assurance that, despite the emergence of this powerful "other", he — his conscious self — remained an active participant. The voice Konevskoi heard with such delight was his own. Indeed, this "other" merged with his conscious *self*, rendering the two "selves", as it were, a single whole.[10]

Both tone and specific details of this account make clear that Konevskoi addressed it to someone familiar with its underlying assumptions, whether or not he fully accepted them. His companion of the previous summer at Mikhailovskoe and then in the student circle, Semenov shared his interest in questions of *persona* and *consciousness*. As will be seen, later exchanges between them harked back to the central point stressed in this letter, i.e., Konevskoi's core conviction, from which he never wavered: the integrity of the *persona* must be preserved throughout any mystical encounter, and never made subject to another, stronger will.

Five evenings later Konevskoi explored another wild venue, this time a steep mountain path. Fortified by the experience of 7 July, he confidently expected new revelations. Nor was he disappointed. The young mystic — as he now knew himself to be — was drawn irresistibly to sharing "the earth's life." However, this time, as he recorded his experience, the impression of engulfing *quiet* was so overpowering as to induce terror: "And there was terror at the sense that the earth was hanging over an unseen, unheard deep" ("A New Spiritual Frontier [*Novyi dushevnyi rubezh]" SP 1904*, 151). But suddenly, as he descended deeper into the ravine, that *quiet* was filled "a disturbing hidden, troubled murmur" (151). "What is it? And what sort and what unheard beings and forces are silent at the bottom of all that earth-life? And not only are they silent, but they also act, and perhaps they rule our fates..." The fear of the unknown all but overcame him as he sensed below him "an unknowable ocean, which for man is ruinous." Still he continued downward, at every step feeling more intensely "how two kinds of existence moved toward one another, infinitely distant in essence from each other." At last he could go no further: "And I felt that, if I were to stir or move the least bit forward, or back, or to one side — I would discover the force of that quiet abyss" (152).

Not without reason, then, Konevskoi entitled this account "A New Spiritual Frontier." Although written as a sequel to the account of his first mystical experience, it is less conclusive and more disturbing than the previous one. Perhaps the most notable difference between the two experiences and the narratives describing them lies in their differing emphases. Central to the first is the manifestation, in all its vivid reality, of another self within. In the second, it is his contact with a deeper mystery: the hidden life of the universe that both beckoned and repelled, leaving him transfixed on the brink of still further discoveries.

Another piece, presumably also written during Konevskoi's wanderings in the Thuringian forest, is undated. ("Shame before Mother Earth *[Styd pered mater'iu zemlei])" MD* 114-117)[11] The locale is similar, but is approached from a different, earthier point of view. This prose sketch is notable, if only because it reflects a side of Konevskoi not so far represented. It begins again with a steep descent toward a stream that runs far below. However, this descent occurs, not at dusk, as on the other occasions, but in broad daylight, thus allowing full scope to his powers of observation. At first the focus is on visual detail: "In the ravines are monstrous hollows and caves. Their sides are overgrown by ancient dark-green moss, ferns and some kind of delicate grasses, like clumps of hair" (114). Sunlight, when perceptible at all, penetrates into the dense foliage as if through stained glass in a Gothic cathedral. After this nod toward Christian motives, another theme takes over. Initially perceived as being "like a cool underground chapel," the ravine is now a damp wilderness where

> [i]n some places giantic roots have eaten into the steep thighs of the ravines. Yes, and here snuggle and hide the dark brown children of earth's bowels — plodding and diligent laborers — long-bearded gnomes, goblins, dactyls, corybantes — these priests of the loins of the vast monstrous mother — Cybele (*MD* 114-115).

As the explorer goes deeper into this wild, mysterious place, the imagery changes. The dominant metaphor is now an erotic one, with the great earth-mother Cybele as the central figure. The "steep thighs of ravines" that surround his descent are densely covered, as we have seen, with dark moss, fern, and grass "like clumps of hair." This humid concavity is redolent of the presence of the "loins of the vast monstrous mother" — at once seductive and terrifying.

Epithets that punctuate these passages — "monstrous, hideous" — express the speaker's mixed awe and repulsion. So likewise does the image of Cybele that emerges. This is hardly the figure created by a Greek sculptor for the goddess's temple in Athens or the deity to whom Pindar built a temple in Thebes.[12] This "mother" is a barely personified entity, scarcely distinguishable from the raw material of nature. Konevskoi's horrified fascination before this elemental near-nothingness finds expression in the word "*hyle*" the "prime matter" of the ancients. The earth-mother's sole personifying features are "loins and thighs." Yet she inspires terror and wonder: "O, what terrifying wild nooks with hideous disfigurements hide in the twists of the innermost parts of this dark, rude divinity..."(115). Contemplating this divinity, he senses himself approaching the very borderline between being and non-being.

From this point, the meditation takes a turn foretold in the title: *why does man feel discomfort before exposure of the sexual origins of life?*

> Is this not why man is ashamed of the details of the act by which he is born on earth, — that these details remind him, shapely creature that he

is, encased in well-marked forms, of those dark elements that he has called unclean, — because there is no uniform surface, but they are made up of all sorts of elements, *soiling* one another? Yes, and the human *persona* is ashamed of that crude — senseless in his view — decay that burdens every creature afresh with necessary rot (*MD* 115).

The presumption that shame necessarily attaches to the details of the "act by which he is born on earth" has too long a history in Western culture to be remarkable. However, the reasons Konevskoi adduces have more to do with Darwin than with the Book of Genesis. Obviously, the experience he has just undergone, of consorting with nature *en déshabillé*, so to speak, has shaken him profoundly. In those teeming depths he has come face to face with facts he prefers to ignore, facts that remind him of his own origins and their closeness to the inchoate beginnings of all living things.[13] Now he faces the fact that continuation of the human race depends on a specific case of those same burdensome conditions, namely male-female sexual relations: "Man knows that love, attaining the goal of its desire, creates out of itself and another its beloved offspring, and for that, love is condemned to *ruin, debauch* itself and another " (*emphasis IK;* 115).

This revelation of the fatal consequences of Eros is implicitly linked to Konevskoi's on-going ambivalence about the body, with all its vulnerability and intractability. More specifically, it confirms his greatest fear about the body's inevitable decay.[14] The saving difference between life and death, he insists, is that in life movement and change occur around a stable core that can withstand assault and retain its integrity. Death, presumably, is quite the opposite, i.e., it involves total and final disintegration. Once more the argument has come around to the ultimate threat of death: destruction of the *persona*.

Konevskoi's poetic output during the seven weeks he spent in Austria and Germany at first glance resembles a series of travel postcards sent to family and close friends. A few were written in the early, Austrian phase of his journey and, as noted, were enclosed in letters. Several were written during his Thuringian sojourn. Descriptive, meditative, full of wonder, they harmonize, not surprisingly, in mood and theme with the essays written during this time. On 12 July he explored the Inselsberg, the highest peak of the Thuringian forest, and composed lyrics inspired by that superb landscape. Two days later, on 14 July, Konevskoi was in Eisenach, which Baedeker's 1893 English edition called "the finest point in the Thuringian Forest" (Baedeker, *Northern Germany,* 351). Here he paused to write "The Sultry Hour (*Dushnyi chas*)" (and possibly also "Shame before Mother Earth"). This lyric's mystery is uncouched in philosophical meditation; it is about "[t]he smell of flesh in ferment." (*SP 2008,* 92) The heavy, languorous heat of noonday permeates this forested spot, where nature at noonday may force man to confront the fact that decay, change, loss — in a word, death — are necessary elements in the cycle of human existence. But it also allows him to savor one sensuous, pungent moment without any accompanying analytical *thought.*

4. Back to Russia

After his walking trip through Thuringia, Konevskoi visited Bayreuth in order to experience Wagner in the proper setting. Less than a week later, he was on his way back to Russia. With him he carried a bundle of varied experiences — artistic, mystical, but also geographical and cultural; all of these included an element of self-discovery. Setting out seven weeks earlier to explore a world known to him only fragmentarily and secondhand, he expected to find answers to some problems but doubtless to discover others. One of the latter was the question of his identity, a question that was to occupy him in various ways for some time to come. Every Russian traveler carried some awareness of the basic historical, cultural, and psychological divide between Russia and the West — an awareness sharpened and made concrete by first impressions en route. While he showed interest in the more usual travel encounters, the evidence suggests that most of Konevskoi's attention was absorbed by Western art, by Alpine scenery, and by the inner experiences induced by both. Overall, the mood was one of excitement and heightened attentiveness to the newness and variety of what he saw and felt.

By contrast, on the return trip, as he approached the Russian frontier, he was oppressed by the unrelenting monotony, topographical and psychological. After the weeks spent among craggy peaks and medieval German architecture, Russia presented no contrast, no relief, in terrain or, as he found upon reflection, in the Russian spiritual "profile." A lyric written, as he noted, 21 July "beyond Koenigsberg, on the road to the Russian border," eloquently voiced his mood.[15] Viewed from the west, Russia's border represented to him the fatal line that divided Proserpine's dual existence, divided between the blooming earth and the underworld. And he, this "unfortunate son of the swamps," while losing the sun, is fated also to lose his gift of song, or so he fears. The coming months stretch ahead like a barren waste, as he greets his sad homeland: "mute, joyless land!"

After less than a month at home in St. Petersburg, Konevskoi again boarded a train, this time for Kiev.[16] Enroute he saw around him a profoundly middle Russian river-and-steppe landscape, unlike either the mountains and forests he had seen abroad, or the northern Russian setting to which he was accustomed. The resulting sketch, "Elements of Two Peoples'" (3 Sept. 1897 Kiev) was a preliminary effort to analyze the contrasts between "Russian Slavdom" and all that "Germany" now represented to him in culture and spirituality.[17]

To begin with, after his recent exposure to the latter, Russia and the Russian spirit seemed to him unbearably simple. The Russian worldview did not include awareness of an individual self, or of any distinction between "self" and "other." It lived in unconscious belief in all-embracing "oneness." On the other hand, in German thinking there was "self-awareness of the *persona*," along with numerous other subtleties. (*SP 1904*, 156) The Russian Orthodox faith possesses a beauty and simplicity that, while easily seen as idyllic, can scarcely be called mystical. In his present view, then, Russian spirituality must be regarded chiefly with affection and gentle condescension.[18]

Perhaps it was Konevskoi's pride that prevented him from leaving the matter there. He had gone to Europe hoping to learn more about the mysticism manifested in the visionary elements of some contemporary European artists' work. Returning to Russia he was at first unable to discern any native mystical bent in the Russian nature. After a fairly tentative attempt in his essay to deal with elements of national character (language ranks high), he turned toward the future. If, in the past, Russian Slavdom and the Orthodox faith seemed to offer a simple, unreflective worldview, the future could well be different. Indeed, the seeds were already in the ground and a few shoots were visible. Here he referred to the prophetic vision of the great creator of the Karamazovs, Fedor Dostoevskii.

Surely Konevskoi was aware that, in attempting to identify the Russian spirit's distinctive features, he was venturing into a vast and many-faceted debate. Nonetheless, he was not to be deterred. Already in his study "Lyric Poetry in Contemporary Russia," he set out lofty standards for the future of Russian lyric poetry, where the indispensable feature is a genuinely mystical worldview. Now, rather than conceding that, for the foreseeable future, such inspiration must come from the West, he turned his attention to mining Russia's heritage, largely outside of formal religion, for mystical riches he strongly suspected to exist there. Over the next few years much of his most intriguing poetry draws on this theme.

5. "A Wild Place"

If titles alone are counted, Konevskoi's poetic output in fall 1897 was extremely meager (i.e., one). However, that one, the poem "A Wild Place (*Debri*)," was his longest and most ambitious so far (*SP 2008*, 106-110). Dated winter 1897-1898, "A Wild Place" is surely linked to his meditations that autumn, after the return to Russia.[19] If he wondered whether his mystical capabilities had remained behind in Thuringia, "A Wild Place" was a step in a reassuring direction. However, the "revelations" here were of another sort from those recently experienced, drawing, as they did, on *Russian* nature and folklore, with their — at least for a Russian — rather homey familiarity. But Russia also contains darker mysteries lying in its spiritual depths that Konevskoi hoped to plumb.

A common feature of Konevskoi's nature poems is his method of using descriptive detail to anchor the poem, less in its physical setting than in its spiritual one. "A Wild Place" provides an excellent example. The first, eight-line stanza, with its description of the wide open steppe, windswept, its surface all in clear view, stands in strong contrast to the rest of the poem; the purpose is to establish immediately that the speaker is a spiritual denizen of the latter. Lexicon, line, rhyme scheme and other elements all support this goal. The first stanza consists of one sentence of the simplest grammatical construction, each line before the last ending with a comma. Vocabulary here is carefully confined to the standard lexicon. The impression of flat monotony thus created is reinforced by the iambic tetrameter with masculine endings and the rhyme scheme (*abab*), as well.

However, beginning with the second stanza, the impression of two-dimensionality is cancelled by new imagery and new linguistic features, which set the scene for what lies ahead. In the dense oak groves, murmurs and rustling heard by the hero in semidarkness — the lines are full of sibilants — promise mysteries to come. Many words are marked as archaic or as belonging to traditional poetic vocabulary. Meter and rhyme scheme remain constant throughout the poem with few deviations, but their effect is altered at will, as the plot dictates.

The storyline here is of a type found in world literature from epic and fairy tale to modern adventure and narrative of experience: it conveys a call to test or ordeal, followed by revelation and transformation. Deep in the heart of his beloved forest, the young hero of "A Wild Place" is led to a magical crossroad. There commences a fairy tale, replete with the magical signs, events, and characters typical of traditional Slavic midsummer night's highjinks. But when the mysterious light fades, and the glade is empty and still, the hero waits for admission to a deeper mystery: "My spirit is ready!"

In the short concluding section, forest and stream no longer serve as playground of fireflies and watersprites. Instead, nature begins to reveal her truly mystical facets. The telling sign, as in Thuringia, is water — the sound of flowing water, calling the searcher to look deeper. And, as on that first occasion, an inward response is evoked: the stream of cold water flows into the young searcher's inner self from a source deep in nature itself.

The poem's last lines, standing apart at the very end, hint cryptically at further explorations. "Deathless Koshchei still lives": in Russian folklore, the wicked Koshchei possesses the secret of unending life. Countless tales tell of challenges to his secret and to his very existence, mounted by "Ivan Tsarevich — the Tsar's Son." Always victorious, Ivan wins, with the aid of animals, birds, and occasionally humans whom he has befriended during his quest. Many episodes end with Koshchei falling dead.[20] Here, though, "Koshchei" remains "deathless," as do "[the poet's] ancestors." By implication, then, the struggle continues: the presentday Ivan continues his quest to snatch Koshchei's secret from him: the secret of endless life. Presentday Ivan's journey of personal discovery seems ready to follow the sign pointing to the depths of Russian history and legend.

6. *"A Varangian from beyond the blue sea"*

In his essay "Elements of Two Peoples" Konevskoi foresaw the possibility of a future Russia whose mindset would be diametrically opposite to the presently prevailing oblivious serenity. In support of this prediction, he adduced evidence of contrary strains, present and past, in the Russian character. Where did these strains originate? Or were they dormant in the Slavic character from time immemorial? Beginning from medieval Rus', he introduced the wily shape-changing prince Vol'ga Sviatoslavich, who, popular in the epic folk tales called *byliny*, nearly always won out over his plodding earthbound opponents.

Two poems written in spring 1898 offer the first sightings of the Varangian (Norse) motif that would become central to Konevskoi's thinking and creative work, including some of his most striking poetry from 1898 and 1900. The first of these poems, "From Konevets (*S Konevtsa*)," takes a form close to the dramatic monologue of romantic poetry, with the central figure addressing an audience of one or more, often with gestures or movements.[21] Here the opening stanza sets up a productive tension between isolation and engagement: the speaker (outsider, observer, perhaps scout) and the alien land that has captured his imagination. Announcing himself as "a Varangian from beyond the blue sea," the speaker proceeds to describe the panorama before him.[22] The lake below, Ladoga, this "marvel," remains gray and unfathomable, while battles are waged near it and a young nation spreads out beyond.

However, it is the language that entrances him. Surveying the vast prospect from his high perch on the island of Konevets, he is moved to compose a veritable paean to the Russian tongue. This language, "great and abundant," corresponds in rhythm and contour with the broad rich land on which he gazes. The cadence of the first four stanzas is flowing, lyrical, with full stops occurring only at the end of the final line of each. The final stanza is a tableau: this grim Varangian, as he calls himself, clinging fiercely to the rough trunk of an island pine, is transfixed by the vision of the future that lies before him.

When "From Konevets" appeared in 1899 in *Book of Reflections (Kniga razdumii)*, the collection organized by Konstantin Bal'mont, an epigraph was used with it: "Concentrated, I live in myself alone."[23] Though later abandoned, the epigraph nonetheless was well chosen, in that it pointed to this lyric's significance in Konevskoi's ongoing construction of his identity. The choice of "Konevskoi" as his pen name was formalized, with some indecision, sometime during the summer of 1899, when *Dreams and Meditations* was in the later stages of preparation. In a letter to Briusov of 23 June, he used "Konevskoi" in the title. *(LN 98:1:464)* Yet, to Aleksandr Bilibin on 2 July he wrote that the author's "name" would be "Ezerskii".[24] However, the name jotted near the head of a notebook begun the previous December suggests that his attraction to "Konevskoi" began earlier.[25] And Konevskoi it was to be.

"Konevskoi" referred to the island Konevets (Finnish Konivets, Kononsaari), near the western shore of Lake Ladoga, which, in the late nineteenth century, had a direct steamboat connection with St. Petersburg. Very likely Konevskoi visited it in his boyhood more than once, since he often spent time with relatives in the nearby Vyborg district, to which the island belonged. The island's history, like that of the entire region, was a turbulent one, where Swedes and Russians battled, with now one, now the other, prevailing. The monastery, founded by the Novgorod monk Arsenii in the fourteenth century, was rebuilt numerous times.[26] But the Varangian of Konevskoi's poem seemingly was of a different mindset from his more violent fellows. "Grim Varangian" though he called himself, nonetheless he came, not to ravage the land but to explore it, and to master the linguistic treasure he admired. With this latter, surely, he might gain access to its spiritual and material abundance.

Language, especially Russian, viewed from multiple perspectives, was one of Konevskoi's closely held and truly sustaining values. Some two years later, in a letter to Aleksandr Bilibin, he stated forcefully what to him was the absolutely central role of language in defining a so-called "people": "The only thing that unites individuals constituting one people is language [...]. All other features of peoples are either fluid or transitory, or merely political divisions" *(AVL,* 182). He prided himself on being "a man who, by the blood of his ancestors, is in all respects international, or more precisely, multinational, with an absolutely equal division between Germanic and Slavic bloods. Nonetheless, in respect to native language, I am totally Great Russian."

The second "Varangian" poem, "From Generation to Generation (*V rody i rody: I*)," written in spring 1898, in effect portrays the next generation of adventurers, descendants of the Varangians who, as legend holds, were invited to rule over Rus'. (*SP 2008,* 96-97.) These free spirits, following wherever their destiny took them, swept over the steppe with the same fierce vigor as their kinsmen roamed the seas. The manuscript bore an epigraph from Emile Verhaeren: "Mon coeur, où le héros…?" Konevskoi, inspired by nostalgia for times past, at the same time lovingly traces that past's transformation into legend. "Where are you, eagle-eyed generations," the poem begins, who "swept across the steppe in flames like devils?" Their warrior spirit does not fail but is etherealized, as their fate lifts them to another realm, the "city of gold and glass," the realm of popular legend.

"From Generation to Generation" ends as it began, with a question, and essentially the same one: "Mon coeur, où le héros…?" But, whereas, in the first instance, the note of nostalgia seems to dominate, the ending is tinged with wonder and mystery, and open to further meanings. For Konevskoi, the Varangians were symbols of prized values and characteristics that early entered into the Russian bloodstream. Ancient Russia — Rus' — stood for the heroic genius that Konevskoi believed to be inherent in the essential Russian spirit — the spirit that he sought to define and, perhaps, ultimately to make his own.

7. The Literary-Intellectual Circle, 1897-1898

Meanwhile, the "Literary-Intellectual Circle" continued to figure importantly in Konevskoi's activities during his second year at the university. His notebook shows him offering two topics during the autumn term and one in the spring.[27] His presentation on 29 September 1897, entitled "A Page from Summer Impressions: Arnold Böcklin, a Lyrical Sketch about his Painting," was possibly an enlargement of enthusiastic remarks in his letters to Ivan Bilibin and S. P. Semenov. No doubt his talk was illustrated by the reproduction of "Im Spiel der Wellen" that he brought back from Munich (AVL, 155, 162). Presumably it was an early draft of the essay "Böcklin's Paintings. (A Lyrical Characterization)," completed the following June, during his second Böcklin pilgrimage.[28] This essay will be discussed in that context.

His second presentation, which extended over two meetings, bore the title "Contemporary French Lyric Poetry." On 9 November the topic was the poetry of Jules Laforgue, and on 18 November, of Émile Verhaeren.[29] Konevskoi's interest in contemporary French poetry began early. At the end of 1896 he was reading intensively in recent collections by Viélé-Griffin and others; at the beginning of 1897, he read *Poésies complètes* of Laforgue, *Poèmes* of Verhaeren, collections by Henri de Régnier, and more Verhaeren.[30] Laforgue's attraction for Konevskoi may have rested to some extent on sympathy for a poet whose gifts had no time to develop all their promise. One is reminded of the symbolic significance for some Russian critics of such figures as Garshin and Nadson (and later, of course, Konevskoi himself), whom they saw as early sacrificial victims in the coming process of change. Konevskoi characterized Laforgue as "a single fleeting guest, swiftly passing through French letters" (177).

8. Kant's tyranny: The battle over time and space

Konevskoi's third and final presentation for the year in the circle, delivered on 20 March, showed his continued immersion in metaphysical questions. A collaborative effort, undertaken with his fellow student Iakov Erlikh, it bore the title: "The dogma of multiple conditions of consciousness as the chief foundation of the critical theory of cognition."[31] No text is extant. Erlikh, philosopher and musician, was the center of another circle frequented by Konevskoi. N. L. Stepanov wrote: "In Erlikh's circle, philosophical, ethical, and aesthetic questions held first place. The circle had a clearly expressed idealistic and mystical character, with a bias toward pantheism. Spinoza and Leibniz, Schelling and Hegel, Vl. Solov'ev and Paulsen were the most actively discussed names in that circle" (*LN* 92:4:184).[32]

It was probably no coincidence that, at just this time, Konevskoi was laboring over an ambitiously conceived — but never finished — work to which he assigned the weighty title: "The Cornerstones of my Worldview (I-NotI. Finity: Space, Time.)"[33] Dated "February-March-April 1898," this effort clearly heralded the approach of an intellectual and spiritual crisis that had been brewing for several years. The schoolboy who wrote in an early poem ("Fragment") of his desire to "embrace the whole world with my mind in a single instant" found poetic language sufficient at that stage to express his eager impatience. However, three years later, that youthful urgency has transformed itself into something far more knowledgeable and assured, but tinged with desperation.

By the middle of his second year at the university, many factors — lectures on philosophy by the neo-Kantian professor Vvedenskii and his colleagues, voluminous reading, discussions with associates, above all, intensive inner mental activity — brought Konevskoi to a critical point. Often before, he had written down accumulated thoughts to see where they led. Now he probed and tested ideas and theories absorbed, first of all, from Kant, in pressing need to find an answer to the crucial question: could a world view based on Kant's principles support the goals he had set himself? *If not, where was he to turn?*

Konevskoi's starting point obviously was Kant's view of the human subject and its relation to the outside world as set forth in his *Critique of Pure Reason*. Kant saw human perceptions as formed through *a priori* intuitions of time and space. Present from the first instant of existence, this equipment allows man progressively to decode the world outside him. At the same time, it precludes his penetrating further, to the *Ding an sich*, the thing-in-itself, or, viewed otherwise, the All-One. This intellectual barrier had become the object of Konevskoi's resentment and rebellion.

Predictably, then, the central issue of "Cornerstones..." concerned the battle between the *persona* and the limiting effects of the intuitions of time and space. This is the subject of the first and longest of the four sections. But behind Konevskoi's primary question lay another: was there not some way to overcome these limitations on the human spirit, some way to remove the boundary between the individual and the All-One *without losing the self's identity*? One may ask if he seriously hoped to find such a path. The answer is: he did. Moreover, an important loophole presented itself in Kant's own exposition: "As to the intuitions *of other thinking beings,* we cannot judge whether they are or are not bound by the same conditions which limit our own intuition, and which are *for us* universally valid" (*ital. mine*).[34]

Konevskoi pounced upon this remark. "I accept Kant's notion *about the mere formal reality* of space and time, and their common category — causality for individual perception" (*ital. mine*). It follows then, that, since we do not know that other types of thinking beings are similarly restricted, there may be a way around these hindrances for us, too, while still maintaining Kant's basic premises. He set out to find this way.

An essential step to this end was to establish the integrity and continuity of the *persona*, whatever changes may occur. It must be shown that, from his first moments, an infant possesses rudimentary awareness of himself as separate from things around him. If so, not only the *I/not I* barrier, but consequently the *persona*, too, is shown to be present from life's very beginning. Throughout his arguments Konevskoi was careful to show that the findings of contemporary science in no way contradicted Kant. In this particular matter he found support from William James, with whose *Principles of Psychology* (in abridged form) he had become acquainted more than a year earlier: "I totally adhere to the view of the psychologist James, that, with its very first sensation, the infant already senses (though is far from being conscious of it — a big difference!) a borderline or marker between 'I' and 'not I.'"[35]

Another and important facet of his mode of thinking then appeared: a series of counter-factual proposals showed him ready to follow entirely new avenues of investigation. What if the "time-space" limitation did not exist, or could in some way be neutralized? Or what if the very mode of perception might be changed? I.e., suppose the "apparent organs of perception" are removed from the equation, but not the inner self, "not 'I,' not its will to exist, and not consciousness and not thought outside of time." What would remain? "That same consciousness and will: in general — *the nature that acts in prophetic dreams, in visions, in apparition and speech at great distance*" (ital. mine).[36] In other words, the essential "I".

Among the notable figures whom Konevskoi invoked, along with James, to support his arguments were Wilhelm Wundt, Gustav Fechner, Helmholtz, and others, but not Karl Du Prel. Nonetheless, Du Prel's influence was strongly present in his thinking now, as it had been earlier. In fact, his records show him at the beginning of 1898 reading both William James's *Psychology* (in Russian) and Du Prel's *Die Philosophie der Mystik* (read between 21 January and 1 February).[37] The coincidence (if it was one) was well-timed.

The larger part of Du Prel's two-volume work is devoted to the topic of dream and somnambulism in relation to the duality of human consciousness. Many psychic phenomena were already being studied widely in Europe and the United States, and Du Prel made use of contemporary research to establish his own position. Stressing the close links of the dual consciousness to his primary topic, Du Prel wrote in his preface: "If man is being dualised by a threshold of sensibility, then mysticism is possible; and if, furthermore, this threshold of sensibility is a movable one, then is mysticism even necessary" (1:xxv).

Wholeheartedly as Konevskoi sympathized with much of Du Prel's thinking, he chose in the present context to leave the latter's contribution anonymous. Nonetheless, he could not resist mentioning certain examples from the chapter "Dream as Physician" (related there secondhand), where "people in the condition of prophetic dream recall or, more precisely, relive their ordinary waking life." And, if they should be ill, they can diagnose the illness and prescribe the remedy. More than that, "they see clearly the road to the pharmacy, [...] or even to the field or wood where the grasses grow" that yield the necessary healing juices. Remarkable as such cases were, Konevskoi obviously found more significant the condition at which they pointed: "*life outside of time* (at which the manifestations of sleep-life hint) and *life outside space* (which certain conditions of people gifted with mediumistic abilities allow them to experience)" (*ital. mine*). For a moment he exulted in the very possibility:

> In fact, experiencing everything outside of time, i.e., not sequentially but all at once, and outside of space, i.e., without differentiation of 'I' from 'not I', we will already have no cause to fear the restraints of some infinitely more powerful force that deceived us about the dividing line between 'I' and 'not I' and all the notions linked to it.

However, misgivings remained. "The most magical signs of conquest of space — the union of 'I' and 'not I', — is given, of course, in the revelations of Indian magicians." But these mediumistic and somnambulistic phenomena, even if more widely available, nonetheless "do not yet constitute destruction of the barrier between 'I' and 'other'."[38]

In the study's second part, headed "Infinity," Konevskoi turned to another topic, or so it seemed initially. However, before long, the problem of "I/not I" and its accompanying conditions, time and space, emerged once more. Was it possible to conceive a situation in which the "I" might stand, free of these limits, in an independent, ongoing relationship with universal Being? He is forced reluctantly to admit, intimate communication with other beings or with nature offered no guarantee of such relationship.

At this point his underlying anxiety burst to the surface. He now found himself constrained to question the meaning of his mystical experiences of the previous summer. He had hitherto perceived the intimate contact with nature that he felt on those July evenings in Thuringia as the first step in the ambitious journey toward his long-standing goal, "[…] comprehending the World Soul and the meaning of our existence, penetrating by direct sense the secret essence of things so as to receive luminous revelations about the structure and meaning of our nature..." (*LN* 92:4:182). He was now forced to a painful conclusion:

If I should begin to feel in everything I encounter in the world a single life, a single force, that same which pulses in me — I would still not move one inch, if I wished to feel myself, let us say, *merely* that lifestream that courses through the whole world structure — that is simultaneously in the flowerlet, and the she-wolf, and in me, and to be no longer that person confined within these four walls. That is, whatever ecstasies I experience in the face of nature and man — [*the handwriting here changes, now resembling ancient script*] **ecstasies that evoke in me the sense of the tremor of universal life — before me obviously there will always remain something that, even if I should participate in the life of that universal Being, will bar for me the road to that Being, will show itself forever victorious over my powers. That is the force of space and time, constituting the defining property of my 'I' and the fractured state of my perception. The superior law weighing us down is this: the 'I' is inseparable from the 'not I.' Perhaps the force of that law in not omnipotent, but, in any case, no force at our disposal can do away with it.**[39] [*Konevskoi's usual handwriting resumes.*]

There is no escape. After this bitter admission, "Cornerstones …" has two more sections, headed *"Body" and "soul" — "mechanism" and "consciousness"* and (*Life and death*). But, less than one page and two pages respectively, they add little to his effort to overcome these seemingly invincible limitations that so afflicted his sense of his own selfhood.

Sometime in April Konevskoi laid aside this work, never to resume it. By the end of May, he was on a ship crossing the North Sea, where new discoveries lay just over the horizon.

Notes

1. *RGALI*, 259.1.18.5ob.
2. 259.1.18.8ob.
3. 259.1.18.14.
4. Line 23.
5. 259.3.18.
6. *Baedeker's Austria-Hungary*, Leipzig, 1911, p. 162.
7. 259.1.18, 25ob-26ob.
8. The Glaspalast, designed for the German industrial exhibition of 1854, was subsequently used for all important art exhibitions mounted in Germany, until Berlin built a similar structure in 1886. (Maria Makela. *The Munich Secession. Art and Artists in Turn-of-the-century Munich.* Princeton, N.J.: Princeton University Press, 1987, pp. 5-9).
9. "Contemporary Dutch Painting" and others. *Dreams and Meditations (MD)*, 99-105.
10. This account, slightly altered, appeared first in *MD*, 110-112, then in *SP 1904*, 148-150, under the title "A Hair Away from Another Life Within." Konevskoi's footnote to the title on the first page almost certainly was written well after the actual experience. It reads: "We use that expression [*zadushevnyi*] in the sense in which it is understood by Vl. S. Solov'ev, to mean the manifestation of another consciousness belonging to the human *persona*. That consciousness appears involuntarily in all cases of hypnotism and sonambulistic trance; it is deliberately induced in the mystery ritual of many ethnic religious rites that suspend certain conditions of normal time and space in perception." This note underlines the continued importance to Konevskoi's thinking of somnambulism, mediumism, and, specifically, of Baron Du Prel's theories about a "second self." The reference to "mystery ritual of many ethnic religious rites" points to an interest that developed later, which will be discussed below.
11. "Shame before Mother Earth," was not included in *Poems and Prose (SP 1904)*.
12. *Br-Efron* 39:41. Spb 1895.
13. Just here he finds another instance of man's unfreedom. The burden imposed by body on spirit is a frequent subject of lament by Konevskoi. See "Genius," 10 June 1899. *SP 2008*, 138.

[14] So far nothing in Konevskoi's biography gives a clear indication of his personal attitude and feelings in sexual matters. However, based on what we know, it seems safe to surmise that these were uneasy, perhaps confused, and tinged with fear. His relationship with Anna Nikolaevna Gippius a year and a half away will answer some, but not all, of these questions.

[15] *SP 2008*, 188.

[16] "Journey to the Ukraine" (presumably to visit his friend Aleksei Veselov). *RGALI* 259.1.6, ll.41ob-42. During the journey from St. Petersburg on 17-18 August he finished reading the first and began the second volume of Schopenhauer's *Die Welt als Wille und Vorstellung*. On the return trip he finished the second.

[17] *SP 1904*, 153-159. A second composition, "The Vladimir cathedral in Kiev" (*n.d.*), a brief descriptive piece, appeared in *Dreams and Meditations* only. (Pp. 123-126.)

[18] These remarks about Russian Orthodoxy and the tone in which they are made reveal the extent to which, especially after his trip west and his deepened exposure to certain modern trends in European art and thought, the meaning of such terms as "mystery" and "mysticism" had been modified in his thinking.

[19] "A Wild Place,"(1897/98 Peterburg). *SP 2008*, 106-110. As epigraph he selected two quatrains from "Les (*Forest*)," one of the poet Kol'tsov's "Dumy", *PSS, SPb.* 1911, 122-123. Konevskoi later made Kol'tsov the subject of an extended essay, to be discussed in a later chapter.

[20] This migratory tale appears in three versions in: A. N. Afanas'ev, *Russkie narodnye skazki*. (5 vols. Ed. A. E. Gruzinskii, 4th ed., Moscow: I. D. Sytin, 1914) vol. 2. pp.165-188. Many variants exist, as this edition's commentary indicates.

[21] *SP 2008*, 94-95. The primary modern practitioner of the dramatic monologue was, of course, Robert Browning, of whose poetry Konevskoi was an admirer.

[22] It might be noted that, according to the legendary account of the founding of the Russian state, a party of Varangians, led by Riurik and his brothers Sineus and Truvor, came to settle the northern Slavic lands at the invitation of Slavs who famously informed them, "Our whole land is great and rich, but there is no order in it. Come to rule and reign over us." Given Konevskoi's fascination with these Norse founders (he claimed to be descended from Sineus), it

is easy to imagine a rather whimsical scenario in which this particular "Varangian" played the role of scout for other Varangians to follow. However, that Varangian's attraction to the language almost to the exclusion of all else would have made him less useful as advance observer.

23 The other contributors to *Book of Meditations*, besides Bal'mont, were Valerii Briusov and the artist Modest Durnov.

24 To borrow the name of the protagonist of Pushkin's unfinished polemical *poema* "Ezerskii" would suggest a character and fate very different from those that became attached to "Konevskoi." Whatever thematic inspiration Konevskoi drew from Pushkin's work emerged later in his own unfinished poema "The Milieu [*Sreda*]" (*SP 2008*, 162-163.)

25 *RGALI* 259.1.6, notebook No. 4. The article on the monastery in Brokgauz-Efron called it "Konevskii or Konevetskii". (Br.-Efr. 30:946.) V. Ia. Morderer has reported that the name "Konevetskii" occurs "in a make-believe encyclopedia (1893), which he compiled and dedicated to the history of an imaginary country Rosamuntiia". *RGALI* 259.1.3. 54(ob)". *LN* 92:4:177. n.56.

26 Brokgauz-Efron relates: "Near the hermitage is the 'Horse-Stone,' an immense slab of granite; here, according to tradition, before the arrival of Arsenii, a horse was offered to the spirits to secure their good will" (vol. 30. S. Petersburg, 1895: 946).

27 *RGALI* 259.1.6.35.

28 "Zhivopis' Beklina (Liricheskaia kharakteristika)," *SP 1904*, 160-169.

29 "Leading the Protest of the New Poetic Movements (Laforgue's Poetry)" (*SP 1904*, 170-189). A larger work, in which these two were obviously to be included, was never completed. Indeed, only "Laforgue's Poetry" was published, and that posthumously, under the above title. Both are mentioned in correspondence with Briusov in 1898 and 1899. However, by summer 1899, Konevskoi was more interested in translating Verhaeren. No more is heard about the Laforgue study until 2 October 1900, when he offered it to Briusov for the almanach *Northern Flowers*. Though apparently accepted, it was published only in 1904, in *Poems and Prose*. Considerable evidence exists to show that Briusov's later interest in Verhaeren, which led to extensive translations and even a personal relationship with the poet, stemmed from Konevskoi's enthusiasm. (*LN* 1:98: 511, 514, 519, 525.)

30 *RGALI* 259.1.6.27ob-29.

31 259.1.6.48ob.

32 For more on Erlikh, see also 98:1:459n.2 and 539. Friedrich Paulsen (1846-1908), German panpsychist, professor at the University of Berlin, biographer of Kant. His *Einleitung in die Philosophie* (1892) was translated into several languages during the 1890s, including Russian.

33 *RGALI* 259.3.9. "Kraeugol'nye kamni moego mirovozreniia."

34 Emmanuel Kant, "Transcendental Doctrine of Elements," *CPR, Sec. I, 4*.

35 *RGALI* 259.3.9.20ob, note xx.

36 Page 15ob.

37 259.1.6.53. Since Konevskoi became acquainted with both works earlier, these notebook entries probably indicate an intensive re-reading. *Psikhologiia (Text Book of Psychology)* was the Russian translation of James's abridged version of his *The Principles of Psychology*, made in 1895 by I. Lapshin, a lecturer in philosophy at St. Petersburg University and used during Konevskoi's first year at the University.

38 Page 16ob.

39 Pp.17ob.-18.

Chapter 3

A Love Affair with the World's Waters

1. "At Sea"

The end of May 1898 marked the close of Konevskoi's second year at the university, a time of strenuous intellectual effort and relatively modest poetic output (with two important exceptions to be discussed below). After what might be called the fiasco of his effort to establish "The Cornerstones of My Worldview," he was eager to get away. The end of the spring term (and another cash gift from his "Austrian aunt") made it possible to refresh his spirit by once again heading westward, this time by sea.

On 31 May, he was crossing the Baltic on the steamship "Elbe." The lyric "At Sea (*V more*)", which he composed on this first sea voyage, was a chant of freedom, an exultant cry of liberation from bonds that had become intolerable.[1] With one grand verbal gesture, he cast overboard the baggage of secondhand images and ideas absorbed in the half-light of what he calls "domestic captivity." A chant of freedom, this is, moreover, a declaration of love for water and wind that, from then on, became his life-sustaining elements.

The exhilaration in these lines is unmistakable. Gripped by a totally new physical and emotional experience, he seemed to have abandoned his previous mode of dealing with the world and now looked toward a completely new horizon. His earlier delight in study and close philosophical reasoning was dimmed for now by exhaustion and frustration, to be replaced by direct apprehension of the external world in all its splendor.

Among the "joys of life" once enumerated for his friend Aleksei Veselov, "creative work" had received relatively little attention of late. Now he was ready to repay that debt with interest. Once before, in the early lyric "Resurrection," he had hailed a joyful new beginning: "Heaven, earth... What marvelous sounds!" Now, in "At Sea," he turned to a similar task with equal zest and more finished skill. The long hexameter line strengthens the impression of wave motion, and the dense consonant structure slows the lines. The thick, hushing *zh, sh, shch,* etc., and the explosive *p* and *b* suggest a spirit struggling to escape. The emotional momentum carries over to the next stanza, where it rises to a climax with the triumphant shout "the sea!" For the time being, at least, the strenuous mental exercise that until recently absorbed him has been set aside. Instead, his creative energy has burst into play: plans, ideas, inspirations revel freely there, where thought lies quiescent: — *Requiescant in pace.*[2]

"At Sea" signaled the beginning of Ivan Konevskoi's ecstatic relationship with the world's waters. However, except for a few brief prose attempts to capture the sea's various moods during the crossing (apparently the weather was good), his attention during the voyage seems to have dwelt chiefly on other features. Also in prose he chronicled his journey up the Rhine, through the Alps at the St. Gotthard Pass, and as far south as Lago Maggiore.[3] Yet, in a less direct, but potent, fashion, the sea continued to weave its spell.

2. The World of Arnold Böcklin

A major force in this was the work of the Swiss painter Arnold Böcklin, in particular his marine paintings, which had enchanted Konevskoi a year earlier in Munich. The Böcklin collection in Basel drew him now to the artist's birthplace, high above the Rhine. While in 1898 its Böcklin collection was still smaller than that in Munich's Schack Gallerie, Basel's State Museum nonetheless held some of his major works.[4]

When Böcklin turned seventy in 1897, the art world in Germany mounted a celebration of impressive proportions. Munich, for several decades one of Europe's leading art centers, that year boasted several major

Böcklin exhibitions, which drew devotees and art tourists from various parts of Europe and notably from Russia. Already by 1890 the art lover's pilgrimage to Germany and to Munich in particular was an established ritual among Russia's cultural elite. Aleksandr Benois's memoir relates how, in 1890, he embarked on his first solo trip abroad, to Germany, with a major goal of seeing "as many pictures by favorite artists as possible, with Böcklin at the head."[5] The opportunity to view all these works fed many an eager amateur's curiosity, including Konevskoi's.

The opportunity for a return visit to Böcklin's works helped crystallize Konevskoi's perception of the late-blooming Swiss painter's vision. At the same time, certain key elements of his own inner vision began to take definitive shape. Equipped with notes and drafts from the previous summer, he set about writing "Böcklin's Paintings (*Zhivopis' Beklina*)," subtitled "(A Lyrical Characterization)." This remarkable essay later became the centerpiece of *Dreams and Meditations*, the record of his spiritual journey, 1896-1899. Its subjectivity, not uncommon in art criticism of the time, was doubtless intensified by its author's deep intuitive sympathy with both paintings and painter.[6] In any case, "Böcklin's Paintings" contains a rich assortment of clues to the new direction in which Konevskoi was about to embark.

"Turn to his paintings — and, wherever you gaze, there breathes the broad expanse of God's world." To Konevskoi, Böcklin's paintings offered an open universe, abundant, endlessly varied, in constant motion, with sea and wind as images of nature's utter freedom and unpredictability:

> From sea to sea, fresh, free air spreads. You feel how, across the whole face of earth, in wide streams flows quivering life. And the whole intoxicating joy of being speaks to the heart in that soaring movement and gripping excitement. [...] Böcklin's land is a land bubbling with milk and honey, and at the same time it is open, open to all winds (*SP 1904*, 161).

In Böcklin, Konevskoi found a powerful ally in his struggle against those limitations on human powers of perception imposed from without. Böcklin's figures exist, not in any specific time or place, but in an elastic blend of the historical and mythological past, or in an indeterminate present, whose broad vistas open into an endless future. This universe, moreover, is full of unpredictable phenomena. Especially is this true of his marine paintings: "In his 'Play of the Waves (Im Spiel der Wellen)' Böcklin takes images from all ages and milieus" *(SP 1904,* 164).

Early in his essay, Konevskoi defined what he saw as the key feature of Böcklin's vision: "Seventy-year-old Böcklin is younger than the majority of contemporary artists, and among them he listens most keenly to the *flight of the future*" (*SP 1904,* 160-1; *ital. mine*). His meaning here is worth examining. A year earlier, setting off on that eventful first journey westward, Konevskoi was guided by a goal that was closely intertwined with his ardent pursuit of artistic experience: he meant to learn all he could about the "new mysticism." Some of the new "artist-mystics" whose works he had already encountered, particularly the new French and Belgian poets, seemed to him to have far outstripped their romantic forebears on the mystical paths of discovery. However, it now appeared that none was so fearless an explorer, so willing to go beyond the bounds of accepted reality, as Arnold Böcklin.

Nor was Konevskoi alone in this perception. Writing at the time of Böcklin's death in 1901, Zinaida Vengerova, well-known Russian chronicler of European modernism, analyzed his work, particularly his seascapes, with sympathy and penetration. Of "Im Spiel der Wellen" she wrote: "This is no fabricated fairytale, but indeed it is the moving power of the element, assuming for a moment palpable form. [...] All this fairytale-like symbolism is full of deep meaning, because it is created with a deep feeling for nature, a powerful love of life and an understanding of the constructive force hidden in being" (*Education [Obrazovanie],* 55).[7]

Two years later, another critic, Aleksandra Chebotarevskaia, friend of Viacheslav Ivanov and sister of Anastasia, wife of Fedor Sologub, published in *Russian Thought* a lengthy and highly informative article on Böcklin's career.[8] In a vein close to Vengerova's but with a prophetic note added, she wrote of his treatment of nature in the works of his prime:

[H]e anticipated the ancients and departed fully into the art of the future when he endowed elemental beings with human forms, only slightly symbolized. [...] The paintings by Böcklin have immense cultural-historical meaning. In them he intuited the age's yearning — a pantheistic striving for the coming to life of the elements (*RM,* 126).

However, Konevskoi's ideas anticipated theirs by several years. We have seen how his thirst to penetrate the secrets of the universe attracted him early on to pantheism. On that memorable evening in Thuringia the previous July, he felt himself penetrated by a mysterious force, another personality, unquestionably emanating from nature itself. Yet he could claim, "I am not the powerless slave of that new nature that had entered into me. That nature instantly merged with me, formed one closed circle with the whole of my conscious self" *(SP 1904,* 150). The notion of an individual actually uniting with the oneness of nature, *while at the same time maintaining its own identity,* was a staggering one. How exactly this was to be accomplished was for him an on-going puzzle and challenge. Meanwhile, Böcklin's conception of nature as, in Vengerova's later formulation, "the moving power of the element, assuming for a moment palpable form," opened possibilities thus far unimagined.

That Böcklin's worldview was pantheistic was generally accepted. But add to the mix the notion of panpsychism, and a whole new layer of meaning is revealed: the entire universe becomes vibrant with a shared *conscious* life. Panpsychism, the belief that mind or consciousness is present throughout the universe, has ancient roots, going back to animism and, in presocratic Greek thought, to hylozoism (belief that matter is animated or that matter and life are inseparable). After a long hiatus, interest in panpsychism reappeared in the seventeenth and eighteenth centuries with Spinoza and Leibniz, then with Gustav Fechner, physicist and psychologist, under whose aegis it reached its peak in the nineteenth century. Fechner's version of panpsychism held that, not only humans and animals, but plants, stones, indeed every object in the universe, in varying degrees possesses an inner psychic life. Thus, where the conventional pantheist looks forward joyously to losing himself in the All-One, the panpsychist anticipates continued existence as an *individual* participating in the all-pervasive *conscious* life of the universe. Obviously, this view's implications for Konevskoi's quest were considerable.

Konevskoi's acquaintance with panpsychism probably came through readings and discussions in the circle gathered around his fellow student Iakov Erlikh, with special attention to the work of Spinoza and Leibniz, Schelling and Hegel, Vl. Solov'ev and Paulsen (*LN 92:4:184*).[9] The Berlin Neo-Kantian Friedrich Paulsen authored, among other works, a popular *Einleitung in die Philosophie*. This work gives a lucid account of the way in which pantheism converges with the notion of panpsychism. Together, as presented in Paulsen's *Einleitung*, these two ideas come across as the only reasonable alternative to atomistic materialism.[10]

One of Paulsen's major premises requires an unbroken continuity running from top to bottom of the scale of being. "The organic and inorganic bodies form, not two separate worlds," he insists, "but a unitary whole in constant interaction" *(Paulsen, 99)*. Psychic life must possess the same continuity, rising from the very bottom upward.[11] Of a hypothetical opponent Paulsen says, "He assumes that organic bodies arise from pre-existing elements [...]. Why does he not make the same natural assumption in this case as well, and say that an inner life was already present in germ in the elements and that it developed into higher forms?" (100) Thus panpsychism would guarantee an interconnected psychic life throughout the universe. A better channel for exploring the *"world structure*,*"* in Konevskoi's understanding of the term, could scarcely be devised.

While Böcklin's marine paintings fit admirably into this scheme, they seem to have stimulated Konevskoi's thinking in another, not unrelated, direction, as well. Very soon after his 1897 visit to Munich, he wrote the essay called "Personifications of Forces (*Olitsetvoreniia sil)*," in which he probed what might now be called evolutionary biology.[12] No doubt the recollection of those seascapes, with their strange, exuberant inhabitants, urged him to speculate boldly about nature's thus far unexplored possibilities. Like virtually all his contemporaries, Konevskoi was unaware of the discoveries three decades earlier by the Austrian monk Gregor Mendel, which would before long lead to the science of genetics. But as an attentive browser in the Brokgauz-Efron encyclopedia, he could easily have read there an authoritative, signed statement of the current scientific position (or lack thereof) on the question of heredity:

> Until this point, not only is there no satisfactory theory of heredity that would explain mechanically the basic process of transfer of hereditary features, but till now it has not been established precisely which characteristics of an organism are passed on to descendants, and which are not.[13]

Considering this hiatus in scientific knowledge, Konevskoi felt free to pose his own provocative questions. Nonetheless, the opening proposition of "Personifications of Forces," is disconcerting:

> Is it possible to say in advance, as with the result of a mathematical theorem, that from a living seed will grow grain, bush, tree, but not a particular organism with features and structure by chance resembling the human? Or, finally, that there will grow only a tree, or a plant of some sort, but not a tree and in addition some organic being? (*SP 1904,* 143)

He readily admitted that, in the future, science might be able to answer such questions. However, as of now, some of the current hypotheses seemed to allow the most astounding conclusions. For example, he easily found support for his own suppositions in evolutionary theory, in accordance with which, he asserted, "the notion of the beginnings of animal life in plants is completely natural, as is that of the existence of intermediate forms between the two." And after all that, why should we not admit "the possibility of the development of so-called fantastic beings from a vegetable seed and from other, moving and productive forces of nature?" (*SP 1904,* 146) In short, why should nature be limited *at all* in its forms? And why are the Kantian forms of perception — time, space, causality — immutable, and, as such, "secure from sudden disappearance or replacement by new forms?" (*SP 1904,* 143)

Rather than bow to these limitations, he chose to posit another, parallel sphere where such rules have no force — such as the universe of Arnold Böcklin. Like many young painters, following a long tradition in European art, Böcklin began early to paint subjects and figures from Greek mythology. However, his renditions soon took on a character untraditional to a degree that threatened to end his career almost before it began. Not many years before his phenomenal rise to popularity in the nineties, certain of these paintings, notably "*Im Spiel der Wellen*", were the center of a public scandal. This large, colorful, action-filled canvas, which hangs in the Neue Pinakothek in Munich, was perhaps Böcklin's most controversial work.[14] When first exhibited, it caused an uproar in the press and among the public. What for some viewers was lighthearted erotic play was for others crudity, even pornography. Equally offensive to many was the earlier "Triton und Nereide" (1874). Like a large number of Böcklin's paintings, excluding portraits, this one implies a narrative or pre-narrative. It shows a moment of repose (or exhaustion) for the two on a rock amid the waves, following what Konevskoi imagined as a dizzying cascade of events epitomizing the "riot and confusion of life…" (*SP 1904*, 163).[15]

But, though Böcklin's idiosyncratic representations of myth were condemned for their alleged indecency, they provoked outrage for other reasons as well. Some serious critics demanded to know: what *right* had he to paint as he did? Departing from accepted classical models, Böcklin portrayed his centaurs, nereids, and tritons with features both animal and human, which for some were both too realistic and too closely integrated into one *persona*. As Chebotarevskaia astutely observed: "Such beings as human-fish or human-bird will always evoke in viewers a feeling of dissatisfaction, if the artist paints them with realism, as portraits, fully represented" (*RM*, 126). These beings displayed human-like emotions and behavior. Though belonging unmistakably to another species, they were, in fact, disturbingly human.

Perhaps equally disturbing to many viewers was the emergence of what Chebotarevskaia called "so far unknown, but entirely possible, organic beings" (*RM*,121). Certainly, some of Böcklin's subjects, if not totally unheard-of, are at least unexpected. Water, the elemental source of all life, is the natural progenitor of new, unknown forms, and his sea paintings are rich in examples of "intermediate" forms of being: tritons, centaurs, nereids, and other unnamed types. Neither the sea-centaur in "Im Spiel der Wellen", his large forward appendages replacing hooves, nor the diving nereid, with small fins sprouting on her ankles, nor indeed the goggle-eyed polyp (or something else?), peering over the triton's shoulder, conformed to common mythical representations.

In "Personification of Forces" Konevskoi argued that all such beings, whose appearance is unpredictable by any known scientific laws, nonetheless must be recognized as "centers of personal consciousness and personal organisms, in which are freely concentrated the creative forces of the universe" (*SP 1904*, 147). If this basic hypothesis holds true, he thought, the possibilities for exploring the universe are virtually unlimited. Man may not only *not* be nature's *last* word, he may not be the *only* one; here, now, in the past, in the future, or in another sphere entirely, there may exist some beings not subject to the restrictions of time, space, or causality. Furthermore, if panpsychism is a viable theory, the communicating chain of *personae* may be virtually without limit. Konevskoi's intuition of another, unknown universe — future or coexisting with our familiar one, peopled by beings both like and unlike ourselves, more profoundly linked with nature, but *personae* in the full sense of the word — had overpowering implications.

3. *"I think and sometimes believe…"*

A 9 October letter to Aleksei Veselov suggests that for Konevskoi the summer of 1898 was even richer in mystical experience than the previous one had been.[16] The correspondence between the two since Veselov's departure for Kiev two years earlier was more or less regular. However, writing after a lapse of several months, Konevskoi noted that their spiritual paths seem to have sharply diverged. "You," he wrote, "more and more withdraw from earthly life, while I more and more strive to touch her and feel her pace and her excitement" (*AVL*,173). The pace and excitement that attracted Konevskoi certainly was not the "buzz and rush" of urban life. While during his two journeys, he spent appreciable amounts of time in

Salzburg, Munich, Cologne, and Heidelberg, only Cologne received more than a brief mention in his travel notes, and then only its churches and points of historical interest. Clearly, the life that mattered to him was the life that circulated through Böcklin's world at all levels. His task now was to learn more about this life and, above all, to learn how to share in it more closely.

Three months earlier, in the lyric "At Sea," Konevskoi joyfully declared his spiritual emancipation and his eagerness to cast his lot with the free elements of nature and all that they signified. But now, thoughts of another, disquieting sort had overtaken him. Analyzing the effect on his rational powers of his most recent encounters with nature, he sensed that a fateful, perhaps irrevocable, step has been taken:

> This past summer, as last year, I roamed about a good deal, so that much of my strength was spent on exchanges with nature, with her soul. With great alarm I often notice that reception of waves of elemental, nonhuman life into my nature erases, threatens to erase much — much that is firmly conscious, much powerful logical thought (*AVL*, 173).

These experiences were exhilarating yet profoundly disturbing. His account of them is stylistically marked, not only by its solemnity, but by the complexity that sometimes occurs in Konevskoi's writing when his thought outstrips his syntax (and his handwriting). The phrase "I think and sometimes believe," three times repeated, at least provides a central structure. Its first occurrence begins an effort to clarify — for himself, first of all — what exactly has taken place. What is the inner *mechanism* of this experience, or rather, of its first stage, i.e., "exchange with nature, with her soul"? What part of his being is it that penetrates the heart of nature? (173) Konevskoi is rendered incoherent by his effort to formulate an answer.

The second use of the phrase "I believe..." develops the line of thinking begun the previous summer in Thuringia, when, for the first time, he was made aware of "another self" actively operating within him. At that time, he wrote to Sergei Semenov that the condition in which he found himself was very close to "mediumistic" *(AVL,* 163). Now, drawing on Du Prel's *Der Spiritismus* for classic examples of mediumistic powers, he proposes that the force at work is "that other consciousness" that appears in the sleep of the somnambulist or in telepathy, communication at great distances, that "inner life of our *persona* of which Du Prel speaks" (163).

Obviously Karl Du Prel's little book contributed importantly to Konevskoi's inquiry into the hidden potential of the self. Though no real evidence has emerged to show that Konevskoi was interested in spiritualism as such, he readily used its "findings" insofar as they supported his main thesis, i.e., the existence of an expanded, potentially unlimited "second self". The quest for this, in turn, was linked to his developing notions of mystical pantheism and of the poet-mystic. His letter to Veselov concludes, apparently (the text is incomplete), with the assertion that, on occasions when, in nature and absorbed in composing poetry, "I think and believe there arises in me the voice of that unknown 'I,' [*sic;* text ends here.] (*AVL,* 174.)

In this final passage, the opening phrase omits the qualifier "sometimes", suggesting that his recent experiences have brought him to a new level of certainty about his status as poet-mystic. "Creative work," first among his cherished "joys of life," is now causally linked to his mystical-pantheistic experience. He now dares affirm that his poetry, like all genuine mystical utterance, possesses the quality called "prophetic"; and that, emerging from a source beyond the poet's everyday consciousness or sensibility, such poetry draws its meaning from unknown depths. His ever more intimate contact with nature, he asserts, has brought him to this state.

Konevskoi's long-term goals altered very little from the time when he spelled them out so forcefully for Veselov in the *gimnaziia*. But from a schoolboy's phrase-making, however sincere, his desire to probe the secrets of the universe developed into a quest that by now had taken on form and urgency. The mountains, whose magnificence and power dominated his imagination during much of his first visit, were joined by the sea, first revealed to him in Böcklin's seascapes. His second journey westward revealed within him an affinity with the sea that amounted total surrender. Böcklin's "open universe," mysterious, constantly changing, full of unpredictable phenomena, was for him the very image of the universe. At the same time, he realized that this was only one model. There could be others. From this point forward, Konevskoi was constantly on the watch for further models that might offer new ways of "penetrating the "universe."

4. Rus'

After the memorable sea voyage that brought him to western Europe, the return to Russia by land was a disorienting experience that left Konevskoi searching for his proper coordinates. Like many other Russian travelers, he found himself facing the question: "What, after all, does it mean to be a Russian?" Most obviously there was geography. After his sojourn among European mountains, lakes, and rivers, there now lay before him this vast land-mass he scarcely knew. Following a short stay at home in Petersburg, he again departed, this time for the area of middle Russia southeast of Moscow. A year ago, after his return from Europe, he traveled to Kiev where Veselov now lived. Two years ago was the memorable trip to the Nizhnii Novgorod fair. This year the destination was the home of his classmate Baron Boris Nol'de. To Alekandr Bilibin, who was to accompany him, he explained their travel plan, which included a stop with relatives who lived on Lake Seliger, before moving on for a longer visit with their friend (*AVL*, 172). The home of his relatives on Lake Seliger had a particular historical attraction that he explored at a later date. However, further in this journey he found another fragment to be added to the image of ancient Russia — or Rus' — forming in his mind.

Though not covering a great distance, the journey broke new ground by introducing him to an unfamiliar area with historical associations. Riazan', once a medieval princedom, an embattled outpost of ancient Rus' sacked by the Mongols, was now merely a provincial city. Nonetheless, in the only lyric he wrote there, Konevskoi sounded the theme of ancient Rus', introduced to his poetry a few months earlier in "From Konevets." He called it "Drought (*Zasukha*)" (*SP 2008*, 104). To be sure, a faint trace is all he finds here of a past quickly swept away by hot winds from the steppe. Despite the historical myths here embedded, the impression is of something long gone, leaving an empty horizon.

Nonetheless, "Rus'" is the name by which, with increasing frequency, Konevskoi referred to his native land. For him "Rus'" represented that image of the Russian spirit that he sought to identify and, perhaps, to assimilate. His interest in this matter clearly had biographical roots, as well as spiritual and mystical ones. His maternal line offered an ethnically and historically rich background. According to Brokgauz-Efron, the Anichkovs descended from a prince of the Great Horde, Berka or Berkai, who transferred his allegiance to the Grand Prince Ivan Kalita in 1301 and received the baptismal name Anikii.[17] Their rank as military gentry thus bore an ancient pedigree, considerably pre-dating that of the Oreus line, at least insofar as historical records reveal.[18]

Konevskoi identified strongly with his paternal ancestors and their ancient traditions: those seafaring forebears, the Norse adventurers who roamed the seas in search of booty and adventure. After his son's death, General Oreus wrote to Valerii Briusov about Ivan's interest in the Varangians: "This tribe interested the deceased because our family name was of Swedish origin, and it is extremely likely that among our ancestors were participants in the bold sea raids of the Vikings and the berserkers" (*LN* 98:1:542). According to another source: "Ivan Konevskoi was proud of his Swedish ancestors, 'Varangians,' recalling that his clan descended from the legendary Sineus" (*LN* 92: 4:181).[19]

After his second return from western Europe, Pre-Petrine Russia became more and more an object of Konevskoi's curiosity. In early September 1896, after their memorable visit to the Nizhnii Novgorod exhibition, Konevskoi, his friends the Bilibin brothers, and Sergei Semenov spent a few days in Moscow. This was the beginning of Konevskoi's fascination with Russia's ancient capital and all that it preserved of Russia's earlier history, especially as reflected in art. Their visit to the Tretiakov Gallery, across the Moscow River from the historical center, was the highpoint for Konevskoi. He described the building as elegantly set in gardens and surrounded by shrubbery and high walls. "This hidden location gives to the whole place a special mystery and charm, just like a fairytale castle in a dense forest" (259.1.16.41ob.).

Inside the Gallery, his enthusiasm did not diminish. Each painting — of those he thought noteworthy — was recorded. Among them was Viktor Vasnetsov's 1880 painting "After Igor' Sviatoslavich's Battle with the Polovetskians" (259.1.16.43ob.). Some two years later this same subject is recognizable in Konevskoi's "From Afar (*Izdaleka*)." (*SP 2008, 114-115*) Written in the form of a dramatic monologue, it shows a mortally wounded warrior, left lying on the field of battle, as he calls to his comrades to return and build a memorial, a *kurgan*, over his body to preserve his memory.

In Vasnetsov's painting the field is littered with corpses and weapons, while the sun sets behind the Karpathian mountains. But the focus is on the body of the young warrior in the foreground, over which a bird of prey hovers. Konevskoi's poem evokes the same setting at the start — the young warrior's body, the birds of prey, the distant mountains and fog — but the focus is on the warrior's thoughts and emotions. From events of the near past — the "great, glorious battles" — they move toward death, with all its indignities. Short, sometimes broken, sentences mimic the gasps of the dying warrior, while the pungent vocabulary conveys the ebbing life and poetry still within him. Time passes, the battle has ended, his comrades are far away or dead. The *kurgan* will never be built.

Like "From Generation to Generation," the preceding poem in Konevskoi's growing anthology of lyrics on the theme of Varangian-Rus', "From Afar" is basically about death and the remembrance of heroes after death. The earlier poem opened with the heir's nostalgic question, "Where are you, generation with the falcon's eye…" The answer was already known: did they not ride on heroically in the traditional *byliny*, "into a city of gold and glass?"[20] In "From Afar" the point of view is that of the dying warrior, who narrates his own heroic story. He fights; he falls; still feeling himself part of the warrior-fellowship, he awaits burial with honor. Yet in the final quatrain he welcomes "night, sightless and mute." And as the sands run out, he faces death serenely, even prophetically, still hoping that the record of his life and deeds will endure.

Worth noting is the alternating metric pattern between odd- and even-numbered stanzas; reading the stanzas in separate series (1-3-5, 2-4-6) creates the effect of two separate strands of narrative. The dactylic line of four/three feet in stanzas 1., 3., and 5. evokes nineteenth-century romantic-heroic ballad models, while the iambic pentameter of stanzas 2., 4., and 6., associated with the same period's romantic and civic elegy, serves to elevate the vision of the hero's fate.[21] Moreover, observing the warrior's death from this dual perspective may allow sympathetic penetration of his inner self, while keeping his heroic actions well in view.

The dedication of "From Afar" to his close friend Ivan Bilibin opens a window on another of his boyhood friendships where common interests formed a significant bond. A year older than Konevskoi, Bilibin studied in the faculty of jurisprudence at St. Petersburg University. During his stay in Munich in 1897 Konevskoi sent him a long, enthusiastic account of his artistic adventures there. The following summer Bilibin was in Munich, working in the studio of Anton Azhbè. By that fall 1898 he was back in St. Petersburg, in Princess Tenisheva's school, studying under Ilya Repin. By this time he and Ivan Bilibin were both deeply attracted to Old Russia, though for very different reasons.

5. "The Sea of Life"

In October 1898, back in St. Petersburg once again and presumably engaged in his university activities, Konevskoi nonetheless found time to compose "The Sea of Life" (*SP 2008*, 111-112). It might be read as a fanciful, even playful, commentary on the previous summer's sea voyage and its exhilarating, liberating effect on his spirit. It also takes him back to childhood reading that showed him newly imagined worlds that could be entered at any moment, leaving behind the burdensome limitations of time, space, and logic. The eight rollicking quatrains combined the delight of wonder books remembered and the exotic words and pictures they evoked, with the more sophisticated pleasure of turning those images and sounds into poetry.[22]

It is the sea again, entrancing, magical. Lines of amphibrachic tetrameter and trimeter, swelling and subsiding with their alternating feminine and masculine rhymes, hypnotically convey the sea's motion.[23] Frequent amphibrachic words, reinforcing the waves' motion and rise to a crest.

Inevitably those marvelous oceans of Konevskoi's early years were overlaid by Böcklin's richly imagined seascapes teeming with life and activity, so recently imprinted on his mind's eye. Böcklin's mysterious villas by the sea flicker in these watery reflections. Indeed, as the poet turns the pages of those early books, the past summer's recollections, inspirations, and serious thoughts intertwine with earlier memories. The fourth stanza evokes early days, when he often found his mind distracted by roving fancies and sometimes more serious, daring thoughts.

Then, in lines ringing with a child's excitement at the watery world lying before his imagination, he renews the jubilant embrace of "At Sea." With delight he relives the countless adventures on which these splendid books once launched him: southward, to land's extremities where the araucaria tree grows. In another part of the globe — another exploit: the biblical whale, its round eye fixed on him as it surges out of the depths, offers to make him another Jonah.

Meanwhile, in a cascade of alliteratives, the journey goes on, across the sea's immense spaces toward the north pole and the fabled land beyond the north wind, Hyperborea. Now Konevskoi turns to the classical legend of this perfect land of perpetual sunlight, loved by Apollo. There, a happy race of people, the Hyperboreans, live a thousand years in their paradise, until, weary of existence, they throw themselves from a high cliff into the sea. Here, adopting direct address, the poet exhorts a tribe of Hyperboreans, progeny of the sea god Nereus, to follow him. "Into the world of death, blessed, marine [...] To taste voluptuous repose!..." The inducement he offers could be taken as a manifestation of decadence, uncharacteristic of Konevskoi though that be. Nereids are not usually found in northern seas. But they do occur frequently in Böcklin's sea paintings. Indeed, with this final stanza, the poem modulates into a new key, with several features that lead us back to Böcklin.

In the whole corpus of Arnold Böcklin's works, some of his finest paintings treat the theme of death and the hereafter in varied guises. The most famous and mysterious of these is doubtless "Die Toteninsel"("Island of the Dead"). But another important and highly relevant is his richly imagined "Gefilde der Seligen" ("The Field of Bliss"), where a noble centaur arrives at an idyllic island, bearing his beautiful companion, there to share the inhabitants' bliss, which is understood to be, unlike that of the Hyperboreans, unending. Of "The Field of Bliss" Konevskoi wrote: "The artist has worked a miracle. He has revealed the prototype of such a fulfilled condition that, the longer one looks at it, the more clearly it tells the heart that, indeed, all fullness is achieved, nothing else is needed" (*SP 1904*, 167).

However, pictures of serene, unending bliss were far from Konevskoi's own vision. "I am yours, your kinsman, sacred monsters!/ Drawn to the unknown south,/ I strain my gaze into watery immensities/ And see the half-world of the sea." This triumphant claim points to the liberated imagination's power to explore "other" universes, future or possibly coexisting with this one, where "other" beings may bring "other" powers to bear on mysteries as yet unheard of. The symbolic (or real) locale for such discoveries is, of course, the sea.

Notes

1. "V more," *SP 2008*, 97. A friend remembered him on a later journey, pacing the deck, reciting this lyric. Sergei Makovskii, *Portrety sovremennikov*. Moscow: Agraf, 2000. P. 425.
2. "May they rest in peace." (Lat.)
3. See *Dreams and Meditations*, pp. 129-148.
4. "Kentaurenkampf," "Das Spiel der Najaden," "Vita somnium breve," and others. Igor Grabar' wrote, in his 1901 review of Böcklin's works in *World of Art (Mir iskusstva)*, no. 2: «In Basel are held ten works of Böcklin, of which six are first class... [All] of them express the most varied sides of his genius" (91).
5. *Moi vospominaniia v 5-i knigakh*. "Nauka": Moscow, 1980. Two vols. Vol.1: 2:516.
6. "As an art critic Konevskoi adheres totally to those methods, to that philosophical-aesthetic and impressionistic style, that is cultivated by the *World of Art* critics (S. Makovskii. S. Diaghilev, and others)" (*LN* 92:4:186).
7. Zin. Vengerova, "Arnol'd Beklin. 1827-1901." *Obrazovanie*, Feb. 1901, 49-55.
8. A. Chebotarevskaia, "Beklin i ego iskusstvo." *Russkaia mysl'*, 1903, 5, 109-137.
9. During autumn 1897 Konevskoi gave prolonged attention to Spinoza's *Ethics*. (259.1.6.50ob) Also see his letter to Aleksei Veselov (*AVL*, 171).
10. Paulsen's *Einleitung* was first printed in German in 1892. The English translation, *Introduction to Philosophy*, which appeared in 1895, contains a preface by William James.
11. In support of his argument for continuity of psychic life, Paulsen mentioned recent studies of such an intermediate form, the protista, and even the "soul-life of the protista." (Paulsen, 95-96n.)
12. *SP 1904*,143-147.
13. "Nasledstvennost'," Brokgauz-Efron. Spb. 1897, 40:641.
14. Of all the seascapes of Böcklin, this apparently was Konevskoi's favorite. Generally it was the marine paintings and the life they portrayed that won his complete approval. Captivated by their humor and high spirits, coupled with eroticism and sheer energy, he described with gusto the

playful antics portrayed there: "In all respects remarkable, [...] his marine pictures, saturated with the ancient pagan joy of sparkling waves, inhabited by dreamy, sensuous nereids and boisterous tritons with green scaly tails." In July 1897, he wrote triumphantly to Sergei Semenov back in Russia that he had managed to secure a photocopy of *Im Spiel der Wellen*. (*AVL*, 162; *RGALI* 259.3.21.)

15 One modern critic notes that in this painting viewers might also experience a sense of disorientation resulting from the point of view, which is almost at water-level. Action and figures are in the very near foreground. The perspective and the annihilation of distance, in effect, force the viewer into the action, ambiguous as that is. (Bernd Wolfgang Lindemann, "Le 'frisson' Böcklin. Motifs, iconographie, mise en scène", *Arnold Böcklin 1827-1901*. (Basel-Paris-Munich, 2002, pp. 47-55.) pp. 52-53. A viewer may be puzzled by the green water-serpent, or by the polyp (?) floating nearby, or by the rather wicked expression on the nereid's face as she caresses the glistening serpent.

16 A letter to Vladimir Gippius, dated 2 July 1898, contains an expanded account of the tour. *Ezhegodnik Rukopisnogo otdela Pushkinskogo doma na 1977 god*. Leningrad, 1979, pp. 87-93. Full of enthusiastic and detailed description, like those of the previous summer sent to other recipients, it gives no indication of the mystical aspect of the journey.

17 The Brokgauz-Efron article "Anichkovy" further relates that on that solemn occasion the Metropolitan blessed Anikii with a richly jeweled ecclesiastical symbol, the *panagia*, and other gifts, some of which are "believed to be, to this day, in the possession of the Anichkov family" (Br.-Efr., Spb, 1890, 2:786).

18 The Oreus family traced its lineage back as far as the seventeenth century and claimed Swedish origin, though several members held prominent posts in Finland, and recent evidence points to the possibility of their Finnish descent. See: Ben Hellman, "On Ivan Konevskoi's Finnish Roots," *Aspekteja. Slavica Tamperensia V*, Tampere, 1996. Pp. 95-100.

19 The *Primary Chronicle* identifies Sineus as Riurik's brother, who became ruler of Beloozero. *Povest' vremennykh let*. 2nd ed. D. S. Likhachev and V. D. Adrianova-Peretts, eds. St. Petersburg: "Nauka", 1999, p. 13.

[20] While no existing texts pre-date the eighteenth century, byliny are commonly regarded as epic songs orally transmitted from early Rus'. Their heroes, the *bogatyrs*, and their exploits were part legendary, part historical.

[21] M. L. Gasparov, *Ocherk istorii russkogo stikha*. Moscow: "Nauka", 1984. Pp. 165-166.

[22] Unclaimed sources embedded in this delightful poem are several. For example, it is difficult to believe that Konevskoi overlooked Jules Verne's *Twenty Thousand Leagues under the Sea* (1881), with its giant squid and other wonders that enchanted so many of his contemporaries. Almost surely, too, he knew more about current thinking about Hyperborea and the Hyperboreans than he chose to reveal here. (*Br.-Efr*, 16: 722. Spb, 1893.) However, their significance for him lay in their final plunge into the sea. Again, he recalls "the dead brigs/ Deep beneath the waters' cover." Little as he valued Bal'mont as a poet, Bal'mont's volume *Quiet* (*Tishina*), published in August 1898, with its initial poem, "The Dead Ships," could at least have suggested the phrase for inclusion. (According to his reading notebook, Konevskoi did not read Coleridge's "The Rhyme of the Ancient Mariner" till sometime in 1899. [*RGALI* 259.1.6.74ob.])

[23] This pattern became the most common used in nineteenth-century ballads. (M. L. Gasparov, 121.)

Chapter 4

Two Meetings

In the latter part of 1898, Ivan Konevskoi made two new acquaintances, each of whom, in very different ways, was to have a profound effect on his life and his poetry. The first was Anna Nikolaevna Gippius, of the famous Gippius family, whom he met soon after his return from Riazan'. The second was Valerii Briusov, whose acquaintance he made on 12 December in St. Petersburg. The relationship with Briusov, primarily literary in nature, generated an active correspondence and numerous mutual visits. Moreover, Briusov's contribution to Konevskoi's posthumous reputation can hardly be overestimated. The relationship with Anna Gippius is much less well documented, and was much shorter in duration. Nonetheless, though a great deal is left to surmise, her personal impact upon Konevskoi was clearly of major importance to his immediate future.

1. "Marvelous Dryad"

The second of the four Gippius sisters, Zinaida, Anna, Tatiana, and Natalia, Anna apparently differed from her artistic sisters in almost every way: character, temperament, views, and actions.[1] Fiercely independent in aims and mode of life, she graduated from a medical institute in Kharkov in 1903, worked as a doctor in the Caucasus, from 1915 served as an army doctor on the German front and after 1917 with General Denikin's White Army. After 1919 she lived in emigration.[2] At the time of her meeting with Konevskoi all this lay ahead, but her independence and high goals even then were obvious. Konevskoi's first impressions of her, as well as his strong attraction, both physical and spiritual, appear in the poem he dedicated to their first encounter, "Memories of a Meeting (*Pamiati vstrechi*)." (*SP 2008*, 120-121)

Clear-eyed and serious, she radiated vitality, strength, intelligence, and feminine warmth. Her eyes, "green like water," her straight figure, full lips, and fleeting smile hinted to him of a nature both severe and kind. Most important, she was willing to listen to what Konevskoi called, with some reason, his "mad thoughts." Their growing friendship may have been, in part, an attraction of opposites. Inexperienced in relations with the opposite sex, he was overwhelmed by her fresh womanhood, as well as her presumed superiority in every conceivable way. Yet Anna was possibly as much an "outsider" as he. At any rate, common ground apparently existed for a meaningful and, for a time, intense attachment on his side, and possibly on hers as well.[3]

Autumn 1898 was a productive time for Konevskoi's poetry, the beginning of a period that lasted through 1899. Until the very end of 1898 no new poem formally linked to Anna Gippius appeared, though some may indirectly reflect their growing association. However, the year's final work, entitled "Holiday Cantata (*Prazdnichnaia kantata*)," is dedicated to "Anna Nikolaevna G." (*SP 2008*, 136-137) An exuberant, ecstatic chorale celebrating the conquest of time and indeed of every barrier to total freedom, it evidently draws on Nietzsche, a source new to Konevskoi's poetry. The epigraph is from *Also Sprach Zarathustra*: "Lust will aller Dinge Ewigkeit,/ will tiefe, tiefe Ewigkeit."[4]

Konevskoi's acquaintance with Nietzsche began considerably earlier, probably with the lengthy article by V. P. Preobrazhenskii, published in 1892 in *Problems of Philosophy and Psychology*. Though he read this article in spring 1896, he apparently returned to the subject of Nietzsche only sometime during 1898. By the end of 1898 he had begun translating a number of Nietzsche texts. The fact that he dedicated to Anna Gippius a poem so Nietzschean (or specifically, Zarathustran) in content, strongly suggests that he expected a sympathetic and comprehending reception.

The early months of 1899 were rich in poetry linked to Anna. The peak of this came between 2 and 14 February, with a cycle of five poems under the general title "Stirrings (*Volneniia, SP 2008,* 121-122)" at its center. Even without confirmation, it would be difficult to overlook the connection between these lyrics and their emotional subtext. Fortunately concrete evidence is available. A copy of the book *Dreams and Meditations* survives with Konevskoi's inscription: "For Anna Nikolaevna Gippius, strong bearer of thoughts and ecstatic flights. I. Oreus. November 1899. Pb." In addition, Konevskoi's hand inserted dates under the following: "Stirrings" (3-4 February), "Signs (*Priznaki, SP 2008,* 122-123)" (5 February), and "Long Ago and Now (*Davno i nyne, SP 2008,* 123-124)" (6-8 February).[5]

The arc described within the cycle "Stirrings" itself predicts the trajectory of their relationship. An epigraph from Tiutchev, "Love, love — proclaims tradition…" echoes the lines from the earlier "Memories of a Meeting": "I did not love, but how I strove/ To love…". The soaring lines of the cycle's first lyric convey a mood of breathless expectation, till at last, "I passed beyond the edge of dream,/ But even there found you." The next two lyrics continue the upward curve, but with the fourth, the momentum comes to a sudden halt: "Why these new alarms?/ So distressed am I in my soul" ("*K chemu eti novye smuty?*", *SP 2008,* 122).

The fifth and final poem dramatizes these "alarms" with an image familiar to any reader of Hoffmann or Poe (as Konevskoi was): the "double" ("No, I am alone — (*Net, odin ia* —)", *SP 2008,* 122).[6] As he explained to Aleksei Veselov the previous October, he believed in "doubles" as external manifestations of "that inner life of our *persona*" and inseparable from it. (*AVL,* 173)[7] His earliest encounters between nature and the inner second self in the Thuringian forests left him feeling exalted, but at the same time threatened by some unknown force; similarly with more recent experiences. Now framing the question in dramatic terms, he issues a challenge to the lately discovered inner self: "Come forth, my incarnate double!" But like most famous "doubles," this one is unpredictable. And so, the ensuing struggle with "[m]y foe, my most treasured friend" comes to no conclusion, but rather, leaves him "alone — in empty space". Answers, as ever, are elusive.[8]

Meanwhile, two more poems remain of the creative and emotional upsurge that occurred between 2 and 14 February. Of these, "Signs" surely represents the acme of his joyous optimism. The delight that rings through these lines is engagingly naïve and at the same time telling. They conclude: "Can it be, o marvelous dryad,/ That we may share all this together — /Delight of thoughtful glance/ And wine of buoyant youth?" (*SP 2008*, 122-123)

The last poem in this cluster, "Long Ago and Now," stands out from the others for various reasons. To begin with, it is apparently unfinished. The title, along with the numeral "I." heading the text, indicates at least a two-part structure. But a row of dots follows the last stanza, and "I." is not followed by a corresponding "II." Moreover, the "plot," so to speak, breaks off at what seems to be the highest point. Presumably, the events so far related took place "long ago"; there is no "now". The narrative setting is familiar in romantic poetry: the poet, wandering alone in the forest gloom, experiences a revelation of some sort. But there are unexpected features.

Given Konevskoi's vast acquaintance with poetry in several languages, it may be gratuitous to propose a particular source for this one. Nonetheless, one suggests itself: it is Edgar Allan Poe's ballad "Ulalume."[9] A few months earlier, Konevskoi's reading diary shows him reading the "Poetical Works" of Edgar Allan Poe, presumably in English, since the title is so entered.[10] In "Ulalume" Poe's hero is found sadly roaming with Psyche in "the ghoul-haunted woodland of Weir." Strangely, nothing in the setting, either place or time of year, rouses any remembrance of past events, so sunk is he in his mournful state:

> The skies they were ashen and sober;
> The leaves they were crisped and sere —
> The leaves they were withering and sere;
> It was night in the lonesome October
> Of my most immemorial year;

Then suddenly:

> At the end of our path a liquescent
> And nebulous lustre was born,
> Out of which a miraculous crescent

> Arose with a duplicate horn —
> Astarte's bediamonded crescent [...]

Poe's hero, rejecting Psyche's tearful remonstrance, insists that they follow the "Sybilline splendor," until, suddenly, he finds himself at "the door of a legended tomb" — the vault of his "lost Ulalume." Konevskoi presumably had nothing so morbid in mind. Nonetheless, he may have found in Poe's ballad a sympathetic genre to accommodate feelings that were new to his experience. The setting and meter (three-foot amphibrach) recall Poe. Konevskoi's hero, like Poe's, wanders dreamily in the wood at early morning. Then suddenly, not light, but a sound breaks into his mood: the tantalizing call of a shepherd's pipe leads him over hill and dale. And at last: "From the darkness... gazed those eyes and lips." (*SP 2008*, 123-124)

On this rather awkward image, the poem breaks off. Visions of eyes and/or lips by this time have developed a metonymic relation to the person of Anna Gippius herself. In "Memories of a Meeting," a smile flickers "on pale and full lips" while the speaker is transfixed before those "eyes, green like water." In "Stirrings, 3." the eyes are disembodied, but in "Signs" they belong, along with other features, to a woman who is definitely flesh and blood (in fact, "the marvelous dryad"): "Long ago I saw these hands,/ The movements of body and eyes./ Long ago I heard the sound of that laugh, /But now it is more ringing." Clearly, the poet's strong awareness of the "dryad's" physical presence permeates most of these poems. Yet, this awareness is frequently mixed with awe before her strong spirit and a sense of his own inadequacy. The tension thus created was unlikely to endure indefinitely.

From this point the relationship descended through a troubled period reflected in poems leading up to the cycle "Pale Spring (*Blednaia vesna*)". However, without evidence to the contrary, the "trouble" appears to have existed primarily on the side of Konevskoi. Between "Long Ago and Now" and "Pale Spring" twelve lyrics were completed. Several, but not all, sounded a note of self-examination and withdrawal. (One must bear in mind that they were meant to be read by Anna Gippius, and probably to carry certain messages. Yet they show considerable self-knowledge as well.)

Of these, perhaps the most poignant is "Agreement (*Soglashenie*)," (*SP 2008*, 129-130). This lyric might also have been called "Acceptance," yet the tone is less one of submission to fate, than of dignified acquiescence: "I have no happiness, but I am glad of life,/ While still I live."[11]

The cycle, "Pale Spring (*Blednaia vesna*)," which was dated "March-April (1899)," contains no real surprises. (*SP 2008*, 126-128) Its opening lyric sets mood and scene. The familiar hesitant arrival of the northern spring with its sometimes stifling fog is watched from behind walls by one who believes that, for him personally, spring will never come. Six of the cycle's seven lyrics offer variations on these themes. Only number 6 breaks the pattern. Entitled "(*To Her* [*K nei*])," it begins: "Another time,/ In other days, /We'll meet again." In essence its message is: I am not ready. The cycle ends with a painfully etched self-portrait that includes the lines: "Forgotten spirit, gloomy and fearful,/ Child reared among gray elders,/ .../Will you ever emerge from the woods to freedom?" (*SP 2008*, 128)

The penultimate record of the Anna Gippius-Konevskoi relationship comes in a different form: a letter from Konevskoi in June 1899 to Aleksandr Bilibin. Quoting and paraphrasing key passages, it retails a recent exchange of letters between himself and Anna Gippius.[12] Soon after his return from a May visit to Moscow, Konevskoi wrote to his friend Bilibin that he had taken a momentous step: "I sent a letter to the dryad you know, A. N. G. In it I said that 'before finally renouncing personal communication with her, I cannot forego saying a few farewell words.' " He went on to explain his action:

> It is too painful to me to appear before the open, ringing strength of her soul, her body, when those same thoughts and feelings that were expressed in poems dedicated to her and in the letter accompanying them, turn from swift, transparent streams, playing in the sunlight, into huge dirty smokey blobs, and that happens, even though they continue to waft in my soul like filmy, lightsome clouds.

Here was a young man whose commitment to an impossibly ambitious set of spiritual and intellectual goals had heretofore dominated his existence.

But he was also a young man in love, experiencing sexual attraction to a degree that for him was probably highly disturbing.[13] The combined force of her body and spirit, of her whole being, became more than he could sustain. The quality that seemed most to intimidate him was, as he described it, her struggle for "new intuitions of life, for the widening of each instant into eternity, against Time and any kind of limitation. She [...] seemed to me like the fresh and burning breath of primaeval and powerful freedom." On the other hand, he felt himself incapable of sharing the brilliant life of struggle for ideals — ideals that they shared — that he foresees in her future.[14] The letter closes with the naïve hope that, despite all this, "she will not refuse always to consider me her friend."

To anyone tracing in Konevskoi's poetry the intermittent spasms of self-doubt that he underwent between September and June of that year his announcement will not come as a total surprise. Yet, to Anna Gippius it apparently did. According to Konevskoi, she replied "with an expression of unpleasant surprise at my decision to renounce personal contact with her, and at my hope for a friendly attitude on her side: 'this is a contradiction — explain.'" She denied forcefully his contention that his spirit was "murky" while hers was not. "And if that were so, what of it?" Then, adopting a softer tone, she continued with manifest regret: "I am sorry that I will not be seeing you any more: sometimes it is a great comfort to know that another person is thinking and agonizing over the same thing as she is." Yet apparently Konevskoi held fast: "In conclusion I pointed to the genuine necessity, in spite of all, of distancing myself from personal acquaintance."

Whatever its emotional overtones, their dialogue during the previous months apparently revolved around Konevskoi's dominant philosophical concerns. From the moment long ago when he defined his goal as "to penetrate by direct intuition the secret essence of things," his ideas had not changed. (Stepanov, *LN* 92:4:182) But they had broadened and deepened. Since his first circle presentation in fall 1896, his main intellectual energies had gone into constructing a worldview that preserved the individual *persona* from eventual absorption into the All-One. Survival of the *persona*, the integral "self," with its conscious and supraconscious powers, was essential to probing the nature and meaning of the universe. Time and space must be overcome, if the *persona* is to achieve the unlimited freedom required for achieving that goal. These hard-won beliefs Konevskoi attempted early on to share with this new friend, "A.N.G."

A reader is likely to be struck by the attention both parties in this tense emotional exchange nonetheless paid to abstract questions of worldview. After summarizing at some length for Bilibin his emotional farewell message, Konevskoi added: "Into these words were woven certain general thoughts about the essential directions of the struggle with personal limitation and separation of objects (that is with Space and with Time)." Anna's response, otherwise direct and personal, was on the same level, in the same tone. To this Konevskoi answered in kind: "I expounded at length in the most detailed arguments about my worldview."

Yet all this was less abstract than it seems. Their exchange has the ring of an ongoing argument, one central to the relationship. Along with her other attractions, Anna apparently was able to cope with his intellectual flights. She "spoke his language" and seemingly, to a degree, shared his vision. Yet obviously, Konevskoi had not convinced her of the rightness of his reasoning about the *persona* and its potential, though to do so was of prime importance to him. He may even have been sensed an intellectual threat from her, as well a sexual-emotional one. All this pressure became more than he could bear. His penultimate words to her in this exchange were contained in the lyric *"To Her,"* enclosed with his letter: "Another time,/ In other days,/ We'll meet again."[15]

However, by the following November, he had given up that hope. His lyric "Renunciation (*Otrechenie*). *Dedicated to A.N.G.*", dated 5 November, 1899, concludes: "No place remains in my soul for that single hope:/ The ecstasies of first passion will not return." His life, alas, has shattered into fragments, and at times his breast cannot draw breath. (*SP 2008*, 150.)

Recovery was long, painful, and inconclusive.

2. "My friend, Valerii"

On 12 December 1898, Ivan Oreus recited his poetry at Fedor Sologub's "evening" to an audience that included Valerii Briusov and Konstantin

Bal'mont. Briusov's diary recorded that fateful evening: "The most remarkable was the recitation of Oreus, for he is a splendid poet" (*Dn.* 57). In St. Petersburg on a brief visit from Moscow, Briusov lost no time in following up that first contact. Two days later he visited Konevskoi: "This morning I was at Oreus's. A sickly youth, with nervous jerks; he slightly recalls Dobroliubov of former days, but is less attractive. All absorbed in the newest French poets." He added: "We didn't hit it off very well" (*Dn.* 57-58).

The relationship prospered, nonetheless. On 18 December Konevskoi wrote to his new friend: "I am most grateful to you for sending your two collections and the three new poems you copied out for me." He then offered a pointed comment: "I rejoice at the liberation of your poetry from love of exotic and fantastic words, which are always just one step from the display of a circus acrobat" (*LN 98:1:446*).[16] A busy exchange of letters and poems began.[17] From that time until mid-1900, Konevskoi and Briusov were almost continually engaged in one or another literary endeavor of intense interest to both.

> In January, when Bal'mont arrived in Moscow, bringing the latest literary news and gossip from St. Petersburg, Briusov's diary reported: "Most interesting of all were the three notebooks of Oreus, which Bal'mont brought with him. We were all attracted, we read, re-read, copied, learned them by heart".[18] He added: "I wrote him an ecstatic letter, knowing ahead of time that I would receive a reserved reply" *(Dn. 60).* Briusov wrote: I have read your notebooks long since, and I congratulate you. Yes, this is a triumph [...]. That which we say about the pleasures of art, all that was present for me in your poems. Now I constantly repeat single lines, words, rhymes. The loftiest, most adorable I consider the sonnets, and among them "The Son of the Sun," a cycle brilliant in every way, where the concluding speech is amazing, stunning... "May you be forever fiercely alive" — that line is enough to make me love you forevermore (*LN 98: 1. 451*).

Briusov's enthusiasm for Konevskoi's poetry was genuine and unflagging, though he sometimes criticized individual poems. On the other hand, Konevskoi's comments on Briusov's work were occasionally severely critical or even patronizing. Yet, on the whole, from both sides the tone was cordial, even warm; the letters' frequency itself during that time indicates their mutual regard.

However, in mid-March 1899 there occurred a rare clash. This was possibly the only time when either openly challenged the other on their undoubtedly deep differences in several areas. Briusov, presumably irritated by Konevskoi's harsh criticism of the German poet Franz Evers, whom he held in high esteem, used the moment to underline the fundamental difference between them in such matters.

> You love to pass judgment, while I search first of all for the desirable. In everything and in every instant there is that before which one must bow down. The only temple worthy of prayer is the pantheon, the temple dedicated to all gods, day and night, Christ, and Adonis, and the demons. I love old man Homer, and refined Vergil, the rhetoric of Victor Hugo, and the deliberate hints of Mallarmé. There is the highest level, where all differences fade, where all boundaries are reconciled (*LN* 98: 1: 454).

Konevskoi hastened to explain himself: "I deeply sympathize with that 'pantheon' that you refer to, but I cannot love everything that you mention as a divine harmony between striving and realization, as beauty" *(LN* 98:1:455*)*. He then attempted to define his method of taking these "unlovely things" into his creative imagination and transforming them into less alien forms. For the moment, though, he took a generally conciliatory tone in his response. However, as his next move, Konevskoi offered a direct poetic and philosophical response to Briusov's position in his poem "Declaration to Truth (*Slovo k istine),*" dated 29 April 1899, six weeks after the above exchange of letters.[19] It began: "All the great answers have lied,/ Or rather, they've not lied, all are true", but they are completely worn through. In any case, he rejects them all, and Truth as well — unless it comes to him through Beauty. (*SP 2008* 139-140)

As both poets doubtless recognized, this exchange scarcely represented a genuine meeting of minds. In fact, it was quite the opposite. Briusov, agnostic to the core, spoke the fundamental truth about himself when he said: "But I myself loved only the combination of words." Or put another way, no truth is absolute, but all "truths" offer something of value. On the other hand, Konevskoi's worldview assured him that Truth exists, and that it is far vaster than he has yet seen.

In any case, very soon the first signs of sharp disagreement appeared in another sphere. The subject was the nature and purpose of translation. This dispute emerged fully a few months later, and will be examined at the appropriate juncture. Meanwhile, Briusov came again to Petersburg. Though his chief companion during most of his stay was Bal'mont, Konevskoi was not forgotten. In his diary, following the heading "17-22 March, 1899. Journey to Petersburg", Briusov noted: "Twice I was with Oreus. He is the same as ever, and the poems he writes are all the same, everything the same. This is fine but also boring" *(Dn .63)*.

Soon after, in mid-April, Konevskoi announced plans for a return visit: "I hope to be in Moscow in mid-May, and at that time I will acquaint you, both with the translations I have mentioned, and with certain new poems of mine" *(LN 98:1:459)*. Briusov was heavily engaged just then in preparation for his final university examinations. "Therefore I have not even half an hour's free time at my disposal. I will be dead until 1 June. (Won't you postpone your journey?)" *(LN 98:1:461)*. But for whatever reason, Konevskoi did not do so. Instead, as Briusov recorded, "[Oreus] came to my place during that time, recited many poems, and praised himself mightily." Yet, inconvenient as the visit was, Briusov found it rewarding: "The poems are excellent. I expect great things from him" *(Dn. 70)*.

During July they exchanged short letters from their respective holiday locations, Briusov from the Crimea, Konevskoi from Finland. By August Konevskoi was planning another trip to Moscow, which Briusov's diary entry for 21 September duly reported: "Oreus was in Moscow for two weeks. We spent the first days together constantly, which was tiring. We talked about all poems and poets." Then followed several observations that were revealing in regard to both:

> His most unpleasant feature is his excessively authoritarian manner, his pedantic manner of speech — but that is from youth. He speaks assuredly and decisively, even about things that obviously he knows superficially. I argued with him a great deal about Bal'mont, whom he rejects. [...] Afterwards I organized at my rooms a small gathering of poets — Bachmann, Oreus, Savodnik, Lang. Again we argued about Bal'mont, about the novel, is such a form possible or not, about meters and their origin, and about rhymes. As he was leaving, Oreus bade me farewell with great cordiality (*Dn.* 76).

"But that is from youth": in those words Briusov showed the indulgence of an elder brother toward a junior, a very young sibling, who is unaware of the irritating impression he produces on others. A week later, he received from Oreus "an ecstatic letter. Everything here charmed him — Moscow, my poems, Lang, and the guests at Bachmann's" (*Dn.* 76).

This correspondence and Briusov's diary together provide the fullest available record of Konevskoi as he then appeared to someone in frequent contact with him, who shared his interests and who valued him deeply as a poet. One is struck by the frequent difference in tone between these two primary sources, diary and letters. In large part, this is explainable by the difference in genre and, in particular, by Briusov's use of them. His diary was consciously crafted so as to make available to posterity a record of himself as individual and as a figure representative of his time and place. Its tone in many passages is one of irony, sometimes light, sometimes less so. Comments about Konevskoi, as about many other acquaintances (and about the diarist himself), are candid and sometimes sardonic. The letters of each, on the other hand, except for a few passages, maintain the gracious and cordial manner that one expects from writers of their education, time, place, and mutual esteem. Konevskoi's were as a rule considerably longer (in keeping with the volubility of much of his prose). Briusov's grew shorter and less frequent during the second year of their friendship, as his literary activities and responsibilities multiplied, and their common bond became attenuated. But during all of 1899 the relationship remained close and exchanges frequent.

One compelling interest shared by Konevskoi and Briusov was the gathering and publication of the writings of the former St. Petersburg decadent poet Aleksandr Dobroliubov. Briusov's account of his first visit to Konevskoi (December 14, quoted above) ends with the words: "He passed on to me some manuscripts of A. Dobroliubov" (*Dn.* 58). One may ask how Konevskoi came into possession of these manuscripts. Given that the two younger poets have frequently been paired in writings about the period, one asks also what we know about Konevskoi's earlier connection and possible contacts with Dobroliubov. His interest apparently began with the 1895 publication of Dobroliubov's collection *Natura naturans. Natura naturata*. Two of Konevskoi's 1896 notebooks contain poems copied from that source.[20] Early in 1897, his fellow members of the student circle heard positive comments about Aleksandr Dobroliubov in Konevskoi's paper "Lyrical Poetry in Contemporary Russia." However, regarding this promising young poet, "eighteen or nineteen years old" (Konevskoi himself was eighteen), he cautioned:

> There is not yet enough information available to permit the assessment of his worldview. It is possible to say only that in the general character of his moods one sees that unrestrainedness of *persona* and that eccentric *mistikism* (sic), that same, in a word, alternation of extremes as in Mr. Sologub and, in part, in Mr. Fofanov [two others of his select group] (*AVL*, 121).

Though the title *Natura naturans. Natura naturata* struck him as "a somewhat tasteless, pretentious title", Konevskoi nonetheless saw in it a veritable treasury of language and cultural sources, "the poetry of folk songs, fantastic folk tales, spiritual songs, especially from the schismatics, for example, khlysts, in part also from the poetry of the Orthodox ritual and church hymns. Many of his poems, in essence, resemble folk spells. They are truly a kind of poetic magic" (*AVL*, 121). For Konevskoi, this was sufficient reason for keen interest. Moreover, as always, questions of worldview, of depth and seriousness in the pursuit of answers, were for him essential considerations in weighing his contemporaries. What he had seen in the 1895 volume was enough to keep at a high level his appetite for more from Dobroliubov.

During spring and summer of 1899 the effort to collect Dobroliubov's post-1895 poems for publication was in full cry. Briusov and Konevskoi collaborated in locating the manuscripts that Dobroliubov had deposited with various friends before leaving Petersburg for the life of a pilgrim in the north. Yakov Erlikh apparently was the chief of these custodians. As one of Dobroliubov's oldest and closest friends, he took his responsibilities seriously. In the latter part of April Konevskoi reported to Briusov that Erlikh was unwilling to surrender his holdings without direct instructions from Dobroliubov. Nor would he accept Briusov's word that Dobroliubov had expressed to him his wishes concerning publication. Furthermore, upon hearing of this, Erlikh "took the collection of [Dobroliubov's] manuscripts from me with the stated intention of keeping them himself, under lock and key." Therewith, Konevskoi pointed out to him that "copies including several of the most significant poems from these manuscripts remain with me, some on paper, some in my memory"; and moreover, that "copies of all the manuscripts that have been verified remain in your hands, and nothing prevents any of these from being distributed" *(LN* 98:1:457). But Erlikh did not yield. Moreover, facing final university exams, Briusov was prepared to table the whole problem for the immediate future. (*LN* 98:1:461)[21]

At the end of August, Briusov turned in earnest to the task, commissioning Konevskoi to borrow from Erlikh and several others the original manuscripts. (1:466) Finally, in November, he passed on the good news that a publisher for all or most of Dobroliubov's work had been found: "That same S. Poliakov, whose library is full of volumes of 'Mercure de France' and 'Revue Blanche'" (1:475). Sergei Poliakov was busy at that time, along with Briusov, establishing the publishing house "Scorpio", soon to be the first and chief center for the spread of Russian Symbolism. Dobroliubov's *Collected Poetry (Sobranie stikhov)* was one of its early publications. It appeared at the end of March, 1900, with introductions by both Briusov and Konevskoi.[22]

The two introductions are markedly different. Briusov's is entitled "On Russian Versification," and its subject is in fact just that; Dobroliubov is mentioned only in the final sentence. Konevskoi's essay, on the other hand, is entitled "Toward the Study of the *Persona* of Aleksandr Dobroliubov".[23]

True to his practice, Konevskoi interested himself in those aspects of his subject's *persona* with which he most strongly identified. Central to all other considerations, he said, was Dobroliubov's resentment at the limitations forced on human will and consciousness (*SP 1904*, 196). Konevskoi obviously found strong support here for his own struggle with similar problems and questions that plagued him. Dobroliubov, he believed, was on the way to finding means of dealing with them, chiefly by concentration of pure *will*. As Konevskoi contemplated the latest stage of Dobroliubov's spiritual development, he found himself on familiar ground. His own explorations into the nature of mysticism over the past four years helped him to understand — and warmly support — the direction Dobroliubov was following:

> In order to realize his plan of creating his world outside of human feelings and outside human thinking, outside of body and outside of mind, it remained to this man to choose as the most appropriate path *visionary penetration of mysteries, wonder-working, practice of those states of alternate consciousness that were known to pure mystics of all ages, and, earliest of all, to Indian magicians, and further, to neo-Platonists and gnostics, and that was carried on in the monasteries of eastern Christianity under the name "mental labor."* Such is the straight path to rebirth of consciousness through the force of a single personal will. (*PS 1904*, 198. Ital. mine).

This, it should be noted, is a key text for understanding the direction of Konevskoi's own thought at the end of 1899 and beyond.

In *World of Art*, No.1, 1901, a blistering review of the Dobroliubov volume appeared, authored by Zinaida Gippius. Her piece, entitled "Criticism of Love: Decadent-Poets (*Kritika liubvi. Dekadenty-poety*)," consisted of a withering attack on Dobroliubov and the entire decadent outlook, with special disdain reserved for Konevskoi's essay and Konevskoi himself: "By this foreword, anguished, monstrous — but also childishly piteous, totally incomprehensible, I recognize in Konevskoi the spiritual brother of Dobroliubov".[24] A generation later, a presumably more objective critic, N. L. Stepanov, wrote: "The withdrawn, inwardly intense life of Konevskoi, totally occupied by his searches for truths, brought him close to A. Dobroliubov" (*LN* 92:4:186). However, this formulation seems too vague to be of help in establishing what, if any, personal connection actually existed between the two.

Did Konevskoi and Dobroliubov ever meet? Logically, they might have done so. Only a year apart in age — Konevskoi was born in 1877, Dobroliubov in 1876 —, both were enrolled in the philological faculty of St. Petersburg University. They had friends in common: Vladimir Gippius, Yakov Erlikh, and, later, Briusov. But in each case the timing was wrong.[25] In 1896-7, Dobroliubov's mode of life was at its most decadent, very different from that of Konevskoi and his friends. Then sometime in 1897 Dobroliubov withdrew from his previous existence and, in spring 1898, left St. Petersburg to begin his new life as a "holy wanderer," which lasted more or less for the next twenty years.[26] Briusov's first encounter with Konevskoi was in December 1898. All this seems to suggest that no contact between Konevskoi and Dobroliubov occurred before that date, and no evidence has emerged of a later meeting.[27]

Meanwhile, during the second half of 1899 Konevskoi was fully absorbed by the preparation for publication of *Dreams and Meditations*. This project in its entirety is the subject of the next chapter. However, its progress occupied an important place in the letters exchanged between him and Briusov. At about that same time, Briusov was working on poems that a year later would appear in *Tertia vigilia*, his first fully mature volume of poetry. Of all his collections, this is the one in which there appear the clearest marks of his close association with Konevskoi. A. V. Lavrov wrote in his introduction to the Briusov-Konevskoi correspondence:

> Briusov's acquaintance with Konevskoi's poetry at a time when the stage that produced his book *Me eum esse* (1897) was past [...] was an additional stimulus for finding a new, active link with the world and for widening

the thematic and horizons of imagery and ideas in his creative work. This tendency marked the next stage in Briusov's poetic evolution, clearly expressed in *Tertia vigilia*.[28]

The sympathy that grew between the two poets during that time is captured in the inscription Konevskoi wrote in the copy of *Dreams and Meditations* he presented to Briusov. It reads:

> To dear
> Valerii Ia. Briusov
> as a sign of gratitude
> for his love for my poetry
> and
> the kinship of our worldviews.
> I. Oreus
> November 1899, Pet[ersburg].[29]

A good deal may be surmised about the relationship by parsing this inscription. Without doubt, poetry — and, not least, each other's — was the main bond of their friendship. From Briusov's initial reaction to Ivan Konevskoi's reading, this was never in doubt. Moreover, their meeting occurred at a time when Briusov was suffering acutely the need for a literary comrade to fill the vacuum left by the absence of Bal'mont and Dobroliubov. (*Dn.* 41) The extent to which Konevskoi came to fill this vacuum was made clear three years later, when he poured into a letter to Anna Aleksandrovna Shesterkina his feelings on learning of Konevskoi's death:

> Iv. Konevskoi-Oreus has died... He drowned, swimming in the river Aa in Livonia. Nothing for a very long time has hit me harder. This is worse than all my family misfortunes, more painful than all I have suffered this summer. Ivan Konevskoi has died, he on whom I placed more hope than on all the other poets together. Suppose Bal'mont had died, or Baltrushaitis, to say nothing of Minskii or Merezhkovskii — but not him! not him! [...] While he was alive, one could write, knowing that he would read,

understand, and criticize. Now there is no such a one.[...] Without Oreus I am only half of myself.³⁰

As for Konevskoi, there is perhaps a hint in his inscription to Briusov that he, apparently so self-assured and independent in all things regarding his poetry, in fact welcomed the moral support of such an audience, if not its criticism. However, the second line of Konevskoi's inscription that speaks of their "kinship of worldview" is considerably more mystifying. The key text here is doubtless Briusov's *poèma* "To the Tsar' of the North Pole." Begun in September 1898 and completed in May 1900, this work seized and held Konevskoi's attention through every stage of its composition. In early July 1899, he wrote to Briusov from Finland: "I would be very glad if you would send me a copy of your poem about the Vikings. I have been wanting for a long time to read it." (*LN* 98:1:465). Soon after, Briusov sent "Sven of the Fair Teeth," with a note: This is part 1; 2, 3, 4 are not yet written" (*LN* 98:1:466, n. 6). In September Konevskoi wrote to him enthusiastically: "The *poèma* 'Tsar' of the North Pole', especially if it is continued, will grow into such an immense epos that it will show all your unsuspected strength" (*LN* 98:1:469). A month later, when Briusov sent fragments from the second and third parts, Konevskoi responded: "Again you have given me great delight in your poems about the polar lands." Then followed a detailed critique, where he especially admired "the immeasurable breadth of the horizon and the sweep of the air". Over all he marveled at the picture of the human will battling against the universe, which "deadens the heart". (*LN* 98:1:472-473)³¹

During Konevskoi's visit to Moscow in early January 1900, between inspections of ancient churches and icons, time presumably was found to discuss Briusov's *poèma*.³² Four months later Konevskoi again wrote: "From you I await more than ever the continuation of your *poèma* to the Tsar' of the North Pole. I hope that, in its full form, it will constitute the centerpiece of your *Tertia Vigilia*" (*LN* 98:1:498). When *Tertia Vigilia* at last appeared in the second half of October 1900, "To the King of the North Pole" bore on its title page "A Tale from the Time of the Vikings. Dedicated to Ivan Konevskoi."³³ A few days later, Konevskoi wrote to Briusov: "I offer you my gratitude, my friend, for *Tertia Vigilia*, and in particular for the dedication of the *poèma* about the Vikings. I remain of the opinion that this is the finest example of your poetry" (*LN* 98:1:515-516).[34]

Konevskoi's intense interest in "To the Tsar' of the North Pole", which he regularly referred to as "The Vikings", coincided with the development of what might be called his personal "northern myth." Early stages appeared in two poems written in spring 1898, "From Konevets" and "From Generation to Generation (I)," which sounded the first notes of the northern or "Varangian" theme in Konevskoi's poetry. Partly fed by the sense of his own lineage, partly by the larger "northern myth" already flourishing in Russia, Konevskoi's personal myth drew also on his engagement with nature mysticism and his rebellion against all boundaries that confined the human spirit.[35] The recent departure to the north woods of Aleksandr Dobroliubov, the Nansen polar expedition, the publication of a new translation of the Finnish *Kalevala*: all these drew his gaze northwards. Briusov's "Sven" embodied, in superb poetic form, the nineteenth century's nostalgia for certain "Nordic" qualities like courage, manliness and bravery. But for Konevskoi this figure meant far more. Sven's doughty followers thirsted for adventure — battle, bloodshed, booty — for its own sake, and perished as they lived. But Sven himself pursued a single goal and died, having achieved it.

Even setting aside the splendid poetry of Briusov's tale, the mythical Sven's attraction for Konevskoi is readily accounted for. The hero's fixity on a goal only partly understood becomes more intense as the quest goes on. Once he has penetrated the "forbidden retreat," time is overcome, and so, too, is space — the metaphysical obstacles that so tormented Konevskoi. "To the Tsar' of the North Pole" and his long period of watching its progress toward completion greatly nourished Konevskoi's growing personal myth. This cluster of ideas and images, along with his thinking about Varangians, death, life, and the absolute independence of the *persona*, will appear again in the near future. Meanwhile, "Ivan Oreus" was busy defining his identity as "Ivan Konevskoi," author of the collection of prose and poetry that he called *Dreams and Meditations*.

In retrospect, the friendship of these two poets is at times perplexing. The characterization offered by A. V. Lavrov in his introduction to their correspondence stressed the importance of Konevskoi's relationship with Briusov. To Konevskoi, "whose youth as a poet flowed in a 'cloistered' atmosphere, one of solitary meditation, the very fact of a trusted relationship with Briusov was precious above all." Moreover, "Briusov was valuable to Konevskoi as a responsive, interesting interlocutor, reacting sensitively to everything new and notable in literary life, as one of the few experts and admirers of the newest French poetry" (*LN* 98:1:426). But their relationship was hardly one of mentor and pupil. To begin with, Konevskoi had certain advantages over his friend: first, he was multilingual, with easy command of French and German and a sound working knowledge of English. Moreover, his breadth of reading enabled him to acquaint Briusov with such poets as Emile Verhaeren, and not the other way around. Finally, given Briusov's near-adulatory stance before Konevskoi's poetry, their positions vis-à-vis each other as poets achieved, not full equality, but a sort of complimentarity.

The range of their friendship, it could be said, was narrow but deep. Their real bond was their common passion for poetry. Yet, in fact, a vast, if largely unspoken, difference lay between them in what each believed the essential nature of poetry to be.[36] Their eyes were both set on the future of poetry — but "future," too, had different meanings for each and existed, perhaps, in two different worlds.

Looking at the time after Konevskoi's death, and the vacuum that loomed, Briusov promptly set out to collect, preserve, and publish in proper form his friend's work. When he wrote the letter, quoted above, the news of Konevskoi's death was very fresh in Briusov's mind, and his emotion undoubtedly was genuine. However, consistent with all that is known of his character, the real focus of his grief was the disappearance from the scene of a poet who was already of great achievement, with greater to come.

These two relationships, with Briusov and Anna Gippius, beginning within three months of each other in 1898, were portentous for Konevskoi, each in its own way. In his relations with Anna Gippius he encountered a set of emotions, experiences, and challenges, largely new and exhilarating, but also disquieting. Her brand of idealism, her independence of mind and spirit, and, withal, her intensely feminine presence, affected him powerfully. Directly or indirectly stimulated by her person, he wrote a quantity of excellent poetry, Before long, however, he was forced to a choice, which he made — out of fear or conviction, or both. Certainly his break with her was painful, perhaps traumatic. Did it affect him as a poet? A thinker? Was the effect, if any, positive or negative? Given the mere two years between their separation and his accidental death, these questions must join the many about Konevskoi that remain unanswered.

As for his relationship with Valerii Briusov, not only this, but the image of Konevskoi himself, were for a long time known chiefly through Briusov's writings about him: two memorial poems, but also the several versions of his memorial essay, the last published in 1916.[37] However, with the publication of the Briusov-Konevskoi letters in 1991, a rather different and more complete picture emerged, as this chapter has tried to show. Yet Konevskoi's major debt to Briusov surely lies in the latter's persistent efforts to make Konevskoi known as a major poet, issuing finally in the publication of the collected writings in 1904. If Briusov's labor was very largely dictated by his devotion to the cause of Russian poetry, Konevskoi would have been pleased.

Notes

1. Substantial new information is available about Anna Gippius and, primarily, about her younger sisters, whose way of life she rejected as religious-sexual fanaticism. See: M. M. Pavlova, "Istorii 'novoi' khristianskoi liubvi. Eroticheskii èksperiment Merezhkovskikh v svete 'Glavnogo': Iz 'dnevnikov' T. N. Gippius 1906-1908 godov". Intro., ed., notes, M. M. Pavlova. *Erotizm bez beregov*. Ed. V. Sazhin. Moscow: NLO, 2004.
2. "Istorii 'novoi' khristianskoi liubvi", pp. 392, 402, 405.
3. Anna Nikolaevna Gippius's date of birth has now been established by her own evidence, in a letter to her sister Zinaida, as 1875, making her only two years older than Konevskoi, not five, as previously thought. ("Istorii 'novoi' khristianskoi liubvi", p. 392 n. 4.)
4. "Joy wants the Eternity of *all* things, *wants deep, wants deep Eternity*." From "The Drunken Song," secs. 11, 12, penultimate part of *Zarathustra*. (Tr. Walter Kaufmann.)
5. *LN* 98:1:486, n. 4.
6. *SP 2008*, 122. Given his early fascination with Dostoevskii, Konevskoi may well have found inspiration for his imagery in the many intriguing spiritual pairings of his heroes.
7. In support of this belief, he adduced instances from the history of mediumism cited by Du Prel. He apparently found these helpful in explaining the mystical interpenetration with nature that he had lately experienced.
8. One reader close to Konevskoi was misled by the placement of the lyric in a sequence obviously devoted to Anna Gippius. Valerii Briusov firmly rejected the possibility of anything other than an ordinary love affair between the two. He later wrote: "Everything especially dear and close to Konevskoi was organically alien to her: his worldview, his favorite authors, his constant seriousness" (Br./Vengerov 2: 286). Whether Briusov ever met Anna Gippius is not known. Clearly Konevskoi confided very little to him about the relationship, beyond sending him copies of his new poems.
9. *The Complete Tales and Poems of Edgar Allan Poe*. The Modern Library Edition. New York: Random House, Inc., 1938. Pp. 951-954.

[10] *RGALI* 259.1.6.55ob.

[11] In a letter to Briusov two years after Konevskoi's death, his father, General Oreus, wrote: "I understand very well that Vania, by the cast of his mind and character, had little chance of finding so-called happiness in life, and that for him — I hope — it is better there than it would be here" (*LN* 98:1:546).

[12] The available text of this letter appears in: A. V. Lavrov, "Chaiu i chuiu (*I Hope and I Sense*)," *SP 2008*, 48, n. 1.

[13] Nearly two years earlier he had laid down a principle in such matters. In "To Many in Reply (*Mnogim v otvet*)" (24 July 1897) he wrote: "I did not love. I could not capture all the breadth of the spirit/ In one female person". (*SP 2008*, 29). At that moment his new-found intimacy with nature excluded other claims on his attention and affections. Over a year later, the situation obviously had become more complex.

[14] This abject admission of inadequacy seems to suggest, along with all else, a threat to his poetry: his most glowing words and thoughts, when offered to her, turn to "dirty smoky blobs".

[15] In spite of the "farewell" exchange of letters, Konevskoi may still have hoped for further initiatives from Anna's side. At least, he told Bilibin at the beginning of his letter: "I don't know whether this is the last echo, or the first glimmer of something new".

[16] Presumably Konevskoi referred here to Briusov's *Chefs d'oeuvre* (eds. 1, 2, 1895, 1896) and *Me Eum Esse* (1897). The former in particular indulged heavily in the vocabulary and devices singled out. See: Grossman, Joan Delaney, *Valery Bryusov and the Riddle of Russian Decadence*. Berkeley-Los Angeles: University of California Press, 1985. Ch. Two.

[17] Another important common interest was the newest French poetry, about which Konevskoi was much better informed than Briusov. In this same letter Konevskoi again urged Briusov's attention to certain French poets, especially Viélé-Griffin and Henri de Régnier. This was to be an ongoing subject for discussion. During the following month Briusov argued strenuously for the merits of Verlaine and Mallarmé, as opposed to Konevskoi's favorites, including Verhaeren (of whom Briusov knew relatively little). Urged on by Konevskoi Briusov soon came around to his view on Verhaeren,

acknowledged his excellence as poet and in the years following translated his work and generally spread his fame in Russia.

[18] If Briusov's relationship with Konevskoi was substantial and lasting, Bal'mont's ties with him were short-lived and problematic. Early on Bal'mont conceived a scheme to publish Konevskoi's poems, along with those of Briusov, Sologub, Gippius, and others. However, *Kniga razdumii*, S.-Petersburg, 1899, ultimately contained only poems of Bal'mont, Briusov, Konevskoi, and Modest Durnov, poet, artist, and architect. Konevskoi came to dislike Bal'mont's poetry intensely. In a later letter to Briusov he referred to him as "a shallow and lively charlatan" (*LN* 98:1:491).

[19] This poem stands as the final statement in the volume *Dreams and Meditations* and will be discussed in the next chapter.

[20] RGALI.259.1.11.20-30ob; 259.1.6.19.

[21] Finally, the matter was solved provisionally, when in early June a letter mailed from Arkhangelsk granting permission arrived from Dobroliubov. It was from the Solovetskii Monastery and was addressed to Briusov's wife, Ioanna Matveevna. (*LN* 1:464, n.7)

[22] The "Scorpio" edition carries at the head of "Notes" the following: "The publishers do not consider it superfluous to list the manuscripts of A. Dobroliubov that are known to them." Five collections are listed, two held by Erlikh, three by Briusov. These include fragments and complete pieces, prose and poetry; two additional collections are mentioned. The originals of many poems printed here are in these collections. (*AMD*, 67-68, 2nd numeration [187-188]).

[23] Aleksandr Dobroliubov, *Sochineniia*. Reprint; introduction by Joan Delaney Grossman. Berkeley, 1981.) This volume includes both the 1900 *Sobranie stikhov* and the earlier *Natura naturans. Natura Natura*, as well as Dobroliubov's poems that appeared in the almanachs *Severnye tsvety*, 1901, 1902, and 1903. Also included are the two essays, Konevskoi's "Toward the Study of the *Persona* of Aleksandr Dobroliubov" ([pp. 123-127]), and Briusov's "On Russian Versification" ([pp. 128-134]).

[24] Z. N. Gippius, "Kritika liubvi," *Literaturnyi dnevnik*. 1899-1907. St. Petersburg, 1908. Reprint: Wilhem Fink Verlag: München, 1970. Pp. 55-56. Konevskoi responded fiercely with "Ob otpevanii novoi russkoi poezii (Obshchie

suzhdeniia Z. Gippius v No. 17-18 *Mira Iskusstva* 1900 g.) (*Requiem for the New Russian Poetry [General Judgments by Z. Gippius in No. 17-18 World of Art 1900]*). *Severnye tsvety na 1901 god (Northern Flowers for 1901)*. For texts and a full discussion of these polemics see: A. V. Lavrov, "Ivan Konevskoi—polemist," *Russkaia literatura*, vol. 1, 2008, pp. 211-221.

[25] IRLI 377.2. Arkhiv S. A. Vengerova. V. V. Gippius. "O samom sebe".

[26] In "Put' Aleksandra Dobroliubova" (*Tvorchestvo A. A. Bloka i russkaia kul'tura XX veka. Blokovskii sbornik III* [Tartu 1979]), K. M. Azadovskii wrote: "Dobroliubov's 'withdrawal' occurred in spring-summer 1898. However, the crisis that led to his decision to 'withdraw' occurred earlier" (p.128).

[27] Some evidence exists of Dobroliubov's awareness of and interest in Konevskoi, sometime after he abandoned his first Petersburg phase. The incomplete opening line of an undated letter from Dobroliubov to Konevskoi reads: "From A.M.D.: Dear youth! If you actually have submitted yourself or —" (RGALI.259.1.1.1). However, a letter from "A.M.D." is no assurance of personal acquaintance, since, in the early 1900s, Dobroliubov wrote to many literary personages — not necessarily alive at the time — , urging them to follow his example of withdrawal from society. (Azadovskii, 138) Konevskoi's name occurs in a letter from Dobroliubov to Belyi, probably written early in 1905. There he offered, among other pieces of spiritual advice, the following: "You are continuing Konevskoi, be a worthy heir. Forget his errors, but better, choose the best from him" (Azadovskii, 139). It would be interesting to know what Dobroliubov considered Konevskoi's "best" qualities or actions to be, and what were his "errors".

[28] A. V. Lavrov, "Perepiska s. Iv. Konevskim. Vstup. stat'ia". *LN* 98:1:429.

[29] *LN* 98:1:427. Reproduction of Konevskoi's inscription to Briusov in a gift copy of *Dreams and Meditations*, November, 1899.

[30] *LN* 85:646-647. Briusov's relations with A. A. Shesterkina were extremely close from 1900 to 1902. In his frequent letters he shared intimate feelings and moods. Among the summer's misfortunes to which he referred were his wife's stillborn child and her subsequent illness.

[31] Some of Konevskoi's suggestions were duly adopted by Briusov. *LN* 98:1:474, nn.1-5.

[32] *Dn.* 80.

[33] This dedication was later removed, but, from the second edition on, the entire volume was headed by the dedication: "In Memory of Ivan Konevskoi and Georg Bachmann, two departed."

[34] Nonetheless, he did not refrain from adding: "Alas! an extremely ambiguous impression is created by the final Voice."

[35] Nilsson, Nils Ake, "Russia and the Myth of the North: The Modernist Response." *Russian Literature*, XXI-II, 15 February 1987, 125-139. Otto Boele, *The North in Russian Romantic Literature*, Amsterdam-Atlanta, 1996.

[36] Konevskoi was generally measured in his comments on Briusov's poetry, rarely expressing great enthusiasm. The obvious exception is "Tsar' of the North Pole" and one or two others that appeared in *Tertia Vigilia* (1900). Briusov's first collection *Chefs d'oeuvre* may have been known to Konevskoi when he wrote "Lyric Poetry in Contemporary Russia", but it scarcely would have met his criteria for inclusion.

[37] The first was published in *World of Art*, November 1901, No. 8-9, the last in the classic *Russian Literature of the Twentieth Century*, edited by S. A. Vengerov. (See also "Introduction.")

Chapter 5

"Dreams and Meditations"

Throughout the spring of 1899, letters from Konevskoi to Briusov were accompanied by a stream of new poems for the recipient's admiration and comment. Along with these came Konevskoi's prose translations of poems from several languages, accompanied by his pronouncements about his preferred method of translation, with which Briusov strongly disagreed. Finally, in late June, after packing notes and manuscripts, Konevskoi left St. Petersburg in search of quiet, cheap lodging in nearby Finland. His goal for the summer was preparation for publication in book-form of his writings since 1896.

But he had another objective as well. Writing to Aleksandr Bilibin on 2 July, his first day in Nevvola, Konevskoi alluded to vexations of the past month that made his move from Petersburg necessary, including "a mood of great, though quiet, spiritual disorder" that has dominated him for some time (AVL, 175). To Bilibin he could write as if no explanation for his depression was needed. Only a few weeks ago he had shared with this close friend (presumably not for the first time) the intimate details of his relations with Anna Gippius and their break-up. But beyond this source of suffering, he indicated others, including imprisonment "in the burnt lime of the swampy capital" (AVL, 174).[1] However, the Pension Lang, where he now resided, offered a suitable retreat for regaining his emotional balance.

The past months, he reported, had brought on "a great decline of spirit and creative strength." But a partial distraction arose in the shape of his project to publish his work. This plan was made possible by the generous biennial gift from his "Austrian aunt," the same who previously had supported his travels. "This time I've decided to use it for a complete edition of my lyric poetry (in verse and in prose), with the addition of many translations from foreign languages into prose" (*AVL*, 176).

The plan sketched here shows that, although Konevskoi had already mulled the project for some time, the form was not yet final. Nor was the author's pen name decided. To Bilibin he wrote: "The collection's title will be: *Dreams and Meditations of Ivan Ezerskii: In Passing I-V — Thoughts During Travels — Boecklin's Paintings (a lyrical characterization) — In Passing VI — Translations of Poems in Prose*" (*AVL*, 177). To Briusov ten days earlier he gave the title as "Dreams and Meditations of Ivan Konevskoi."[2]

The decision to use a pen name was made, at least partly, at the behest of General Oreus, who, though generally supportive of his son's projects, nonetheless could not countenance use of the family name in association with the new poetry.[3] At the same time, this circumstance gave the young poet a unique opportunity to shape further the new identity he was forming. The Varangian who made his first appearance in the lyric "From Konevets" was linked to a geographical location, the island of Konevets, which had its own historical connotations. (Had that Varangian been named, he would fittingly have been called "Konevskoi.") Since that surname apparently was Ivan Konevskoi's invention, he was free to attach to it the meanings he chose, drawing on the Varangian/Old Russian heritage to which he felt himself entitled. Moreover, the name might serve — as in fact it did — as the center around which a poetic myth was created. The name "Ezerskii," on the other hand, carried its own identity, imparted by Aleksandr Pushkin.[4] While Pushkin's Ezerskii was of noble lineage, the hero himself was a mere cog in the Emperor's bureaucratic machine and represented the decline of the old noble stock. Konevskoi would take up that theme in his late, unfinished narrative poèma "Milieu (*Sreda*)," but apparently he chose for the present to defer it.

Dreams and Meditations can be viewed as a spiritual diary, including, inevitably, a strong element of self-examination, coupled with efforts at self-definition.[5] In his 1916 retrospective, possibly reflecting on his own autobiographical writings, Briusov wrote: "He constantly returned to self-definition […]. And from these self-definitions emerged a distinct image, perhaps not fully the one that showed Konevskoi as he was in reality, but the one by which he represented himself to himself" (*Br./Vengerov* 2:289). In any case, Konevskoi was unquestionably right in regarding this undertaking as a summing up of the road he had covered thus far. In accomplishing this task, he arranged items to produce a very personal, subjective narrative with only periodic nods at chronological accuracy. Numerous themes weave through the sections, and toward the end of the final section his conflicted relationship with the physical world, including his own body, assumed particular prominence. This enterprise, too, was part of Konevskoi's passionate, ongoing effort to penetrate the mysteries in, around, and beyond him, which was consuming his artistic and spiritual energies at the end of 1899.

1. "Le sourire ètrange de la Vie"

The overall effect of *Dreams and Meditations* is idiosyncratic, though by no means chaotic.[6] Size and type of print vary, seemingly at random. There is no table of contents. Instead, the title page provides large headings, with subheads dated to mark what Konevskoi considered in retrospect to be epochs in his life. Where dates do occur — usually at the beginning and end of sections, — they are significant.

The collection opens with three poems, all dated, with their own epigraphs and dedications. Together they offer a cryptic outline of the text to follow. Moreover, they encapsulate the past and present of his spiritual journey as he perceived it, and then they project future steps. The first of these, "Dedication (*Posveshchenie*) to Da Vinci's 'Gioconda,'" has as epigraph a line from one of Konevskoi's favorite French Symbolists, Henri de Régnier. It pictures the poet standing, fascinated but uncomprehending, before "Le sourire ètrange de la Vie." Konevskoi's poem, dated 26 June 1898, in Lauterbrunnen, in the Berner Oberland, i.e., near the start of his second European tour, expresses the sense of puzzlement and wonder that accompanied him on this journey. The second, "From 'Eternal Vaults'

(*Iz 'vechnykh svodov'*)", dated 26 September 1898, marks the moment when, having returned from his second journey west, he feels himself poised to enter a new phase.[7] As Briusov later wrote: "These two journeys drew a line between the former lad Vania, who lived in closest intimacy with his old father, and the independent young man Ivan Konevskoi, poet-'decadent,' sought-after guest in certain literary circles" (*Br./Vengerov*, 2:283-284).

However, of the three lyrics, the third is the one that raises the most fascinating questions, both for its content and for its dedication. "A Summons (*Prizyv*). (To Valerii Ia. Briusov)" was one of the latest items added to the collection. "A Summons" calls the addressee to join a quest for "another, broader life" that Konevskoi now suspects must exist in some form, in some "other" state of being.[8] His longstanding rebellion against the limitations laid upon human nature comes to a head in the pathetic human figure at its center, cut off from the great natural universe. Those marvelous instants of oneness with nature that he experienced during the previous summer told him that the barrier was not impenetrable. Yet they were mere glimpses of that "other" state he so desired to attain.

"In Passing (*Mel'kom*)" was the expression Konevskoi chose to convey the notion that these lyrics, rich as they are in content, conveyed "mere glimpses" of life as he had seen it in those few years. "In Passing: I-V" separated its contents roughly by chronology (sometimes adjusted thematically) and genre. "*I. In Cell and in Field* (*V kel'e i v pole*). *1895/96. Winter and summer*" includes poetry written during his early period, beginning with "Resurrection," February 1895. This is followed by "*II. Sonnets. 1896. Late summer and early autumn*," the climax of which is the masterful cycle "Son of the Sun." Here several important future themes are introduced.

The poems and short pieces of descriptive prose in the next two sections cover what may be called Konevskoi's cultural and spiritual awakening. They are gathered under the title "Visions of Travels (*Videniia stranstvii*). III. IV." Epigraphs begin to appear in this section, beginning with Tiutchev's: "This wondrous world…/ With its varied forms/…/Through hamlet, town, and field/ glimmering stretches the road." His first discovery of the Alps, in summer 1897, is aptly introduced by William Wordsworth's "For the power of the hills is on thee..." But the series is capped, unexpectedly, by "From Konevets" (spring, 1898). The Varangian-Rus' theme continues immediately with "From Generation to Generation: I" (April 1898). The final lyric, "Before and After (*Do i posle*)," follows the traveler home with his expanded store of vivid memories.

The fifth section of "In Passing" is devoted solely to the four-part poem "A Wild Place (*Debri*)" (1897/98). Then comes a collection of prose pieces from both summers, "Thoughts During Travels (*Umozreniia stranstvii*)." This is the sum of the meditative descriptions that trace his initiation into mysticism through European art and the forests of Thuringia to Lake Como. They lead up to the major essay, the centerpiece of the book: "Böcklin's Paintings. (Lyrical characterization)." *Dreams and Meditations*, now three-quarters of the way to completion, provides a backward reflection over the road the young poet has traveled spiritually to reach the point where he now stands. This pivotal study of Böcklin, who "keenly listened to the flight of the future," points a course toward that future.[9]

2. "In Passing. Experiences, Combinations, Foretellings"

The final section of *Dreams and Meditations* bears an epigraph from Goethe: "Die Welt ist voller Widerspruch, — / Und sollte sich's nicht widersprechen?" (*Vorklage z. d. Liedern*). For Konevskoi, that fall, winter, and spring of 1898-1899 was a period of change and mingled uncertainty, happiness, self-doubt, and near-despair. Reflecting on the recent past, he saw dreams and disappointments mingling with new experiences, feelings, and challenges, and consequently felt deeply uncertain of the outcomes. The first half of 1899 was the most productive period of his short career as poet, with thirty-five lyrics, including two cycles, written between January and mid-June (compared to fifteen for the rest of 1899, and twenty five for all of the previous year). Of that thirty-five, only two (unfinished) were omitted from the book.

The section opens with a cluster of "experiences," the first of which is "The Sea of Life," with its delightful recollections of childhood fantasies and adventures in reading. Together with the next two poems, "A Solemn Vow

(Obetovanie)" and "Echoes *(Otgoloski)*," it forms a trilogy, through which the poet's *persona* moves from childhood imaginings through adolescent thirst for exotic adventure, to the verge of maturity. His recent journeys figure in "Echoes," both as warm memories and as travels in what the epigraph from Paul Verlaine called "Le pays de mon rêve".

The degree and kind of freedom Konevskoi experienced on those two journeys to western Europe was a major departure from anything he had known before. Not only was he able to go alone where he wanted, see and do what he wanted, his mind itself was freer than it had ever been. Especially was this so during the second summer, when he found himself able to think more freely about very many things, including what freedom itself, in its various forms, truly was.

These and related themes recur among the lyrics in this section, sometimes anchored by folkloric or mythic images. A striking example is "A Dream of Battle *(Son bor'by)*." The epigraph is from Nekrasov, and the all-pervasive "wind" of Nekrasov's lines is the also dominant image of Konevskoi's poem. But resemblance to Nekrasov stops there. Konevskoi's dream-vision takes the poet-figure on a strange journey, where he bonds firmly with the wind, "wandering Vetrilo," and becomes, along with him, a power moving freely outside human affairs.[10] After the long and transforming journey, he awakens to find himself a stranger, alien to human life. The wind sweeps hauntingly through these six stanzas, with their long lines of iambic hexameter. Alliteration and assonance abound, with the "v" of "*Vetrilo*" and "*veter*" — "wind," in Russian — predominating. It is a mysterious poem, revealing and concealing at once.

After his son's death, Konevskoi's father wrote to Briusov of visiting his son's grave in the woods on a windy day: "He loved the forest (remember his 'A Wild Place') — and he is buried in the forest; he loved the wind, finding much poetry in it, — and on that day, in wonderful, clear weather, there was a strong wind blowing..." (*LN* 98:1:536.) Indeed, along with the sea, wind is one of the central elements in Konevskoi's symbolic system. His essay on Böcklin's paintings is filled with descriptions of wind and sea together: "From sea to sea a fresh, free wind plays. It is as if, across the entire face of the earth, in broad streams, quivering life flows." Everywhere is the "world wind...": the wind, the sea, the sky together as living symbols of all that Konevskoi held most essential: freedom, in all its configurations. (*SP1904*, 161, 162.)

A cosmic variant of all this appeared at least once, in "Winter Night (*Zimniaia noch'*)," a lyric written in January 1899 and dedicated to Aleksandr Bilibin (in Konevskoi's eyes the very image of a free spirit).[11] The feeling of free movement throughout the universe, evoked by a starry northern sky, is a magnificently liberating one. But more and more, Konevskoi found his innate passion for freedom clashing with the limitations forced on human nature — time, space, heredity, his own body. And along with this grew his determination to find a way of dealing with that body: subduing or transforming it, or evading the limiting factors by some other means altogether.

The next two poems begin to envision, if only symbolically, freedom from the body and its constraints. The first, "Contempt (*Prezrenie*)," is a recasting of the lyric "From Afar," where the poet imagines himself as the victim of a clash between the forces of Rus' and alien hordes from the steppe. In that earlier poem, his final charge to his comrades is to build a glorious burial mound, beneath which he may rest in peace. In "Contempt" the message is different. Gone are the images of glorious combat, of honorific burial in the field. Instead, the fallen warrior tells those who have found his corpse: toss it away and let the plowing begin! But while his corpse lies rotting, his spirit goes free, seemingly wafted away by the wind.

Following this comes "From Cold Freedom (*S kholodnoi voli*)," where the wind appears in all its symbolic force. Gazing out at the driven clouds and hearing the wind, the poet feels his heart straining to break loose from its restraints and flee to the "world weather," his true fatherland. Yet, despite this ecstatic yearning to be up and away, Konevskoi was still in a quandary about achieving total freedom, even about its true nature. Was freeing the spirit from the power of the flesh a goal to be aimed for, or was it even desirable?[12]

Another, striking item in this cluster is the untitled lyric beginning: "There is a great struggle in my blood." The speaker hears there a reproachful chorus of past generations, his physical antecedents, reminding him of his debt to them — his body — and exhorting him: "Live!" Is he then to be trapped in an existence shared with plants, and animals, confined to the formula "born-reproduce-die"? Does this body, the agent of his moments of intimacy with nature, in the end also pull him into the limited existence of the natural world? That relationship that he has so ardently sought would seem, then, to have its disturbing side. The latter half of the poem provides answers, determined, defiant. In a word, he tells those voices urging him "live" that he has another, higher life live, that of the heart and the spirit. Yet he does not sound totally convinced that his answer is complete.

For this piece Konevskoi chose an arresting epigraph: "*Genus — genius. Vladimir Solov'ev*". In his short article "Genius" written for the Brokgauz-Efron encyclopedia, Solov'ev initially linked the origin of "genius" with the term "genus" (Russian "*rod* — clan, primary group").[13] This entity, expanded to include race and heritage, is the ultimate source from which flows all the layered treasure accumulated from the beginning. The "*rod*," then, as Solov'ev explained it, is carried forward through *both* body and spirit. Konevskoi used Solov'ev's reasoning to support the claims in his final quatrain, where he carefully spells out his heritage: "Not only bone and flesh, taken from bone, flesh — I am an independent and free spirit." Bravely said.

The lyric "Genius" is linked to that just discussed not only by the latter's epigraph. However, the emphasis is different. Far from separating himself from other living things, in "Genius" the poet insists on their close loving kinship: he is of their "breed." Nor, greatly as he still yearns to be free of the weight pulling him ever downward, is he willing to abandon this kinship link for an unknown higher existence. But can he have it all? He thinks he may.

However, immediately following this is "The Quarrel (*Spor*)," where conflict between spirit and body comes to the fore again.[14] The tone now is long-suffering endurance liberally laced with humor. Thus the uneasy, unavoidable and, in the end, fond interdependence of spirit and flesh is ruefully accepted, as his love of earth and life begins to be reconciled with the yearning of his spirit to be free. Penetrating the secrets of the universe is still Konevskoi's goal, but perhaps the body, too, can be turned to advantage. Instead of threatening his freedom, this indissoluble relationship of spirit and body may still provide opportunities worth exploring.

The final poem of this series, "Declaration to Truth," also forms its climax. Already cited in the previous chapter as a response to Briusov's notion of a pantheon of beliefs, it again displays the growing impact of certain of Nietzsche's ideas on Konevskoi's thinking at that time. This poem might have served conveniently as a bridge to the translations conceived as the final section of *Dreams and Meditations*, since, as will be seen, some of Nietzsche's poems played a central part. In the event, however, the translation project remained unpublished. Emphasis was thus thrown entirely on Konevskoi's original writings and the picture they presented of his spiritual profile at that point.

3. The Translation Project

In a letter from the second half of April 1899, Konevskoi revealed to Briusov, perhaps for the first time, the extent to which poetic translation now formed part of his artistic program: "Recently I have translated a great many poems for the first time and brought into order much in my previous translations of Viélé-Griffin, de Régnier, Verhaeren, Swinburne, Rossetti, Nietzsche" (*LN* 98:1:457-458). One possible future project concerned the first-named, of whose poems he had translated so many that "it seems to me it would be possible to put together an entire collection of his poems in Russian" (98:1:458). However, for his immediate purpose, the array of talents needed to be more varied and more inclusive:

> Or perhaps a volume of some poems I have already translated, along with selected long narrative poems [*poèma*] by various poets, such as — aside from Viélé — de Régnier, Verhaeren, Swinburne, Rossetti, Nietzsche, which I have already considered for translation, would have a still more internally coherent character. A collection of such selected works would be marked, it seems to me, not only by profound internal unity, but also by the manysidedness of its expression of truly-*contemporary* poetry: by

"contemporary" I mean that *new*, excellent thing that the poetry of our day has brought to the earlier and just as new, but *different* images of the eternal.

To this list, he considered adding passages from Ibsen, Maeterlinck, Emerson, and Ruskin. He concluded: "In this, I think, a really philosophically-generalizing formulation of 'the contemporary' would be achieved" (98:1:458). Writing several weeks later to Aleksandr Bilibin, he put his purpose more crisply: "The object of the translations is to produce the fullest and most vivid formula of the philosophical meaning of the chief contemporary moods" (*AVL*, 177).

A month later, with publication plans for the entire project drawing closer to realization, Konevskoi set about gathering the manuscripts loaned to friends. On 24 May he gave Briusov careful instructions for returning those he had left in Moscow on his recent visit:

"[I]f you please, on the wrapper of the package write my father's title: "His Excellency (Ivan Ivanovich Oreus)" Otherwise, I fear those sycophants, noting my name, would find it necessary to investigate the contents of so bulky a manuscript, and having done so, would detain and submit it to special review (in particular —translations, for example, — from the forbidden books of Swinburne)" (98:1:462).[15]

On 2 July, writing to Bilibin from Finland, Konevskoi asked him to return the translations loaned him, "among which the excerpts from Nietzsche must serve as the final chord of the whole translation project."[16] The important mission of this section, as he saw it, clearly required careful planning; choice and placement of selections were not negotiable. In the light of this, he again voiced apprehensions about the censor's reaction to the selections from Swinburne, the "great and magical poet," whose poems, destined as cornerstones of the collection, contained "extremely sharp affirmations of pantheism against Christianity" (*AVL*, 177).

Konevskoi's enthusiasm for the English writer Algernon Charles Swinburne focused on just a few of the poet's most famous poems, which pressed hard against — or overstepped — the boundaries of generally accepted morality and belief. Of those poems, the one on which, by all indications, he laid most weight was "Hertha." Many critics have ranked "Hertha" among Swinburne's finest works for its vigor and sweeping lines. Others, particularly among his Victorian contemporaries, found it blasphemous. Konevskoi obviously considered it to be eminently expressive of the "contemporary" spirit. The pagan pantheistic doctrine voiced by its central figure is at times embodied in the earth-mother, at times the world tree of Norse mythology:[17]

> I am that which began;
> Out of me the years roll;
> Out of me God and man;
> I am equal and whole;
> God changes, and man, and the form of them bodily;
> I am the soul.
>
> Before ever land was,
> Before ever the sea,
> Or fair limbs of the tree,
> Or the flesh-colored fruit of my branches, I was,
> and thy soul was in me (1:732).[18]

Near the poem's climax comes Swinburne's version of the "death of God" — the same proclaimed a few years later by Nietzsche's prophet Zarathustra:

> For his twilight is come on him,
> His anguish is here;
> And his spirits gaze dumb on him,
> Grown gray from his fear;
> And his hour taketh hold on him stricken, the last
> of his infinite year (1:739).

The poem's final line contains the apotheosis of "man" heard in so many works of the later nineteenth century in various languages: "Man, equal and one with me, man that is made of me, man that is I" (1:740). This triumphant cry is heard again in another favorite of Konevskoi's, "The Prelude." Man's life is traced through time and change, from youth till the end, with one message: man's soul is the supreme arbiter and guide: "Save his own soul's light overhead,/ None leads him, and none ever led, [...] Save his own soul he hath no star" (1:668).

Two other poems by Swinburne, "Genesis" and "Anactoria," also stood high on Konevskoi's list.[19] "Genesis" is an astringent revised retelling of the Book of Genesis: "Yea, before any world had any light, /Or anything called God or man drew breath,/ Slowly the strong sides of the heaving night/ Moved, and brought forth the strength of life and death" (1:777). "Anactoria" is a dramatic monologue delivered by Sappho. (1:57-66) Apparently for Konevskoi it encapsulated major decadent themes: defiance of traditional morality, sexual freedom, and, perhaps even more, the superior human being's contempt for lesser beings and refusal to admit death's final power over the poet, whose song is supreme. Clearly, then, for the goal Konevskoi had in mind — "the fullest and most vivid formula of the philosophical meaning of the chief contemporary moods," — Swinburne ranked alongside, or above, Nietzsche in importance.

In the same July letter to Bilibin, Konevskoi addressed some cautionary remarks to his friend's budding interest in Nietzsche, which probably was inspired by his reading of Konevskoi's translated excerpts. Konevskoi cautioned that, "if you are going to acquaint yourself with *Zarathustra* in its entirety, you will find few passages worthy of comparison with the two chapters of Part IV that you already know" — i.e., "Noon" and "The Drunken Song (Midnight)".[20]

Konevskoi's first intensive acquaintance with Nietzsche's writings apparently began in December 1898, when he read both *Also Sprach Zarathustra* and *Die Geburt der Tragödie*. By all indications, it was the former that held his attention. However, as the above warning to Bilibin shows, his reaction was not unmixedly positive: quite the opposite. His remarks on *Zarathustra* continue with the disappointed wrath of one who expected better: "Most of the rest is incomparably lower, and indeed like Nietzsche's writings generally, reveals only, as if in passing and randomly, magnificent world horizons", while the rest is not only "senseless" but "boiling over with the commonest street talk, suitable only for vulgarians" (*AVL*, 177). One of the "horizons" glimpsed but not fully expanded was, to judge from his notes, Zarathustra's proclamation of the *Übermensch*. He would soon pursue this topic further.

Meanwhile, Konevskoi continued to gather his manuscripts and ready them for submission to the censor. Before that could occur, of course, there was the matter of money. The plan to publish depended on the generosity of his "Austrian aunt," who in previous years had financed his journeys west. At the outset, the gift of two hundred rubles seemed adequate to cover the printing of the entire collection. Now, in early July, he awaited the final word from the printer. However, when the total cost turned out to be 300, not 200, rubles, the translation section had to be eliminated. (*LN 98:1:464, n.3*). *Dreams and Meditations*, when it appeared late in 1899, consisted of just that — Konevskoi's original work, poetry and prose. The translations, to which he attached particular importance, were left behind.

4. Poems in Prose

For Konevskoi, publication of *Dreams and Meditations* in no way marked the end of his efforts to see his translations in print. Moreover, a new factor entered his calculations near the end of 1899, with the establishment of "Scorpio," the publishing house that one scholar called "a stronghold of the Russian symbolists."[21] One of "Scorpio"'s earliest publications was the collected poetry of Aleksandr Dobroliubov, to which Konevskoi had devoted much time and energy, and in which his essay "Toward the Study of the *Persona* of Aleksandr Dobroliubov" and Briusov's "On Russian Versification" served as forewords. Briusov, now a close comrade and literary adviser of its publisher, S. A. Poliakov, secured the volume's publication.

Yet, however influential the role of Briusov in "Scorpio"'s affairs, Konevskoi might reasonably have entertained doubts about his willingness to assist in publishing the cherished project, the collection of translations. Already the previous June Briusov wrote: "Speaking generally, for me your original poems are dearer, more precious than translations" (*98:1:463*). Whatever his objections, they were not spelled out here, probably because Konevskoi was already well aware of them. Their disagreement on the relative merits of using poetry or prose for poetic translation was profound and probably dated almost from the beginning of their acquaintance. In the already-cited letter of the second half of April 1899, Konevskoi's forceful statement of his position implied an ongoing dispute:

> I continue to insist on my conviction that, [...] in general, truly artistic verbal creation cannot and must not depend on its metric form, so that it becomes plainly inartistic when deprived of that form: the latter case would be a true sign that the metrical form merely masked the inadequacies of its images. Metrical sound deepens the action of the lyric's images; linked with these it is a new exemplar of the artistically splendid. But by itself, without their help, it lacks any such meaning. The construction of images of a word must represent, on the contrary and without any link to sounds, an independent model of artistic action. *(98:1:458)*.

As is well known, both positions have very long histories of support among poets and translators.[22] In an unpublished article from the 1930s the critic and scholar N. L. Stepanov noted that, in defending prose translation of poetry and also in asserting that metrical translation may conceal a lack of ideas, Konevskoi was repeating arguments made by Goethe. However, Stepanov, who had the advantage of firsthand study of Konevskoi's texts, stoutly defended, not so much the principle laid down with such firmness, as the poetic excellence of his prose translations. (*LN 98:1:460 n.9*)

In the same article, Stepanov noted a feature of the poems chosen for translation that guaranteed the "cohesion and unity" of the volume:

> Despite the differences among the poets represented here, the choice of them, as well as the selection of individual works, was made by Konevskoi in conformity with his philosophical and artistic views, thanks to which the translations were linked as closely as possible with his original work. There

appeared in the poems translated by Konevskoi the themes and moods characteristic also of his own lyrics. From the works of various poets he chose the "philosophical lyric," which rendered the "mystical feeling" of the end of the nineteenth century (*LN 98:1:460, n.10*).

Moreover, Stepanov observed, "[t]he very method of translation, the ideological and stylistic accents imparted by Konevskoi, brought the translations close to his own poetry."

Konevskoi's unyielding insistence that, generally speaking, poetry cannot be translated in any way but in prose was countered by Briusov's own statement of principle, with no compromise forthcoming from either side. Briusov's "manifesto" came in his "On Russian Versification". For Briusov the whole question of translation centered on the sanctity of the poetic line. The line was the "sacred matter" of poetry, separated totally from ordinary language. "The line is a particular whole." He then explained the organization of the line: "The unit of measure of the line is the image. The line's size is determined by the number of images, i.e., the important, meaningful expressions it contains. [...] Those lines that are equal in number of images are of equal dimension. These images stand in specific places, such as, at the very beginning, the middle, and the end" (Dobroliubov, 129). His conclusion was admirably concise: "The essence of the line is the equilibrium of images" (131).

However, Briusov's argument did nothing to dissuade Konevskoi from his project. One reason for that may have been that, to Konevskoi's mind, it was irrelevant. He found nothing to quarrel about in Briusov's prescription for the original lyric; translation was another matter. Here he simply rejected Briusov's basic premise that the poetic line is primary, that it cannot be separated into its elements and reorganized without destroying the essential poem. For him the thought-bearing image was primary; if anything is to be sacrificed — and surely, in translation something is — let it be that which is most dispensable.

Upon reading Briusov's essay a few days after the Dobroliubov volume appeared in print, Konevskoi wrote a complimentary note: "Your note 'On Russian Versification,' it seems to me, is true in its feeling for the matter and cleverly generalized and proven" (*98:1:488*). It was a carefully worded response, leaving the matter of translation unmentioned: they agreed to disagree. Yet, in early May 1900, he broached the matter again, with a practical end in view:

> Despite your intention of translating, or, perhaps, already completion of the translations, of course in verse, from [Verhaeren's] poetry, I am pursuing all the more my long-stated aim of precisely rendering his poems into prose. At present, the highly significant program of such translations, which I conceived, is almost completed. And, of course, the idea of a series of translations laid out by "Scorpio" strongly inclines me to hope for the inclusion of my collection in the complex. [He then prodded slyly:] I hope that the publisher of "Scorpio" will not share your uncompromisingly negative attitude toward translation of poetry by means of prose, and therefore I have decided to transmit through you my proposal to publish my volume of translations. I would be grateful if I might learn from you the address of S. A. Poliakov (*LN 1:98:492).*

Briusov's response was diplomatic, if somewhat disingenuous in its disclaimer of power to make decisions for "Scorpio." He also offered a palliative, namely, that S. A. Poliakov (presently traveling in the Crimea and the Caucasus) had expressed the desire to carry out Dobroliubov's plan of publishing translations of "examples of the newest poetry — Russian, French, English, German, Italian, Scandinavian, Polish, Czech...". And perhaps Konevskoi would be willing to add his translations to such a project. (*98:1:496*)

But presumably Konevskoi had already noticed on the foreleaf of *Aleksandr Dobroliubov. Collected Works,* the heading "In press," followed by three items. The third of these read: "Examples of the 'newest' poetry in translations by Aleksandr Dobroliubov and Vladimir Gippius. "[23] He promptly responded: "What you write about S. A. Poliakov's plans concerning translated editions awakens hope in me." However, his remarks on May 14 were less conciliatory: "In any case, if he intends to execute A. Dobroliubov's scheme faithfully, then let him take note of what was passed on to me recently by Erlikh: [...] it turns out that [Dobroliubov] agrees with me entirely in my view that word-for-word prose is necessary in translation of any poetry" (497).

There the matter lay till late August, when Konevskoi heard from S. A. Poliakov. This letter contained a rejection of Konevskoi's proposal for a volume of carefully selected translations, but instead proposed something more limited: "If you would offer us a volume of translations of either Swinburne or Rossetti, it could appear as part of the proposed series."[24] Nothing was said about prose translations, but shortly after, Briusov wrote: "Don't be offended that you cannot come to terms with 'Scorpio.' [Poliakov] is extremely burdened, with so many publications on hand" (98:1:509).

Meanwhile, the almanach *Northern Flowers for 1901 (Severnye tsvety na 1901 g.)* was in preparation and already advertised by "Scorpio." Konevskoi offered several poems, articles, and — as if to keep the subject alive — a sampling of his prose translations: "I cannot resist pointing to the excellent sense of the prose translations, even though unsympathetic to you, even of Viélé-Griffin" adding: "although as to independent publication [...] I await S. A. Poliakov's answer" *(98:1:511)*. But the final answer came from Briusov: "Translations in prose are completely unsuitable to the character of the Almanach" *(98:1:514)*. Moreover, writing in Poliakov's name, Briusov also laid to rest any hope that Konevskoi still retained for publication by "Scorpio" of a full volume of translation. He offered as the reason competing commitments and financial risks and obligations.[25] A month later, on 20 November 1900, Konevskoi accepted with grace the hard realities of the publishing business.

So ended Konevskoi's determined campaign to present Russian readers with a meaningful picture of the contemporary spirit in European poetry. So also were these and later readers deprived of valuable insights into some major changes that occurred in Konevskoi's spiritual profile over the four years covered by *Dreams and Meditations*.

Notes

[1] This unflattering description is one of the earliest expressions of Konevskoi's intense distaste for St. Petersburg, which became more pronounced over the next two years. (See Ch. 8.)

[2] *LN* 98:1:464, n. 2.

[3] *LN* 98:1:546-547.

[4] A. S. Pushkin, "Ezerskii," *Polnoe sobranie sochinenii*, 10 vols. 4: 339-348. Moscow: Akademiia Nauk, 1956.

[5] By several accounts, self-scrutiny was one of Konevskoi's outstanding characteristics from boyhood on. In an early notebook, with apparent gratification he recorded a remark of his favorite teacher F. A. Luter: "More than the others, you pay conscious attention to your actions" (*RGALI*.259.1.4.4ob).

[6] Briusov noted the publication in his diary for December 1899: "Oreus has printed *Dreams and Meditations*. The publication's exterior appearance is poor. Oreus's poetry I consider among the most remarkable of the turn of the century" (*Dn*. 78). The run of 400 was slow to circulate, to judge by the book's rarity in Moscow soon after publication. On 31 January, Konevskoi informed Briusov that "two days ago I gave the book dealer 'New Time' ten copies" for potential Moscow readers. (*LN* 98:1:480) However, it reached enough of these to produce negative reactions among most of Briusov's Moscow circle, as he faithfully informed Konevskoi. (1:481). In another class entirely was the intensely hostile review by his former friend and comrade Vladimir Gippius, (*Mir iskusstva*, NN. 5-6, 1900) of *Kniga razdumii, Mechty i dumy,* and *Sbornik stikhotvorenii B. V. Nikol'skogo*. Konevskoi's stinging response appears in "Ivan Konevskoi. Pis'ma k Vl. V. Gippius". *Ezhegodnik rukopis'nogo otdela Pushkinskogo doma na 1977*. Publ. I. G. Iampol'skogo (Leningrad: "Nauka", 1979). Pp. 79-98. Many years later Gippius remembered painfully how "roughly I parted from Oreus" and called it "one of my grievous sins" (p. 85).

[7] The source of the quoted words in the title, "Eternal Vaults", is "Brozhu li ia (If I roam)", Aleksandr Pushkin's dark meditation on death's inevitability: "We all shall descend to the eternal vaults." Konevskoi deliberately and

predictably reverses direction, from the darkness toward hope of the world bathed in light.

8 Reference is to Konevskoi's inscription in the published *Dreams and Meditations* (see previous chapter). The links of their supposed "kinship of world view" are easily traced. "Summons" was dated 3 May 1899 and probably was added as the book took shape during the summer of 1899. One indication of Briusov's reaction to that may lie in his poem "To the Scythians (*Skifam*)," written late in 1899. It was discussed, most likely, along with "To the Tsar' of the North Pole," during Konevskoi's visit to Moscow in early January 1900, and in mid-January Konevskoi asked for a copy. (*LN* 1:478). With Konevskoi's dedication of "Summons" already in his hands, Briusov may have responded with an answering set of images: a narrator hero, moving easily across time to assume large-than-life form in idealized settings and actions. The rough draft bears a note "Poems of the Past and the Future (*Stikhi o bylom i budushchem*)." (Briusov, *SS*, 1:592.)

9 "Böcklin's Paintings. (Lyrical characterization)." *SP 1904*, 160-161.

10 The standard dictionary definition of *Vetrilo* is "sail (archaic, poetic)". However, "*veter-vetrilo*" is found elsewhere, particularly in folkloric usage, as a personified natural force. A notable example is in *The Tale of Igor's Campaign*, where Prince Igor's wife, Yaroslavna, beseeches the wind to return her husband to her: "O, vetre, vetrilo!"

11 See the sonnet sequence "Son of the Sun," dedicated to Aleksandr Bilibin and the discussion of it in Chapter 1.

12 A few months later, in September 1899, during a visit to Moscow, Konevskoi began a friendship with a longtime friend of Briusov's, A. A. Lang (A. L. Miropol'skii) whose strong esthetic and mystical leanings appealed to him and presumably added to his own thoughts on this matter. While there he wrote a short meditation that likely shows the influence of their discussions. ("On the Matter of Freedom (*K delu svobody*)," 11-17 Sept. 1899. Moscow. *SP 1904*, 221-222). A few months after Konevskoi's death Miropol'skii's spiritualistic work *Lestvitsa, poèma v VII glavakh* was published by "Scorpio." It was dedicated to Ivan Konevskoi.

13 Vladimir Solov'ev. "Genius (*Genii*)," Br.-Efron 15:228.

14 Its epigraph is: "*Kein Subject ohne Object.*" Schopenhauer Kantiani.

15 Konevskoi had reason for concern. Beginning from the publication of his first volume of *Poems and Ballads* (1866), Algernon Charles Swinburne (1837-1909) aroused outrage for his atheism and sensual extravagance, along with praise for technical brilliance. Banned in Russia at that time, even later, in the 1900s publication of his works was severely limited. See: *Vesy* N 2, 1905, p. 66.

16 These were selections from *Also Sprach Zarathustra* and from *Dionysos-Dithyramben*, as published in *Gedichte und Sprüche* (1898). (*LN* 98:1:461.)

17 "Hertha." Algernon Charles Swinburne, *Collected Poetical Works*, vol. 1. London: William Heinemann Ltd., 1927, pp.732-740. For information on the mythical sources of the figure "Hertha," see: *Dictionary of Northern Mythology* (Rudolf Simek, tr. Angela Hall, Cambridge: S. Brewer, 1993.) "A supposed Germanic earth-mother." Misreading for "Nerthus" (145)."Nerthus is a Germanic goddess whose cult on a Baltic island in the 1st century Tacitus (*Germania*, 40) reported in detail." (Simek, 230) She was worshipped as Mother Earth. "Yggdrasill (ON, 'Odin's horse'). The name of the world-tree in Eddic mythology." "The ideas are those of nineteenth-century evolutionary science and positivism, their vehicle is that of Norse mythology" (Cecil Y. Lang in *The Pre-Raphaelites and Their Circle*, 2nd ed., University of Chicago Press, 1975, p. 516).

18 Swinburne, *Collected Works*, v.1, pp. 732-740.

19 These four poems constitute the Swinburne selection in the bound manuscript Konevskoi entitled "Sbornik perevodov proizvedenii Zapadno-Evropeiskikh pisatelei [...] *(Collection of Translated Works of Western-European Writers)*," 236 pp. *RGALI.* F.259.1.9.

20 Writing to Briusov in the second half of April, 1899, Konevskoi listed many of his recent translations, including: "From Nietzsche I have translated two of the most splendid examples of his lyric poetry, lost in the rubbish of the sixth part of 'Zarathustra': 'Noon' and 'The Drunken Song'"; (*LN* 98.1.459). Note 18 (p. 461) lists in full the selections from Nietzsche that were included in the projected volume of translations.

21 N. V. Kotrelev, introduction, "Perepiska s S. A. Poliakovym, (1899-1921)". *Valerii Briusov i ego korrespondenty* (*LN* 98:2:19).

22 H[ugh] K[enner], "Translation," *Princeton Encyclopedia of Poetry and Poetics*, enlarged ed. Ed: Alex Preminger; assoc. eds. Frank J. Warnke, O. B. Hardison, Jr. Princeton, N. J.: Princeton University Press, 1974, 866-868.

23 There is no indication that these titles ever appeared in print.

24 *Pamiatniki kul'tury. Novye otkrytiia. 1988.* P. 23 ("Pis'ma A. Miropol'skogo k I. Konevskomu". Publ. I. G. Iampol'skii).

25 In the first draft of this letter Briusov conveyed Poliakov's answer in blunt terms: "'Scorpio' is obliged to concern itself, not only about the demands of Russian poetry, but about its ['Scorpio''s] existence, i.e., in other words, about the demands of the buyers." He continued with specific details of concern to a business proprietor. (*LN* 98:1:515, n.5.)

Chapter 6

The Power of the Word

1. *The Real Finland*

For Konevskoi the second half of 1899 was primarily a time of emotional convalescence and regrouping of forces. June was the lowest point. The rupture of relations with Anna Gippius, combined with inner conflicts associated with that event, as well as other, unspecified tribulations, brought him to a state that he described to Aleksandr Bilibin as "unspeakable weariness," leaving him entirely unable to write. (*AVL*, 174) While even in his darkest days, Konevskoi apparently never lost faith in his inherent worth as a poet, yet to be without a breath of inspiration, to be unable to create, was an unbearable condition.

At last, at the beginning of July, relief came in sight. He escaped to a modest Finnish pension, "Pension Lang," reasonably close to Petersburg but yet in "the real Finland." On his first day there he wrote enthusiastically to Bilibin: "The horizon unrolls around a high crest of uplands and loses itself at one side in a pine forest, scrubs, hills, and gullies, on the other — in a wide shining lake, on a third, finally, directly into the sea" (176). Here, within a short distance of both Lake Saima and the Gulf of Finland, Konevskoi began to experience true peace of spirit. Here also he found a secluded place to complete work on *Dreams and Meditations*.

However, the stay in Finland was shorter than originally intended. In late August he wrote to Briusov:

In spite of the charming effect of the region, inner reasons resulted in my early departure and spending the remainder of the summer mostly near Pbg., at "Lesnoi," (with one of my relatives [uncle Nikolai Grigorievich Diakonov]). In view of the fact that my relative will remain there during the fall and winter, I will spend there three or four days a week. I'm very happy about this.

Next week I think I'll come to Moscow and spend some time there. (*LN* 98:1:467).

One notable feature of Konevskoi's letters during this time was his eagerness to avoid St. Petersburg. It is easy to suppose an unwillingness to encounter Anna Gippius, to be forcibly reminded of happier times with her. (Nonetheless, we remember his writing to Bilibin that, while he had initiated the break, he still harbored hope of a counter-move of some sort from her. This hope might well have kept him within easy distance of the city.) Yet the fact that he attributed his inner restlessness to a *plurality* of causes hints at other possibilities, as well.

One of these is suggested in Briusov's 1916 biographical-critical article about Konevskoi. Looking back fifteen years and more, Briusov wrote of the unusually close relationship between General Oreus and his son, living in intimate fellowship after the mother's death, and then of the estrangement that occurred as the son matured:

> Enjoying this friendship, the father believed that he and Vania shared the same convictions, identical views on all things, a common faith and common ideals. The old man failed to notice that, from very early on, influenced by those conditions in which he himself placed his son's life, their paths began to follow different ways, so that, unnoticed, they diverged greatly from one another. [...] The elder Oreus spoke about this (after his son's death) with great mildness, clearly minimizing the significance of events; but all the same, one felt that, for the father, this was an extremely painful discovery. The general barely looked at those collections of poems that the future poet read to satiety, and never opened the notebooks in which the son wrote down his "Dreams and Meditations" [...] and, of course, knew nothing of

his spiritual experiences. [...] Some chance event, some casual conversation all at once opened the old man's eyes to the reality (*Briusov/Vengerov* 2: 282-283).

As Briusov remembered it, there was no open break, "they remained, if not friends, at least comrades" (2:283). And if the father could not refrain from attempting to show the son his errors, his efforts met firm resistance. He then quickly yielded, resolved in no way to interfere with his son's freedom (2: 283).

Valuable in very many ways, this 1916 biography by Briusov is especially notable for the sympathy shown for the senior Oreus throughout.[1] Possibly the fifteen years intervening since Konevskoi's death altered Briusov's perspective. The four-year age difference between Konevskoi and Briusov (born in 1877 and 1873 respectively), in the fifteen years following the younger man's death, seemed in effect to have extended to a generation's distance, at times imparting to Briusov's narrative an almost avuncular tone. In any event, his account of the father-son relationship rings eminently true in broad outline, as well as in many details. It also throws some light on the spiritual turmoil the younger Oreus was experiencing at that time.

The lyrics written before and during his stay in the "real Finland" of his dreams reflect Konevskoi's hopes and struggles for renewal of spirit. Finland's "white nights" of midsummer obviously seemed to him much purer than their relatively grimy Petersburg counterparts. Though his later relationship with the mythic aura of its granite lakes was so far incompletely experienced, "On a Lightsome Night (*Pred svetloi noch'iu*)" (*SP 2008*, 143) proclaims the sense of spiritual liberation he felt.

As creative force begins to return in his Finnish haven, it is reinforced by cultural and biographical connections. Two new lyrics having a special Finnish link are "The Magic Word (*Slovo zakliatiia*)" and "The Exile's Song (*Pesn' izgnannika*)," subtitled "On a Motive from the *Kalevala*" (*SP 2008*, 124-125, 144).[2] Konevskoi read the *Kalevala* between mid-April and early June 1899.[3] This compilation of Karelian folk tales, completed and published in mid-century by Elias Lönnrot, in a time of growing Finnish nationalism quickly came to be regarded as the Finnish national epic. Russian translations of the *Kalevala* were available in the 1880s, but the appearance of a new translation in 1898 may have caught Konevskoi's attention.[4] His interest may also have been stimulated by the immediate prospect of his Finnish sojourn. In any case, the Oreus family had strong Finnish connections, and Konevskoi often spent time in the Vyborg area during his childhood. Later he confided to Aleksandr Bilibin that, while saddened by the fact that "I have no childhood places that I can call 'native,'" he drew sustenance from the Finnish Vyborg region, which "was for a long time the native soil of some of my forebears" (*AVL,* 183).[5]

Konevskoi's interest in folk epos and folk poetry is traceable at least as far back as his first term in the university, when he studied the writings of F. I. Buslaev and Max Müller on those topics.[6] In spring 1899, he transferred from the classical to the Slavic-Russian division of the historical-philological faculty.[7] By then, his views on some matters departed radically from those of Buslaev. For example, in his essay "Epic Poetry," Buslaev wrote: "The formation and construction of [a language] give evidence, not of the personal thinking of one man, but of the creation of an entire people."[8] Later, pursuing an argument with Aleksandr Bilibin, Konevskoi asserted: "I absolutely cannot accept the notion of national pride or, in general, the concept of a people. Of course, this is a kind of convention and an abstraction. The only thing that unites persons who count themselves as part of a people is — language." (See also Ch. 8.) But he qualified this: "language is created in part by great poets, in part by the soulless activities of daily life." The latter is the invention of "all sorts of people, and is unworthy of [...] attention" (*AVL,* 182). On the other hand, these "great poets," creators of the word and of language, invented and discovered the true names of things, thus greatly enhancing their power over reality. Their kinship with prophets, magicians, and shamans of ancient times clearly is not far to seek.

2. The Kalevala Singers

The three main heroes of the *Kalevala,* Väinämöinen, Ilmarinen, and Lemminkäinen, tireless singers of incantations, versed in magical charms, nonetheless often found themselves in need of the specific "word" that would give them power over foes in particular situations. Once traced to its possessor, that "word" might be obtained by guile or trickery, if by no other means. But then, with that knowledge, they could bend men's will and move nature from its usual course. The space the *Kalevala* gives these incantations in relation to that allotted to narrative may seem disproportionate. Yet in many episodes they function as prime movers of the action. Not infrequently, conflicts arose over whose incantation was most powerful, the outcome being determined by a singing contest of sorts. The power over nature and the natural order conferred by this knowledge caused the "knowers" to be formidable figures in any conflict.

It is worth suggesting here that Konevskoi's "Varangian from beyond the blue sea" also operated within this paradigm.[9] The first three stanzas of this seven-stanza lyric are devoted to the Russian language — like the land, "great and abundant." Curiously, the language mimicks and blends with the land's contours: the two seem inseparable. Or, perhaps, language is the dominant one. Or is he who has mastered this powerful tongue in a manner already in possession of the expanse before him?

Now, a year later, Konevskoi's meditation on language's power continued in "The Magic Word." Undated, this poem was placed, in the 1904 edition, between poems written in June 1899 in Vyborg. In essence it is a series of incantations uttered against a darkly sketched northern background: medieval Vyborg, the bleak Finnish taiga, remnants of steppe battles. The speaker's identity is left unclear — defender of Rus' against alien tribes, prisoner in Vyborg's ancient Swedish fortress, kinsman of Kalevan magicians? In any case, all of these, in the broad, inclusive sense used by Konevskoi, were Varangians. Here the speaker believes from the outset that the sole weapon against evil, be it a generic one, is the magical "word." Yet in each new confrontation the omens are bad, the prospect uncertain, evil becomes more terrifying. Will the "word" he holds to his bosom be sufficient? But yes, because his "word" is the all-powerful *name* of his enemy, victory is assured. The suspense that has been building to this point is resolved in the final stanza. There the complex, sensory, magic "word" takes on the extended meaning of language, of poetry. Each of these possesses the same transformational power, when used by an initiate who has mastered its secrets. As will be seen, this mastery became a further, important subject of inquiry for Konevskoi over the next two years, fitting well into his over-arching intellectual and spiritual quest for the roots of all things.

"The Exile's Song" is based on the fatal misadventure of Lemminkäinen, reckless adventurer, womanizer, braggart, most headstrong of the three chief *Kalevala* heroes.[10] The narrative contained in runes 12-15 is by far the most popular of those describing Lemminkäinen's exploits, and one of the most popular in the entire *Kalevala*. As it begins, Lemminkäinen, though he has recently abducted a bride, is eager for more excitement. Lured by the possibility of more booty and sexual conquest, he sets out, disdaining his wife's pleas to remain at home with her, as well as his mother's warning about his inadequate command of magic. Defiantly claiming to be a consummate magician, he sets off for the gloomy northern place called Pohjola or Sariola. Pohjola, presided over by the old woman Louhi, is the abode of many sorcerers. In response to Lemminkäinen's demand for her daughter, Louhi lays down three challenging tasks. On his way to attempt the third task, to shoot the swan of Tuonela, he is pushed into the River of Death by a wretched cattle herder he has offended. His attacker then conjures up a water dragon, whose poisonous stings are fatal to his victim. Then he cuts him into many pieces and hurls him into a whirlpool.

But the defining episode is still to come. Made aware by an agreed-on sign of her son's sorry fate, Lemminkäinen's mother makes use of her deep knowledge of magical charms to lead her at last to the place where he perished. She not only retrieves the dismembered pieces from the River of Death with a long-handled rake, but painstakingly reassembles them into the shape of a man. At last, with the aid of a helper-bee, who searches the world for the salves needed for the final healing touch, she restores her son to life. Then, with maternal curiosity, she demands an explanation. Briefly, he tells his distressing tale and confesses his mistake. Predictably his mother exclaims, "Woe is the foolish man!" After scolding him roundly for his reckless behavior, she easily recites the antidotes to the evil charms that brought about his catastrophe. And then, without further delay, she turns her wandering lad homeward.

According to Finnish folklorist Anna-Leena Siikala, the noted *Kalevala* scholar Matti Kuusi called Lemminkäinen "'the most purely shamanic of the male heroic figures in Finnish epic poetry,'" and the journey to Tuonela, the classic journey to the other world, 'the most fundamentally shamanistic theme of our cultural history'" (Siikala 20).[11] Certainly, the Lemminkäinen narrative and the *Kalevala* as a whole are replete with incidents and images that folklorists and anthropologists have identified as part of the shamanic worldview. "According to shamanistic modes of thought, the beginning of all things, the origins of all phenomena and their fundamental essence are continually in existence in the other world, accessible to the shaman" (*Siikala,* 158). Illumination gained during the shaman's ecstatic journeys to the other world is expressed often in charms, images, and rituals. In a society based on shamanic beliefs, then, the individual chosen by the spirits to be shaman serves as an intermediary between two worlds and wielder of power over nature — therefore, an essential figure in the community.

Granting his interest in things Finnish and things mystical, one yet must ask why Konevskoi selected this episode with this hero from the *Kalevala,* and what he made of it.[12] The name Lemminkäinen is never mentioned in "The Exile's Song," but the character and the chain of events are unmistakable. Yet Konevskoi's poem is of a different genre, perspective, tone, and focus. Lyric rather than epic, the tale is narrated by the onetime daredevil-braggart, now returned, chastened and much wiser, to his ancestral home. Like some Karelian "Ancient Mariner," the protagonist unburdens himself by recounting his experience of death and resurrection.[13] Beginning at the end with his happy return, he spares himself nothing in reliving the experience.

In the *Kalevala*, Lemminkäinen's exaggerated notion of his own prowess as a magician is underlined by the fact that he perishes, not by the hand of some great magician or warrior, but by the trickery of the wretched cowherd Soppy Hat. In Konevskoi's version, the river itself — "Death's Domain" — lures him into its murky depths. What follows is related in gruesome detail: his breast, his shoulders, his face are pierced by poisoned darts, his veins are torn. But he saves till last his greatest and most humiliating punishment: no longer the singer of charms, wielder of magical words, his prophetic tongue is now impotent.

Then comes the turning point: his mother discovers the fragments; with miracle after miracle, the restoration is rapidly accomplished. The mother's prodigious labors and her profound command of magic receive full credit. However, his focus is on his own misdeeds and their consequences. That ill-advised sortie to the realm of the dead was an abysmal failure. The would-be magician, though mercifully restored to life, is stripped of his precious powers, and he has still to complete the journey home. But, at last, the goal comes in sight, and healing is complete: "My dead thoughts wakened,/ When I knew my father's wood."

The *Kalevala*, like most major folk epics, is composed of many episodes, clustered around a few heroes and repeated with variations and contradictions. One feature of other narrative genres that is often absent from the folk epic is character development. Certainly it is lacking in the case of Lemminkäinen, who in the last few episodes of the *Kalevala* is still called "young" and "jolly." Konevskoi's "exile," by contrast, has learned from horrendous experience; he looks back on his earlier self (whatever the actual time lapse might be) as a callow, self-promoting braggart. The story told by the returned one emphasizes the drama of folly and forgiveness, death and return to life.

One prototype for "The Exile's Song" that comes readily to mind is the parable of the Prodigal Son in the Gospel of St. Luke.[14] In that parable the son, after wantonly squandering his riches, returns, naked and starving, to offer himself as a laborer on his father's farm. But the father, who welcomes him home as beloved son, is as forgiving as is Lemminkäinen's mother. There, perhaps, the parallels cease.

However, a different New Testament prototype for the Lemminkäinen narrative appeared in a major work by the Finnish painter Akseli Gallén-Kallela: "Lemminkäinen's Mother," painted in 1897.[15] That painting, along with other *Kalevala* illustrations, was soon exhibited in Helsinki and beyond, helping to win an international reputation for their creator. In Gallén-Kallela's rendition, Lemminkäinen's corpse lies on the bank of the black river, in one piece, but tinged with decay, bearing little resemblance to the brash adventurer he had been. Symbols of death are everywhere — eerie black-and-white flowers, skulls, an evil-looking swan. But the spotlight is clearly on the mother. Haggard face turned skyward, she rests her hand on her son's reconstituted but lifeless body, while her grief-stricken but powerful gaze seeks to compel help from the heavens. Only faint rays of light and a tiny golden bee in flight suggest a positive ending. Yet, even with this difference, comparison to Michelangelo's sculpture of the *Pietà*, the mourning mother of Jesus, was all but inevitable.[16]

In his memoir for winter 1897-1898, Aleksandr Benois wrote of his and Lev Bakst's growing friendship with the leading Finnish artists, including Aksel Gallen (later known as Akseli Gallén-Kallela), whom the Finns "considered their national genius, a great epic poet in the visual arts."[17] Diaghilev, Benois, and the rest of the St. Petersburg "World of Art" group, then in the process of formation, considered establishment of links with foreign artists extremely important to their mission. Benois wrote:

> This alliance of ours with the Finns was a means of expressing that "cosmopolitanism" in art that our group prepared itself to serve, with the very rise of our conscious attitude to artistic activity. [...] Indeed, Finland in relation to Russia was something like "abroad," part of Western Europe (2: 187).

In January 1898 Diaghilev organized the Russian-Finnish exhibition.[18] Gallén-Kallela participated in that and in the first World of Art International Exhibition a year later, both in St. Petersburg.[19] Konevskoi's notebooks show him to be a frequent visitor throughout his university years to St. Petersburg art exhibitions, and certainly to these. This attention was of a piece with his earlier fascination with contemporary European painting during his journeys in Germany and Switzerland in the summers of 1897 and 1898. We have seen how, during those visits to the galleries of Munich and Basel, he studied works by the English Pre-Raphaelites, the Swiss Arnold Böcklin, and others, to absorb elements of what he later called, in an important article in 1900, "mystical feeling."[20]

In September 1896, just before entering the university, Konevskoi, with the two Bilibin brothers and S. P. Semenov, traveled by Volga steamship to the annual Nizhnii Novgorod fair, where, among the many attractions, was the All-Russian Exhibition.[21] In the art section, a few Finnish artists' works also appeared. Among Konevskoi's cryptically registered impressions there was a remark that suggested puzzlement at certain of these: "surmise about Aksel Gallen's illustrations from the *Kalevala*."[22] However, by the time he saw Gallén-Kallela's work again, his artistic sophistication had increased markedly. Moreover, the intellectual and spiritual questioning that underlay his interest in art was becoming more sharply defined. Gallén-Kallela's *Kalevala* illustrations, displayed in St. Petersburg early in 1899, may well have played a significant role in shaping Konevskoi's interpretation of the folk epic. Specifically, "Lemminkäinen's Mother" may have suggested Konevskoi's radical reworking of the story that became "The Exile's Song."

Death-and-rebirth is the essential storyline in all three versions of that tale, the *Kalevala*, Gallén-Kallela's, and Konevskoi's. In the *Kalevala* the restored son, nothing learned, looks forward to pursuing further lusty adventures, for which his mother indulgently prepares him. Gallén-Kallela's interpretation narrowed and deepened the artistic and moral focus, moving magic elements to the background. The moment pictured is one of tension between the mother's inner strength, infused by maternal love, and the powers from which she implores her son's healing. At this moment her son, the bumptious, one-time womanizer and singer of charms, plays no active role; he is a corpse, and nothing more.

Following Gallén-Kallela's lead, Konevskoi recast the magic adventure tale into a lyric genre capable of great moral significance. However, for him, the protagonist's reckless clash with death was merely preliminary to the real drama: the loss and retrieval of his prize possession, the "word." This treasure, with its intimate links to nature and its power over its hidden resources, was gone from him, seemingly beyond recall. Only a long and difficult journey brought him to the place of his origin, his "father's wood." There the dead thoughts at last awakened: rebirth occurred.

3. The Magic Word

A brief paragraph entitled "The Word (*Slovo*)," dated 1900, showed Konevskoi attempting to articulate further — this time in prose — his deepest thoughts about the essence and power of language.[23] Much of this was expressed in the lyric "The Magic Word," particularly in its last stanza, which begins: "O prophetic word, word that is power [...]!" Now, in essay form, he probed the mystery further, in hope of reaching something like a concrete definition:

> In the word, the infinitely large is combined with the infinitely small. All the fullness and breadth of thoughts, strivings, awakenings, sympathies, images, sounds, aromas, touches, sensations of contraction of muscles, of warmth and cold — are concentrated, compressed into these tiny fragments, into conventional auditory signs.

The paragraph's second major assertion dealt with the source of the word's "magic power," stressing the paradox of the word's meaning — firm, solid, specific, yet able to contain limitless shades. By the end of the piece, however, he had fallen back on the purely metaphoric: "In the word we contemplate heaven and the rainbow, as if in a faceted crystal."

The most notable addition of this brief piece — to his terminology, at very least — comes in the first sentence: "The words of oral speeches and languages are invented by *prophets, seers, and magicians*" (*italics mine*). In his 5 June 1900 letter to Aleksandr Bilibin, where he protested vehemently against the notion of language as the creation of "the people," Konevskoi credited that feat to "great poets."[24] In "The Word" he goes a step further. Or do these categories — prophet, magician, wonderworker, and poet — overlap? This was a question he intended to answer.

Four years previously, during the summer of 1896, Konevskoi labored to clarify for himself what was meant by the "new mysticism" (see Ch. 1). His early reading of Tiutchev, Fet, of Maeterlinck, Rossetti, and many other European poets convinced him that a genuine poet-mystic's primary goal is to achieve through his art an understanding of the universe's inner being. To this end, the modern mystic takes advantage of whatever means his contemporary culture has to offer: pantheism, spiritualism, psychiatry, and other resources that may enhance his power to penetrate levels of being.

After his second, hugely rewarding journey to Western Europe, Konevskoi's attention, as we know, turned to his own roots in Russian history and spiritual culture. At this time, too, his fascination with language and the word was reaching its zenith. Among the protagonists of his Varangian/*bogatyr* poems, two figures stand out as phenomenally knowing about the word's power over nature. These are the Varangian from Konevets, and the magician-warrior Volkh, whose easy mastery of nature rivaled and exceeded that of the lusty heroes of the *Kalevala*. Volkh's legendary life and exploits, as interpreted by Konevskoi in "The Elder Bogatyrs (*Starshie bogatyri*)" (1900), drew together elements of great and growing importance to him as he plotted the next stage of his own life-exploits. (See Ch. 8.)

"You have probed the universe" ("The Magic Word"). The connection between these discoveries about the mysteries of language and the life plan that Konevskoi laid out years before becomes apparent here. He wrote then, with conviction but in the awkward phrases of a *gimnazist*: the supreme joys that make life worth living are "*creative work,* comprehending the World Soul and the meaning of our existence, *penetrating by direct sense to the secret essence of things, so as to receive luminous revelations* about the structure and meaning of our nature…" (*italics mine*).[25] Ponderous though it was, this formulation predicted closely the direction Konevskoi's thought would take during the next five years, as he worked to establish his character as poet-mystic-thinker.

4. Stanzas on the Persona and the Poet

Beginning from his earliest writings, Konevskoi worked to expand and refine his notion of the poet. In the 1896-97 essay "Lyric Poetry in Contemporary Russia," he made very clear his belief that Russian poetry in the mid-nineties totally lacked a philosophical foundation that included consideration of the structure of the universe and man's place in it. Moreover, poets capable of addressing problems of death and the survival of the individual *persona* were woefully wanting. Yet these matters were basic to Konevskoi's thinking from the outset. His search for arguments to support his position moved him steadily onward, as he took from various philosophical teachings and mystical beliefs that which served his needs in attaining his proximate and longterm goals.

Over the next two or three years, after completion of *Dreams and Meditations*, which defined the poet Ivan Konevskoi as he then was, one particular problem pursued him relentlessly. The heavy burden imposed on the spirit by the recalcitrant earth-bound, space-bound body, with its inevitable dissolution in death, troubled his thoughts and appeared often in his poetry. Was the true *persona* simply a disembodied spirit, unencumbered by the body? Did it then lack the rich resources at the body's disposal, except during their brief time together?

Konevskoi found this problem facing him on different but interlocking levels: theoretical, imaginative, and personal. The everyday experience of bodily demands shared with all human beings was especially troublesome to a philosophically-minded post-adolescent who was also a poet of distinction. Several of the poems written during the latter half of 1899 reflect this preoccupation vividly. One of these, the two-part "Surges *(Poryvy)*," dated 23 July, rings with poignant longing for deliverance.[26] The contrast of "there, here, above, below," established early in "Surges I," is heightened by images of distant horizons and lofty treetops that deaden earthly complaints, and swelling verbs that mimic billowing wind. Yearnings for freedom and peace of spirit are thus joined with Konevskoi's favorite images of wind and sky and linked to free living things like flights of birds. To emphasize the body-spirit tension, there are religious overtones — church slavonicisms and vocabulary that suggest traditional Christianity's body-soul opposition — hovering like a shadow in the background. The last eight lines take on a pleading tone that says, "I know, the strong ones keep up the struggle, but..." Meanwhile, the speaker waits for the moment when he will be swept away by the spirit of the elements. *(SP 2008,* 145) But in part II, action is the key: reason is disdained, and passionate action exalted over all. Yet, however much "Surges II" differs in form, imagery and tone from part I, the theme of freedom from bondage is central to both.[27]

After the collapse of his attempt to establish "The Cornerstones of My Worldview," Konevskoi appears to have thought his way to a different approach to formulating a philosophy. The volume of translations on which he lavished so much care during most of 1899 was designed to set forth, not his own worldview — at least, not explicitly, — but the worldviews of the truly visionary spirits of the contemporary age. His definition of "contemporary" was carefully honed to include only a chosen few. Among these he singled out a yet smaller set, where Swinburne and, on a slightly lower level, Nietzsche held pride of place.[28]

Konevskoi's fascination with Swinburne, discussed in the previous chapter, surely was fed by the sonorous cadences and daring ideas most resoundingly expressed in his "Hertha": "Man, equal and one with me, man that is made of me, man that is I." In these lines, Konevskoi believed he found strong support for his argument for the independence of the *persona*, along with its interpenetration with the universe. Indeed, Swinburne's prime position in Konevskoi's master scheme presumably rested on his brilliance as an exemplar of those contemporary positions that Konevskoi intended his collection of translations to represent.

The struggle to make a divided nature whole, already present in "Surges I-II," took another form in the pair of poems written immediately after: "Stanzas on the *Persona* I-II" (24 July — 3 August). The epigraph from Swinburne — "between…deeds and days" — is taken from his "Genesis": "Then between shadow and substance, night and light,/ Then between birth and death, and deeds and days/…/ The divine contraries of life began."[29] One of Swinburne's favorite devices, balance and opposition, is used throughout his poem to trace the "divine contraries of life" that are resolved only in death. While this is not Konevskoi's thesis, an image appears in stanza 12 of "Genesis" that may have suggested his pairing in "Stanzas on the *Persona* I-II": "For in each man and each year that is born/ Are sown the twin seeds of *the strong twin powers*" (*ital. mine*). Such an image may have aided Konevskoi in his reflection on the poet's dilemma: "I am held in thrall by two creators./ One — that demon of wondrous words. [...] The other — that spirit unrestrained./ Ever forward, pressing forward" — the spirit that must engage in every battle, who must know what lies beyond every border. And I, says the poet, am made up of both. Examples of balance and opposition carry on through many stanzas. There is a moment when the "spirit unrestrained" seems victorious — but not yet... The struggle goes back and forth.

This densely written, deeply felt effort at self-understanding comes to no final resolution. "Creative work" (understood as art) is the apparent winner in the fight for the speaker's soul. But that other spirit's singleminded drive for action and boundless knowledge is only temporarily restrained. In "Stanzas II," the speaker examines the possibility of bringing the two "creative forces" together, but, again, there is no clear victory.

Whichever way that Konevskoi turned, dividedness of one sort or another threatened to divert him from his self-set tasks. Coping with such problems while keeping his primary goals in sight was a task that would absorb him for the foreseeable future.

5. "All Clear"

Meanwhile, at the end of this summer of 1899, so full of inner turmoil and vexation, Konevskoi's poetic stream did not dry. Instead, it ran, as it were, in two separate channels. Among the poems written then, Valerii Briusov's favorites were the two parts of "Autumn Voices (*Osennie golosa*)," for which he professed his undying admiration.[30] In these, Konevskoi's characteristic imagery and spiritual posture showed at their lyrical best. In a singing, soaring final quatrain, Part I gathers the images of flight in the survey of the human panorama from above — detached yet fascinated —, and, throughout, there is the all-encompassing, magical image of wind. (*SP 2008*, 148) Here is the tissue of symbols that became Konevskoi's distinctive signature. It continued to gather significance as his vision unfolded.

In a different vein are three poems that announce the approach of a new degree of maturity. This, at least, was Konevskoi's assessment of the point he had reached, and to some extent it was accurate. Briefer, more compact than most other lyrics of the period, each has its astringent note, tempered by a particular feeling — irony, loss, renunciation — but without self-pity or nostalgia. The first is "All Clear (*Proiasnenie*)," dated 23 August 1899. The poet stands on some forgotten path, looking back over the swirling visions of earlier, marvellous years, spread like a banner in the air behind him. Now, at this moment, as they emerge into the noise and light of "real" life, they are seen for the fading magic they are, and a satisfying sense of closure ensues: "The pattern is complete, the spirit whole. The blood has ripened. Ripened, too, the mind." (*SP 2008*, 147-148).

On the same theme, but given a twist of irony, is "Gratitude (*Blagodarnost'*)." (*SP 2008* 149-150) "Should I not thank you, O demons of rebellious thinking! [...] I have again entrusted myself to my wily mind": it is the voice of one who has learned a lesson or two the hard way. The third lyric, unlike the other two, is laden with intense, though restrained, emotion: "Renunciation (*Otrechenie*). Dedicated to A. N. G." The last and perhaps most effective of the lyrics inspired by his relationship with Anna Gippius, "Renunciation" truly marks the end of an epoch in Konevskoi's life. A love poem it is, but, unlike the others, it bears a note of pain, nostalgia, but, above all, finality. "Yes, time passes, but not the way it once did": resignation to what cannot be changed is another sign of adulthood. (*SP 2008*, 150.)

Whatever its vicissitudes, the year 1899 was the most productive of Konevskoi's brief career: fifty lyrics, plus a published collection of prose and poetry.[31] However, it left his inner conflicts unhealed, with no formula for wholeness achieved. For the past four years, Konevskoi had worked intensely to bring his life and his innermost core, his *persona*, into conformity with his concept of the poet-mystic as he thus far understood it. The start of the new year and new century found him, then, if not totally restored to spiritual health, at least ready to push ahead along paths he was eager to explore.

Notes

[1] This is fully borne out by the tone and content of the general's letters and Briusov's implied responses. Oreus Sr. repeatedly told Briusov that he left everything in his hands in the editing and production of the volume (*Stikhi i proza*), with the exception of the use of the family name. Nonetheless, although he asks Briusov to burn the manuscripts afterward, this was not done. (*LN* 98:1:548).

[2] "Pesn' izgnannika (*The Exile's Song*)" appeared in *Literaturnyi sbornik, izdannyi studentami imp. S.-Peterburgskogo universiteta v pol'zu ranennykh burov* (Spb. 1900), edited by Prof. I. N. Zhdanov (*LN* 98:1:520 n.3), an anthology of students' writings "in support of wounded Boer soldiers." The Boer War in South Africa broke out in October 1899.

[3] *RGALI* 259.1.6.78.

[4] The first complete Russian translation of the *Kalevala*, that of L. P. Bel'skii, appeared in 1888 and was often reprinted (in some cases, revised), most recently in 2003 (Sankt-Peterburg: "Azbuka-klassika"). A second Russian translation, that of È. G. Granstrem, came out in 1898. Granstrem's earlier version "for young people" (in prose form, but in fact in trochaic tetrameter), was in its third edition by 1880. In 1999, in observance of the hundred-and-fiftieth anniversary of Lönnrot's second and definitive version of the *Kalevala*, there appeared a new translation by Eino Kuiru and Armas Mishin, bilingual, with introduction by Armas Mishin (Petrozavodsk: "Kareliia").

[5] St. Petersburg obviously was not to be considered. At the time of Konevskoi's visits, the Vyborg administrative region included Karelia, but not the more northern section where the tales that make up the *Kalevala* were collected by Lönnrot and his predecessors.

[6] In his notebook No.4 (1896-1897), devoted primarily to lecture notes and reading assignments, Konevskoi wrote: "Buslaev's views on the folk epos. Materials : Buslaev 'Folk poetry', Max Müller 'Views on the Folk Epos." *RGALI* 259.1.17.9.7.

[8] F. I. Buslaev. *Narodnyi epos i mifologiia*. Moscow: "Vysshaia shkola", 2003. P. 25.

[9] "Iz Konevtsa," *SP 2008*, 94-95.

[10] Folklorists have found in the chief Lemminkäinen episode and its variant strong similarities to "journey to the other world" narratives in certain other traditions. (Anna-Leena Siikala. *Mythic Images and Shamanism. A Perspective on Kalevala Poetry. FF Communications. Edited for the Folklore Fellows.* Vol. CXXX, No. 280. Ed. Prof. Sr. Lauri Honko. Helsinki: Academia Scientiarum Fennica, 2002. Pp. 210-319.)

[11] "Shamanism has thus been regarded as representing the oldest cultural legacyof Finnishness" *(Siikala, 24).*

[12] There are, of course, many variants on the story of Lemminkäinen's journey to the other world. However, presumably Konevskoi was concerned with the *Kalevala* version.

[13] By coincidence, perhaps, Konevskoi read Samuel Taylor Coleridge's *The Rhyme of the Ancient Mariner* shortly before he read the *Kalevala*. (RGALI 259.1.6.74ob.)

[14] Luke 15: 11-32. "The seventeenth-century Russian 'Tale of Misery-Misfortune' (*Povest' o gore-zloschast'e*)", with which Konevskoi was surely acquainted, contains the same basic plot.

[15] "Lemminkäinen's Mother." *Akseli Gallen-Kallela, National Artist of Finland.* Timo Martin, Douglas Sivén. English adaptation by Keith Bosley and Satu Salo. Helsinki: Watti-kustannus Ltd., 1985. Pp. 152-153.The painting hangs in the Helsinki Ateneum.

[16] The mother of Jesus, with the dead body of her son on her knees, is portrayed in an attitude of profound grief with no *visual* indication (as in "Lemminkäinen's Mother") of a resurrection to come.

[17] Aleksandr Benois, *Moi vospominaniia v 5-i knigakh*. Moscow: "Nauka", 1980. Vol. 2 (bk. 4, ch. 24) p.188.

[18] Benois also wrote that, had the group *World of Art (Mir iskusstva)* already begun to function, the Russian-Finnish exhibition "would have gone into history as 'the first 'World of Art' exhibition.'" Aleksandr Benois, *Moi vospominaniia*. Vol. 2 (bk. 4, ch. 24) p.187.

[19] John E. Bowlt, *The Silver Age: Russian Art of the Early Twentieth Century and the "World of Art" Group*. Newtonville, Mass.: Oriental Research Partners, 1982, pp. 90, 93.

[20] "Misticheskoe chuvstvo v russkoi lirike" (*SP 1904*, 199-219) is one of Konevskoi's most important statements on the subject.

21 *LN* 92:4:182.
22 *RGALI* 259.1.16.28.
23 "Slovo," is one of nine short prose pieces printed at the end of the 1904 edition. "Mysli i zamechaniia," *Stikhi i proza*. Moscow: "Scorpio," 1904. Pp. 220-232.
24 *AVL*, 182. Of course, since the essay is dated only by year (1900), it could have been written at the same time as the letter, or before, or after.
25 Stepanov, *LN* 92:4:182.
26 In his letter to Briusov dated 28 August, Konevskoi enclosed copies of: "Surges 1-2," "Extreme Meditation (*Krainiaia duma*)," "All Clear," "The Exile's Song," and "Stanzas on the *Persona 1-2*." Briusov's response was cryptic: "In your recent poems, I am more pleased by your usual devices" (*LN* 98:1:469).
27 The passionate insistence of these lines reminds one of Konevskoi's current intense interest in the writings of the two poets Nietzsche and Swinburne, who, despite their obvious differences, were at one in their views of man's potential greatness and the littleness of man's laws and creeds.
28 In November 1899 he wrote to Briusov after reading a recent collection by Verhaeren: "Verhaeren is one of those, if not the first, who will fulfill the assignment at which Nietzsche failed — to be the prophet of our present century and its leader toward coming days. Viélé-Griffin and Swinburne are his equals, but more withdrawn from presentday life […]" (*LN* 98:1:474).
29 "Genesis" (Swinburne's *Collected Poetical Works*, vol. 1, London: William Heinemann Ltd., 1927), p. 778.
30 *LN* 98: 1: 475. Nonetheless, they clearly evoked in him a lightly veiled boredom. Briusov's constant quest for the new, especially in form, which was for him and others among the Moscow symbolists a central criterion for poetry, sharply differentiated his critical standard from that of Konevskoi. This led to his apparent relative lack of interest in the philosophical content and direction of Konevskoi's poetry. In the same letter Briusov wrote: "I don't understand the essence of 'Gratitude' (perhaps the first two lines) and 'To Those Who Serve (*K sluzhiteliam*)'."
31 This total includes several cycles of varying length.

Chapter 7

Abolishing Death (1)[1]

The start of the new century found Konevskoi still relentless in his pursuit of the goals he laid out as a *gimnazist*. The chief and all-encompassing of these continued to be the abolition of death and the ongoing survival of the *persona*. Success in that should entail, as he had grandly put it, "penetrating by direct sense to the secret essence of things," and, ultimately, participating in the boundless life of the universe.[2] Buried here, but becoming daily more visible, was his conviction that, to achieve these ends, it was necessary somehow to get inside the universe — in effect, to become co-extensive with it. Only thus could true immortality be ensured. The only individual capable of such a feat, he came to believe, was the poet-mystic *in his fullest realization*. This Konevskoi aspired to be; if that required total self-transformation, so be it. The months ahead found him investigating new means to that end.

1. *Der Übermensch*

By the mid-1890s every moderately well-informed Russian reader possessed some information, accurate or not, about Friedrich Nietzsche. Both kinds were available from many sources. The first substantial account of Nietzsche's work in Russian was the article "Criticism of the Morality of Altruism" by V. P. Preobrazhenskii, which appeared in the November 1892 issue of the journal *Problems of Philosophy and Psychology*.[3] Vasilii Petrovich Preobrazhenskii, at that time twenty-eight years old, was already an active member of the journal's editorial committee. However, the editorial note accompanying the article revealed a strenuous debate in the editorial offices before it was accepted. Even so, its publication presumably represented a courageous decision by the journal's co-founder-editor, Nikolai Grot, supported by some others. Dissenting members of the committee made certain their views were resoundingly heard:

> The editorial committee has decided to print for Russian readers an exposition of the moral doctrine of F. Nietzsche, which is troubling in its ultimate conclusions, with the aim of showing what strange and sickly phenomena are being generated at the present time by a well-known tendency in Western European culture.

While crediting him with a certain talent, Nietzsche's critics went on to single out grave deficiencies in his moral and religious outlook:

> Blinded by hatred of religion, of Christianity, and of God himself, [Nietzsche] cynically preaches full indulgence to crime, to the most terrible debauchery, and moral decline in the name of an ideal of the perfection of individual representatives of the human race, while the mass of humanity is blasphemously considered the pedestal for the glorification of "geniuses" like Nietzsche himself, dissolute and unrestrained by any limits of law or morality.

Outraged moral feelings led some further:

> And what a great and instructive lesson is presented by the fate of this unfortunate pride-filled individual, who has landed in a madhouse by reason of an *idée fixe*, that he is the Creator of the world. Genuine horror is evoked by the great and deserved punishment of this unfortunate godless one, who has imagined himself a god.[4]

Finally, the committee promised for the next issue "a more detailed analysis of the philosophical side of Nietzsche's teaching" by three members of the staff. These appeared, as promised. The most negative was by

P. E. Astaf'ev, "The Genesis of the Moral Ideal of the Decadent"; Nikolai Grot's critique, entitled "The Moral Ideals of Our Time. (Friedrich Nietzsche and Lev Tolstoi)," was moderate and conciliatory. The third, by the respected philosopher L. M. Lopatin, by far the shortest, criticized the author's positive tone toward his subject: "'Morbid Sincerity': Notes on V. P. Preobrazhenskii's Article 'FN.'"[5] Very possibly, concern about the censor's reaction prompted some to write in the terms they did. Nonetheless, two of the articles have the ring of righteous indignation. But if the committee's note was meant to mute the impact of Preobrazhenskii's exposition of Nietzsche's thinking, it failed. If the more openminded and scientifically inquiring members like Nikolai Grot hoped to launch a discussion on a broader scale, their hope was gratified. As the debate about Nietzsche in the Russian "thick journals" proceeded for the next few years, the discussion in French, English, and most of all German spread in Russia as well, among an ever more diverse public.[6]

Ivan Konevskoi's first serious encounter with Nietzsche's teachings seems to have come in spring 1896, when, shortly before he completed *gimnaziia,* and three and a half years after its first publication, he read that same article by Preobrazhenskii.[7] His notebook for that period showed him reading through the 1892-1893 set of *Problems of Philosophy and Psychology* in an extensive sweep, beginning with the opening statement by Nikolai Grot, "The Journal's Tasks," to the end of that volume, including Preobrazhenskii on Nietzsche.[8] However, his main objective seems to have been, not information about Nietzsche, but rather acquaintance with that interesting journal, which he continued to consult from time to time.

Very little in Konevskoi's reading and thinking in spring and summer 1896 suggests interests attuned to Nietzsche. In fact, according to N. L. Stepanov, quite the opposite was true: "Konevskoi's circle of comrades in the *gimnaziia* was distinguished by its religious-philosophical cast of mind, and in this regard, no significant difference between his family setting and the *gimnaziia* existed."[9] Stepanov concluded, moreover, that "Konevskoi came to the university with his worldview already formed in its basics. Therefore, the university merely strengthened and developed those aspects of ideology, those interests, that had already taken shape in the *gimnaziia*" (*LN* 92:4:183). This assertion may hold for the year 1896-1897, but it is questionable thereafter.

Nietzsche's name appeared on the 1896-1897 schedule of the student circle, of which Konevskoi was secretary. The first presentation, on 29 September, was listed as "About Nietzsche," by V. R. Menzhinskii.[10] However, no further show of interest emerged there, and some time elapsed before Konevskoi himself apparently felt the need to learn more on the topic.[11]

Meanwhile, among his many discoveries of that year was the monthly journal *Cosmopolis,* launched in London in January 1896 and continuing through November 1898. Its prospectus announced: "COSMOPOLIS has no rival in its chief purpose, which is to present English-speaking and Continental readers with a tri-lingual review composed (in equal parts) of English, French and German text by leading writers." No translations were accepted. Its British publisher, T. Fisher Unwin, promised that it "will be published simultaneously in London, Paris, Berlin, Vienna, Amsterdam, and New York." Supplements in several other languages were planned, but only the Russian supplement appeared. *Cosmopolis* was published in St. Petersburg from January 1897 till December 1898, surviving one month longer than the main publication.[12] Notebooks show Konevskoi to have been an early reader of the journal, and his interest apparently increased with the addition of the Russian supplement in 1897.[13]

The first appearance of Nietzsche's name in *Cosmopolis* came in the European edition in May, 1897: "Quelques Lettres Inédites" of Nietzsche, introduced by Henri Lichtenberger. If Konevskoi saw this item, he made no note. However, a year and a half later, in October, 1898, two articles on Nietzsche in the European edition drew his attention. "The Literary Movement in Germany. Friedrich Nietzsche and His Influence," by John G. Robertson, opens with a survey of recent European writing on Nietzsche, starting with the 1888 essay of Georg Brandes, which, as Robertson said, "marks the beginning of Nietzsche's career as a European personality."[14] Robertson undertook to impress on the reader Nietzsche's stature in European culture as "an intellectual force of the first order," and even "'one of the greatest spiritual forces which have appeared since Goethe'" (Havelock Ellis). In the same issue, Stanislas Rzewuski's "La Philosophie de Nietzsche" approached the subject with the same exalted enthusiasm: "Nietzsche proclame avant tout le culte de la vie" (139), a claim that presumably appealed to Konevskoi.

In the meantime, publication of Nietzsche's works proceeded apace in Germany. By 1898 C. G. Naumann Verlag in Leipzig had published twelve volumes of the complete works, with individual volumes available separately in soft cover. In addition, as John Robertson informed his readers, that publisher "has just supplemented the handsome edition of Nietzsche's works [...] with two dainty little volumes containing 'Also Sprach Zarathustra' and 'Gedichte und Sprüche.'"[15] The latter volume, which came into Konevskoi's hands sometime that year, was a selection of short passages from juvenilia, works in print, and some fragments, ending with "Bruchstücke zu den Liedern Zarathustras (Dionysos-Dithyramben)."

Konevskoi's intensive reading of Nietzsche began in December 1898, with *Die Geburt der Tragödie* (no notes taken) and *Also sprach Zarathustra*, where many items were marked "NB".[16] Of these two titles, it was the latter that made a major impression. As we know, by the second half of April 1899 he had already included Nietzsche in his plan to publish a small body of his translations of what he considered the best of "truly contemporary poetry." (See Ch. 5.) The importance Nietzsche assumed in Konevskoi's scheme apparently rested on a very narrow base — a handful of lyrics and aphorisms, chiefly from *Zarathustra*. Nevertheless, along with Swinburne and his verses, Nietzsche's position was to be central in a unified body of work, meant to present "the fullest and most vivid formula of the philosophical meaning of the chief contemporary moods."[17]

Thus far, however, Konevskoi's acquaintance with Nietzschean texts was limited, for all serious purposes, to *Also Sprach Zarathustra*, and his enthusiasm there confined to a few lyrics. Having previously sent Aleksandr Bilibin his handful of *Zarathustra* translations, Konevskoi warned his friend against plunging indiscriminately into the rest:

The greater part of the remainder is incomparably lower, and, moreover, like Nietzsche's work in general, in my view, it merely opens, in passing and by accident, as it were, *majestic world horizons*, and then, like its general flow, is not only senseless, i.e., without harmony in the distribution of its parts, but, worst of all, it circles constantly around extremely trivial and specific points of view and boils with the commonest street talk that belongs in the mouths of vulgarians.[18]

Konevskoi's outrage at Nietzsche's casual way of dropping rare pearls into the sludge of an unkempt, undignified writing style was swelled by distress over Nietzsche's apparent willingness to cheapen his *persona* and message. After particularly flagrant examples reflecting on the "Prologue," he concludes, "[this] I cannot forgive him" (*AVL*, 177). The reason for his vehemence is obvious: the "Prologue" contains the crucial passage that, for Konevskoi, as for many others, was the core of Nietzsche/Zarathustra's message:

Behold, I teach you the overman [*übermensch*]. The overman is the meaning of the earth. Let your will say: the overman shall be the meaning of the earth! I beseech you, my brothers, remain faithful to the earth, and do not believe those who speak to you of otherworldly hopes![19]

Nevertheless, Konevskoi ruled the "Prologue" out of his translation project. He aimed for a distinctive, unifying note to sound through his entire collection and, presumably, within each poet's segment. The two pieces mentioned in his letter to Briusov, "Das trunkne Lied" and "Mittag" — "The Drunken Song" and "At Noon," — fulfilled that purpose royally.

Walter Kaufmann called "Das trunkne Lied" "Nietzsche's great hymn to joy [that] invites comparison with Schiller's — minus Beethoven's music."[20] Over and over it intones Zarathustra's maxim: "But all joy wants eternity — / Wants deep, wants deep eternity." A maxim closely related to this in Nietzsche's thinking is: "Love life, love the earth!" These two loves, he insists, are inseparable:

Have you ever said Yes to a single joy? O my friends, then you said Yes too to *all* woe. All things are entangled, ensnared, enamored; if ever you wanted one thing twice, if ever you said, "You please me, happiness! Abide, moment!" then you wanted *all* back. All anew, all eternally, all entangled, all ensnared, all enamored — oh, then you *loved* the world. Eternal ones, love it eternally and evermore; and to woe, too, you say: go, but return! *For all joy wants — eternity*".[21]

The motives in "The Drunken Song," here drawn together, echo the climactic passage of "At Noon." Zarathustra, falling asleep in the shade of high noon, speaks to his heart: "Still! Still! Did not the world become perfect just now? What is happening to me?" Now again he murmurs: "What happened to me? Did time perhaps fly away? Do I not fall? Did I not fall — listen! — into the well of eternity?" And then once more: "Did not the world become perfect just now? Oh, the golden round ball!" (276-278). The circle is now complete: noon, the moment when the world turns, has arrived, the recurrence begins.

Although Konevskoi considered "the overman" to be Nietzsche's most splendid inspiration, the poems he chose to translate dwell primarily on the "eternal recurrence." It is possible that he grasped intuitively the close relationship between the two concepts. But what was his understanding of "eternal recurrence"? For Nietzsche this was a terrifying, abysmal thought, but probably a true one. Only the most superior individual, i.e., the *übermensch,* could contemplate it with equanimity and even welcome it. One Nietzsche scholar, Richard Schacht, has elucidated the link between these two central concepts as follows:

> Nietzsche's motivation for introducing this idea [eternal recurrence] and making so much of it in *Zarathustra* is thus inseparable from two of his most basic concerns: with the idea and possibility of a total 'affirmation of life' and of the world (as they are, rather than merely as one might wish them to be), and with the emergence of an enhanced form of life strong and rich enough to stand as a 'justification of life'.[22]

In Nietzsche's juxtaposition of these images and ideas, Konevskoi may have recognized something very close to his own concerns. There is no evidence to suggest that he made any effort to penetrate further Nietzsche's doctrine of eternal recurrence.²³ Rather than finding it terrifying, he was satisfied to find in it that same "affirmation of life" that so splendidly echoed his own ruling idea: abolition of death and ongoing survival of the *persona*.

2. What is Noble?

Writing to General Oreus after learning of his son's death, Konevskoi's close friend N. M. Sokolov offered this bit of consolation: "He loved the expression 'noble,' he found in it a deep, mysterious meaning, his soul was able to embrace all the rich content of that word."²⁴ Sokolov may or may not have been familiar with *Beyond Good and Evil* or the particular significance it had for Konevskoi. In any case, he could safely assume that Oreus Sr. was not, and that he would take the word in its generally accepted meaning.

However, just half a year earlier, Konevskoi had spent a solid month absorbing some of Nietzsche's most controversial teachings. During most of December 1899 he buried himself in reading *Beyond Good and Evil (Jenseits von Gut und Böse)*.²⁵ As was often the case, he was less intent on mastering Nietzsche's thought than in following a line of particular interest to himself and applying it according to his lights. Thus, after the tantalizing glimpse of the *übermensch* given in *Zarathustra*, it was of tremendous importance to him to learn more. Whether or not he was aware that Nietzsche actually intended *Beyond Good and Evil* as a restatement, in a different style, of the content of *Zarathustra*, Konevskoi seems to have found it useful for elaborating his own interpretation of Nietzsche's great idea.²⁶

Three of the last four parts of this nine-part work offer, cumulatively and by repetition, a fair guide to where Nietzsche's thinking was leading. In Part 6, "We Scholars," he provides a working definition of the "higher man" and his leading qualities. "Today the concept of greatness entails being noble, wanting to be by oneself, being able to be different, standing alone [...]. 'He shall be greatest who can be loneliest, the most concealed, the most deviant, the human being beyond good and evil, the master of his virtues, he that is overrich in will'" (6:212:329). Then, in Part 7, "Our Virtues," he introduces a new note — the importance of suffering — and a new phrase, "the enhancements of man":

The discipline of suffering, of *great* suffering — do you not know that only *this* discipline has created all the enhancements of man so far? That tension of the soul in unhappiness which cultivates its strength, its shudders face to face with great ruin, its inventiveness and courage in enduring, persevering, interpreting, and exploiting suffering, and whatever has been granted to it of profundity, secret, mask, spirit, cunning, greatness — was it not granted to it through suffering, through the discipline of great suffering? (7:225:344).

Finally, in Part 9, "What Is Noble," the noble being is given the place of honor that belongs to him: "The noble human being honors himself as one who is powerful, also as one who has power over himself, who knows how to speak and be silent, who delights in being severe and hard with himself and respects all severity and hardness (9:260:395). [...] Profound suffering makes noble; it separates" (9:270:410).

These pieces of wisdom held meaning for Konevskoi, although their first artistic fruits were less than striking. Early in January 1900 he wrote to Briusov:

I can tell you about several new poetical writings. But I cannot make up my mind to include them in the body of my genuine poetic creative work. They are written primarily for clarifying for myself several basic themes of action. Therefore even the title given them is very reasoned: Understandings. I may note that these are 'understandings' of Nietzsche's thought about the 'will to power,' expounded by him in the book *Beyond Good and Evil*.[27]

Enclosed with that letter were two pieces.[28] Insofar as poetic quality was concerned, his apologetic tone was justified. Nonetheless, he felt it important to cast in verse form whatever new insights he obtained into Nietzsche's concept of the *übermensch* — itself likely in the process of refinement. The main trophy Konevskoi took from his reading of Nietzsche was, as Briusov correctly observed, the *Übermensch*. (*Briusov/Vengerov* 2:90).[29] The ideal poet-thinker-mystic forming in his mind over the last several years was still a work in progress. To this task the *Übermensch* conceivably had something valuable to offer.

3. Mystical Feeling in Russian Lyric Poetry

Perhaps for Konevskoi the real beauty of Nietzsche's conception lay in the fact that the *Übermensch* was an elastic notion. From age seventeen, when he wrote "Resurrection," Konevskoi knew his mission was to be a poet. At first this meant a zestful creative urge to explore and embrace the totality of human life, rich and varied as he suspected it to be. When that certainty merged, as it soon did, with a passion to penetrate the meaning and structure of the universe, his vision of the "poet" unfolded rapidly.

Konevskoi's early introduction to mysticism (to his mind, the contemporary poet undoubtedly must be a mystic) produced a tremendous urge to test his own capacity for mystical contact with nature. At the same time, he was glad of any models encountered in history, legend, literature, or scientific or pseudo-scientific theory that might serve as subjects for contemplation. It is not surprising, then, that to his fascinated gaze, at least for a time, Nietzsche's *Übermensch* seemed a specimen writ large of that goal of overcoming human nature, the limitations of which Konevskoi well knew to weigh heavily on the spirit.

The first months of 1900 were slack and unproductive. In mid-March Konevskoi wrote Briusov: "I have no new poetry to send you" (*LN* 98:1:485). By early May things were even worse. But, as he looked forward to leaving Petersburg, his condition improved. Moreover, despite the mood of lassitude, Konevskoi was hard at work all spring. On 5 April he told Briusov: "Lately I've been burdened with writing on the topic I've chosen for history of the language: 'special features of language in Tiutchev's poetry, compared with the poetry of Pushkin'" (98:1:488).[30] This was one of several university requirements for that year and the next that he managed to define so as to make them serve his own purposes.[31] In November 1900 he laid before Briusov the larger scheme he had in mind:

> This year I have hoped to finish a study of the creative work of A. Tolstoi as my officially required composition. I have written many drafts, have composed the final version of the introductory sections (where I wrote about the worldviews of Tiutchev, Pushkin, Baratynskii, Kol'tsov, Fet, as

phases of thought preparatory to the philosophy of [Aleksei] Tolstoi), but this is relatively, of course, very little and, in working out even the basic ideas of the study, it is possible to foresee introduction of many substantial revisions and new notions (98:1:517-518).

This ambitious project depended on the willingness of his supervisor, Professor I. N. Zhdanov, to accept his essay on Tolstoi as the required composition. If this was granted, only one more major paper stood between him and the completion of university course work. However, as subject for that work he will choose, "not A. Tolstoi, but some uncomplicated poet (I had in mind Shcherbina)."[32] The envisioned major study of Aleksei Tolstoi was thus put off till a time of less pressure. (518) Unfortunately, that time never came.

The fullest information about Konevskoi's plans appears in a letter from Nikolai Mikhailovich Sokolov to Briusov on 27 December 1901. Reporting on his efforts to gather material and recollections about Konevskoi from their mutual friends in preparation for the edition Briusov was planning, Sokolov wrote:

> From conversations with *all* of Oreus's friends, I've confirmed my conclusion that the center of our deceased friend's interests was poetic creation in the widest sense of the word, which fact was expressed especially sharply in his letter to Semenov written just before his death, and in the unification of all his interests in the unfinished work about the lyric poetry of our poets of the first half of the [nineteenth] century (98:1:520n.4).[33]

Aside from the intriguing reference to the "letter to Semenov written just before his death" (see Ch. 9), there is no real surprise in Sokolov's letter. It confirms the fact that, in Konevskoi's judgment, Aleksei Tolstoi was the culminating figure in the line of early and mid-nineteenth-century Russian mystical poets — a judgment as personal and selective as many such in Konevskoi's critical writing.

Though we might regret that the planned study was not completed, the essay "Mystical Feeling in Russian Lyric Poetry" provides a good sense of what Konevskoi's finished work might have been, even without the essay on Tolstoi. "Mystical Feeling in Russian Lyric Poetry" was first printed in the posthumous 1904 "Scorpio" edition. It was dated 1900, i.e., four years after the summer of 1896, when Konevskoi first wrestled so intensely with the meaning (or meanings) of the "new mysticism." (See Ch. 1.) Four years later, with the benefit of much reading, thinking, and experience, he produced a definition of "mystical feeling" that enabled him to identify with certainty the poets he would treat as "mystical." In his introductory paragraph he wrote:

> By the term "mystical feeling" is meant a special sense of all that is hidden from ordinary human *causal consciousness* and average personal instinct and perception. It is a sense of the *persona*'s presence in states of consciousness that lie outside the usual conditions of perception of objects. It is the uniting of personal consciousness with the sphere of its objects' existence, the enlargement of the sphere of self-awareness (*SP 1904*, 199).[34]

This definition is compactly organized in three phases, each contained in a single sentence. The first enunciates a basic principle: mystical feeling has to do only with what is "hidden from ordinary human *causal consciousness*"; i.e., ordinary reasoning based on causal connections has no role here. The second stresses two elements specific to Konevskoi's conception of mystical activity: positive involvement of the *persona,* and focus on *altered states of consciousness.* The third offers a powerful synthesis, in which almost every word underlines the element that was all-important to Konevskoi: *extended personal consciousness.*

The essay deals first with Tiutchev, less extensively with Pushkin, Baratynskii, and Fet, and, finally, at some length, with Kol'tsov. The founder of this line of poets, Tiutchev is viewed as an "original" in Russian poetry: "He sprang up in the life of the Russian spirit without any preliminary influence, and revealed a *persona* of a quality completely unknown hitherto in Russian poetry" (199). This sketch of Tiutchev is essentially a fable. The young poet is seen less as a "child of nature" than as a kind of metaphysical *tabula rasa,* open to and waiting for messages from the universe around him. And they come. When night falls, and all about him becomes strange, "in the poet's soul arose words unique of their kind, because with astonishing and terrifying directness and nakedness they spoke the ancient secret thought of humanity — the sense of the abyss, the essence of life" (201).

Tiutchev's poetry — or Konevskoi's reading of it — figured prominently in his early attempts to grasp the nature of mysticism. Certain poems had an important role in his first mystical experience three years earlier. Yet, on one vital point, the nature of pantheism, Konevskoi had doubts about their fundamental agreement. From the start, he himself rejected the commonly held tenet that pantheism involved ultimate dissolution of the individual in a universal oneness. For Konevskoi it was unacceptable that Tiutchev, with all his authority, should subscribe in his pantheistic-mystical poems totally to this notion. To show the confusion in Tiutchev's views, Konevskoi undertook to demonstrate the inherent contradiction that he found in his basic philosophical conceptions. For him, he claims,

> everything that exists outside and inaccessible to human consciousness and beyond it is the *abyss, eternity, infinity*. At the same time, this poet cannot believe that in this eternity-infinity there is no 'I' and 'not I' […], no multiplicity, no time, no motion. In the abyss, according to Tiutchev, there is storm, chaos and the 'life-creating ocean.' In it individual entities rise and disappear, but that process has no beginning or end. Tiutchev sensed the eternity of movement, the movement of eternity, i.e., moving from point to point and from instant to instant, eternity existing in space and time.

Therefore, Konevskoi concluded, Tiutchev's "prophetic contemplation of the world structure resolves into nothing other than this inner contradiction, yawning forever" (*SP 1904*, 204).

Tiutchev's meditations, as far as Konevskoi was concerned, dealt almost entirely with the workings of the universe. By contrast, in Pushkin's poetry, he found only "moments" of attention to the mystical sphere of being. Much as he valued his poetry, in Konevskoi's view Evgenii Baratynskii contributed little to the strain of mystical poetry. The only name in the canon of Russian mystical poetry of the early and mid-nineteenth century that can balance Tiutchev's is that of Aleksei Vasil'evich Kol'tsov.

4. The Overman and the Poet

The unexpected name in this otherwise predictable list is not Aleksei Kol'tsov the singer of village love, wide open spaces and liberty, but Kol'tsov the author of the less popular and less critically valued philosophical "meditations (*dumy*)." In November 1900 Konevskoi wrote to Briusov with satisfaction that he had finished writing the essay on Kol'tsov with special fullness and polish, "because my characterization of the heart and mind of Kol'tsov *presents a complete exposition of my personal notions*" (ital. mine).[35]

Here, indeed, is a prime example of what has been called Konevskoi's "monocentrism." (*LN* 98:1:431). All poets are examined first for their philosophical worldviews; in his favorites he finds his own views reflected. Yet, this critical method, if it can be so called, was not the narcissistic exercise that it at first appears. Rather, he sought out those elements that resonated with his own imagination and thought and set out to decode them, as the ultimate goal of his endeavor. In the case of Kol'tsov, as will be seen, Konevskoi's analysis amounts to a veritable personal manifesto.

Konevskoi's article on Kol'tsov has never been published in its entirety.[36] It appears only in abridged form in "Mystical Feeling in Russian Lyric Poetry." Some of the differences are significant. In the original, unpublished text, the first section deals extensively with Kol'tsov's songs and personal lyrics. Besides showing Konevskoi's enjoyment of the songs, it serves an important purpose in building the hero's character as the bold, dashing adventurer of the steppe, in whose songs, "through the forms and tones of ancient oral Russian songs, a solitary spirit, supplied with exceptional drive and force of personal will and power in battle, makes itself felt" (line16). In the abridged version, a single sentence suffices. From there, the printed text moves directly to the "Meditations."

In both versions, Konevskoi represents Kol'tsov's career as poet as a smooth progression from the earlier lyric songs to the later meditations.[37] While this is not chronologically accurate, it supports the image of the passionate young singer who matures into the thinker who struggles painfully with the great questions of life, death, and his place in the cosmic order. Portrayed as a fighter from the start, the poet is seen evolving into a rebel against fate and then against the universe itself:

> Here, in the presence of the deafening breath of the world tempest, he was swept by a tremor of terror before the new gigantic forces that threatened him, and by the nothingness of his human body, will, intellect. The world structure seemed to him a savage enemy and opponent, an unknown monster, a soulless mass that pressed on man with crushing weight.[....] And so he was fired by the dream of measuring his own powers against the crushing might of world forces (*SP 1904*, 212).

To demonstrate the poet's painful struggles and how he dealt with them, Konevskoi chose "The Question." But, while paraphrasing the text, he also made important revisions. Kol'tsov's original begins in a chiding tone, spoken as if by the poet's wiser self to his foolish, headstrong one: "How dare you call out to the sun: Listen, sun! Stand still, don't move!" The speaker rebukes the wayward one for his arrogant attempt to bend the powers of the universe to his own will: "How dare you…?" Then, abruptly, the wiser self speaks to his own weaknesses, crying out in desperation: "What can I do with my unruly will, my sinful thought, my fiery passion?" The poet's lament continues for another thirty lines, asking, in effect, "How long, Lord, how long?"

Kol'tsov's wiser self thus turns out to be, after all, a common mortal, an "everyman," whose humility alone saves him. Konevskoi, however, will have none of this. He envisions "his" poet differently: no "everyman," he is instead a superior human being, trapped in this crass material world that attempts to crush him. Even though helpless and humiliated, he yet proudly insists that the almighty powers bend to his demands. Konevskoi makes this interpretation abundantly clear by the simple process of rewriting Kol'tsov's lines as he paraphrases them:

CHAPTER 7

> He [Koltsov] dared to call out to the sun: "Stand still, don't move"; he dared to look on the sea so that it might "turn to stone," so that, with his *bogatyr's* strength, he might halt the globe in its turning — and his efforts achieved nothing. His personal spirit, awakening in him with monstrous passion, entered into mortal combat with the Earth surrounding him (213).

But the two poets' thoughts unite as a truly hideous question comes to Koltsov, one that Konevskoi finds all too familiar. Kol'tsov writes: "What will happen after death? Will I remember where I was before? Or what, as a human being, I thought? Or will I forget everything beyond the tomb? Will I lose reason and memory?" (Kol'tsov, 94) Konevskoi's manuscript version expands and intensifies this anguished cry with particular fears about the helplessness and infirmities of sickness and old age, "And death, as they say, will take him." Death, followed by nothingness: it is Konevskoi's personal nightmare and the philosophical affront to end all affronts — annihilation of the *persona*. Speaking for Kol'tsov as well as for himself, he says: "These thoughts are blows and insults, unacceptable to his pride. There are no limits to his horror and indignation" (259.3.15.27).

At this point, however, the two poets' attitudes diverge once again. Kol'tsov's final lines bring all the previous tortured questions into focus, putting them to one all-powerful listener, the Supreme Being. When all is said and done, then, for him religious faith emerges as a poignant, powerful presence in his worldview.[38]

Konevskoi, on the other hand, stops short of quoting these final lines. Instead he turns to another "meditation." In its entirety, "God's World" is a paean to the triune God in nature. But Konevskoi bypasses most of the poem and uses only the closing lines: "In life's changes / There is no powerless death,/ There is no soulless life!" In those words, as he sees them, the poet Kol'tsov is saved from despair — not by an appeal to God, but by his own inborn power to contemplate nature and bring the stream of life into himself.

Konevskoi's extremely free adaptations of Kol'tsov's poems clearly went several steps beyond mere interpretation. As it happened, Kol'tsov's worldview as expressed in the "meditations" was uncertain enough in its outlines to allow Konevskoi to shape the texts to accommodate his own views. Moreover, feeling great empathy with the other poet, he obviously felt free to complete, as it were, (or correct) his thoughts.[39] Their common horror of death, bringing with it the threat of annihilation of the individual, provided a strong bond. The difference was that, unlike the earlier poet, Konevskoi insisted that a way ultimately could be found to counter this threat. He proposed to find it.

The next and final step in Konevskoi's reconstruction of Kol'tsov's world view focused on the 1840 "The Poet." For the foundation of his argument, however, he reached back to the shorter version of "The Question," called "Human Wisdom," where the wise self admonishes the other in much severer terms than before, using epithets like "O wise one," "slave of space," "captive of years and time." Finally, he challenges his other self to do the impossible: be all, one and everywhere, be God! Kol'tsov closes "Human Wisdom" with full acknowledgement of God's power and wisdom. However, Konevskoi chooses another tack. By carefully choosing or altering phrases from the "meditation," he frames an argument that leads in a diametrically opposite direction. In his rendering, the crucial passage reads in part: "Let man be all, single and everywhere, in a word, God!" For, if a man can conceive of an "all-in-one" that is both multiplicity and one, *how can he not be this being?* If he is outside that all-one being, i.e., God, then that unity is nonexistent. (*SP 1904*, 214-215. *Ital. mine*).

From this position, Konevskoi wove an intricate set of links to "The Poet," where the exalted figure described earlier reaches its apotheosis. "For the poet there is no power on earth over him. The might of creative *imagination* and *self — inspiration*, artistic and intellectual, is limitless" (*SP 1904*, 215).

"The Poet" itself is a relatively mild statement, embodying Kol'tsov's notions about the poetic imagination, derived second- or thirdhand from German romantic theories, chiefly Schellingian, which he learned from Belinskii.[40] However, his word on mortality in the finale takes on sweep and grandeur: "Marvellous creations of all-powerful thought! The whole world before you vanishes with me..." From this point Konevskoi was able briefly to lift his brother poet to the position he deserved: "One therefore may be convinced that Kol'tsov's poetry contains within itself all the seeds of a worldview that is perfected, fulfilled, in which the *persona* truly achieves all-oneness" (216).

Still, in Kol'tsov the thought of death, to be followed by eternal darkness, produced terror, rather than the towering rebellion against the universe that Konevskoi would have desired. However, in his concluding words, Konevskoi found an excuse for that submissiveness. He reminds the reader that Kol'tsov lived only half a life and was on the brink of a whole new life (and presumably new discoveries) when he died at age thirty-three. Konevskoi, of course, was glad to supplement his spiritual comrade's uncertainties and vacillations with his own increasingly audacious ideas.[41]

By thus fortifying Kol'tsov's thoughts and meditations, Konevskoi had come another step closer to fully envisioning the "poet-thinker-mystic." He also brought him more or less in line with Nietzsche in this task. The contribution of Nietzsche's *übermensch* to the ideal for which Konevskoi strove was already spelled out in his plan for a volume of translations. (See Ch. 5.) With Nietzsche providing a leading voice, the translated poems together were to offer "the fullest and most vivid formula of the philosophical meaning of the chief contemporary moods" (*AVL*, 177). But the ideal was still a work in progress.

Notes

1. Cf. Irene Masing-Delic, *Abolishing Death. A Salvation Myth of Russian Twentieth-Century Literature*. Stanford, CA.: Stanford University Press, 1992. Konevskoi's personal quest for immortality, pursued outside of religious faith, sounds some notes anticipatory of the twentieth-century phenomena.
2. *LN* 92:4:182.
3. V. P. Preobrazhenskii, "Kritika morali al'truizma," *Voprosy filosofii i psikhologii (PPP)*, № 15, Nov. 1892. It was reprinted in 1894, along with N. Ia. Grot, "Nravstvennye idealy nashego vremeni (Fridrikh Nitsshe i Lev Tolstoi)."
4. *PPP*, № 15, pp. 115-116. The editorial note appeared at the foot of the first two pages of the article. Presumably, none of the contributors considered the article's potential to attract rebels from among partisans of the "new art", "decadents", and other "deviants" to the doctrines of Nietzsche.
5. *PPP*, № 16 (January 1893), pp. 56-75, 129-154, 109-114.
6. See: *Nietzsche in Russia*. Ed. Bernice Glatzer Rosenthal. Princeton, N.J.: Princeton University Press, 1986.
7. *RGALI* 259.1.6.10. "End of *gimnaziia* studies 13 Apr. 1896."
8. The contents of volume "1891-1892" were printed on the inside covers and the outside back cover of the January 1894 issue.
9. *LN* 92:4:182. In an earlier notebook, dated "1893-1895", a six-page section headed "Thoughts" expresses sentiments redolent of strictly and explicitly Christian morality. (*RGALI* 259.1.4.14-19.)
10. *RGALI* 259.1.17.63ob.-64. Incidentally, in the Soviet Union V. R. Menzhinskii became a notorious secret police (GPU) chief.
11. Konevskoi's friendship with Vladimir V. Gippius, which began in 1898, when the two frequented the circle of Iakov Erlikh, may have played a role here. In his autobiography "O samom sebe" Gippius wrote that, in 1893, when he was in his midteens, "I was a Nietzschean, not having read one line of Nietzsche and not having heard anything about a single thought of his." A year later he read *Zarathustra*, who became his second teacher, after Dostoevskii and *Brothers Karamazov*. (*IRLI* 377.2. Arkhiv Vengerova, V. V. Gippius "O samom sebe," 10-11.)

12 Interesting information about the Russian *Cosmopolis* can be found in: Rachel Polonsky, *English Literature and the Russian Aesthetic Renaissance*. Cambridge, UK: Cambridge University Press, 1998. Pp. 28-33.

13 Konevskoi's reading notebook shows that in the first year of the European *Cosmopolis* he read a lengthy piece: NoNo. 2 and 3, Ed. Rod, "Le mouvement des idées en France" (first installment and conclusion). When the Russian edition began in 1897, the references scattered on the pages show that he became an even more attentive reader. (*RGALI*, 259.1.6).

14 "The Literary Movement in Germany. Friedrich Nietzsche and His Influence," by John G. Robertson. *Cosmopolis*, Oct. 1898, pp. 31-48.

15 Robertson, p. 42.

16 *RGALI*, 259.1.6.72ob.

17 *AVL*, 177.

18 Both Robertson and Rzewuski stress that Nietzsche's writings have been totally misunderstood by the "crowd." They do not blame Nietzsche himself for triviality and vulgarity, as Konevskoi does. (*AVL*, 177.)

19 The notes from Konevskoi's first reading of *Also Sprach Zarathustra*, in December 1898, show the importance he placed on the "Vorrede," or parts thereof. (*RGALI*, 259.1.6.72ob.) The German word "übermensch" has vexed most translators. The translation used here is that of Walter Kaufmann. A full explication of his preference for the term "overman" and its history and meaning is found in his monograph *Nietzsche Philosopher, Psychologist, Antichrist*. Princeton, NJ: Princeton University Press, 1974. Ch. 11, "Overman and Eternal Recurrence." Pp.307-333.

20 Walter Kaufmann, 236.

21 *Thus Spoke Zarathustra*. Tr. Walter Kaufmann. New York, NY: Penguin Books. IV:10, p. 323.

22 Richard Schacht, *Nietzsche*. (London & New York: Routledge & Kegan Paul, 1985) 261. Schacht discusses the idea that Nietzsche may have been responding to Schopenhauer's supposition in *The World as Will and Idea*, Fourth Book, that no one, knowing what suffering his whole life will bring, would be willing to repeat it. (Schacht, 260)

23 True to his habit, Konevskoi apparently forewent any large attempt to probe, even to understand, to master, an artist's entire philosophy. Thinking for

him was not a process of receiving and adopting another's ideas, but of entering into a dialogue with them. Konevskoi read, not to comprehend another thinker-poet's method of thought, what his arguments were, or what was the foundation of his thinking. Rather, he read, relying on intuition and mystical receptivity, hoping to find sympathetic support and, often, clarification of his own ideas. Certainly this was the case in his encounters with Nietzsche.

[24] From a letter of N. M. Sokolov to Ivan Oreus Sr., enclosed to Briusov in a letter of 29 Aug. 1901 (*LN* 98:1:535). It is possible that the letter-writer knew of Konevskoi's concentrated reading in *Beyond Good and Evil*. More likely, however, he used the word in the usual sense.

[25] *RGALI* 259.1.6.83ob. Note that this reading came just a year after he read *Also sprach Zarathustra*. Therefore, it did not figure in the translation project, but comes in at a later stage, i.e., his fascination with "overman" plus will to power. Konevskoi apparently had read previously a few small selections from *Jenseits von Gut und Böse* and *Fröhliche Wissenschaft*, probably from the small volume *Gedichte und Sprüche*. (*LN* 98:1:461, n.19)

[26] To a correspondent in 1886, the year of its publication, Nietzsche wrote: "Please read this book [*Jenseits von Gut und Böse*] (although it says the same things as my *Zarathustra*, but differently, very differently —)." (Cited from *Basic Writings of Nietzsche*, tr., ed., with commentaries, Walter Kaufmann, "Translator's Preface," *Beyond Good and Evil*, p. 182.)

[27] The letter is dated "no earlier than 12 January 1900." *LN* 98:1:478. Note 1 adds: "The same theme as in the enclosed verses was reworked by Konevskoi into an article under the title of 'On the Matter of Freedom and Power. On Nietzsche's thought "On the Will to Power",' dated: Moscow. September 1899. January 1900. (*RGALI*, 259.3.9.31). Included in the 1904 "Scorpio" edition of Konevskoi's works is the short article "On the Matter of Freedom (*K delu svobody*)," dated 11-17 September 1899, pp. 221-222. Its style and content, as well as title and dates, suggest that it may have been a first draft of the later piece.

[28] These two were later published, along with one more, under the title "Gnomy (Gnomes)" (1-3), *SP 1904*, 153-154. "Gnome" is a Greek term for aphorism or brief reflection.

29 Briusov cited other likely Nietzschean inspirations in Konevskoi's poetry, notably the notion of "man as bridge." His main example was "Kto my? — Nevedomoi prirody perekhody (Who are we? — Transitions of unknown nature)" (*SP 2008*, 156).

30 *RGALI*, 259. 3.11.28-42ob. The editors of the Briusov-Konevskoi correspondence suggested two possible destinations for this composition: one as introduction to an unfinished article entitled "Intersections of Thought in Russian Poetry, Preceding the Thought of A. K. Tolstoi — Tiutchev, Pushkin, Baratynskii, Kol'tsov, Fet," the other as a draft for "Mystical Feeling in Russian Lyric Poetry" (1900). *LN* 98:1:489.n. 3.

31 Another was a paper written the previous October about Evgenii Baratynskii. (*LN* 98:1:473)

32 Konevskoi's essay "N. F. Shcherbina's Worldview (*Mirovozzrenie N. F. Shcherbiny*)" appeared posthumously in the almanach *Severnye tsvety na 1902 g. (Northern Flowers for 1902)*, pp. 194-214, and was reprinted in *Mechty i dumy Ivana Konevskogo* [S.-Petersburg, 1900], Berkeley Slavic Specialties, 1989, pp. 220-240.

33 The plans and manuscripts gathered by Sokolov covered essentially the same topics as were to be included in the unfinished article mentioned in note 30 above. They are listed in: *LN* 98:1:520, n.4. Sokolov himself planned an article about Konevskoi, for which drafts and outlines have been preserved. (*LN* 98:1:534. n.1.)

34 "Mystical Feeling in Russian Lyric Poetry" shows Konevskoi's adaptation of concepts put forth by Du Prel and other psychic researchers as they bore on his by then more finished conception of the poet and his powers.

35 *LN* 98:1:517-518.

36 *RGALI*, 259.3.15.

37 Konevskoi doubtless read all of the *dumy* (fewer than twenty). In both versions of this essay, however, he drew on just six: "Velikaia taina *(The Great Mystery)*" (1833), "Bozhii mir *(God's World)*" (1836), "Tsarstvo mysli *(The Kingdom of Thought),*" "Vopros *(The Question)*" and "Chelovecheskaia mudrost' *(Human Wisdom)*" (1837), and "Poet *(The Poet)*" (1840). Kol'tsov, A. V. *Polnoe sobranie sochinenii.* Ed. A. I. Liashchenko. St. Petersburg: Akademicheskaia biblioteka russkikh pisatelei, 1911. Pp. 60, 71, 96, 92, 94, 137.

[38] This is even more obvious in "Human Wisdom," the variant of "The Question" that was written shortly after it. Pp. 94-95.

[39] He performed this operation earlier on Tiutchev. See above, Section 2.

[40] For a discussion of Kol'tsov's philosophical formation through relations with the Stankevich circle, with Belinskii, and others, see: Iu. V. Mann, "Kol'tsov i filosoficheskaia mysl' ego vremeni." *A. V. Kol'tsov i russkaia literatura.* Ed. I. V. Os'makov. (Moscow: "Nauka," 1988), pp. 37-38.

[41] "Consistency of view was not a characteristic of Kol'tsov, author of the 'meditations.' From negative answer he moved to positive answer and the reverse, while into each answer a bit of the opposite feeling is permitted." (Mann, p. 44.)

Chapter 8

Finland, Novgorod, St. Petersburg

"In a few weeks my father and I will go to Finland, to the shores of Saima, to the Pension Rauha, which Vladimir Solov'ev loved" (*AVL*, 180). Konevskoi wrote this news in early May 1900 to Sergei Semenov.[1] The previous summer in Finland he devoted himself to *Dreams and Meditations* and to the aborted translation project. Now, with that behind him, it was a time for summing up, in preparation for whatever was to follow. As a place for this, the environs of Lake Saima could hardly be bettered. Rich in associations with Vladimir Solov'ev's mystical poetry, Saima now offered a focal point for themes and ideas soon to be woven by Konevskoi into designs affecting the immediate future and beyond.

1. Vladimir Solov'ev

Vladimir Solov'ev's likeness had for some time been discernible in the ideal image of the contemporary poet-mystic taking shape in Konevskoi's mind. Solov'ev's unexpected death in July 1900 prompted an outpouring of tributes, appreciations, and memorials. Among these was a brief article by Valerii Briusov.[2] Upon receiving a copy from the author, Konevskoi expressed amazement at Briusov's choice of poems for mention in his article. With a few exceptions, he found them "extremely unsuccessful parts of that body of poetry."[3] But then came his real attack. Briusov had written of Solov'ev: "His entire philosophy is penetrated by awareness of Christian truth. [...] Poetry flowing from such a worldview is, of course, Christian poetry" (*RA*, 548). Then, moving on to characterize Solov'ev's conception of love, Briusov wrote that, for Solov'ev, love is "a feeling elevating the soul and lifting it above the chains of the flesh." He ended by saying: "Wherever in Vladimir Solov'ev's poetry love is spoken of, either directly or figuratively, it is always to be understood as that higher, mystical feeling" (*RA*, 552).

Konevskoi could hardly have disagreed more with either position. He began by reminding Briusov of his own views on Solov'ev, earlier expressed in "Lyric Poetry in Contemporary Russia." Of Solov'ev's treatment of love Konevskoi had written: "The combination of the forces of frenzy and ugliness with the fruitful forces of harmonious arrangement make themselves felt with special boldness and vividness in that poet's most manly song of love, 'We came together not by chance (*My soshlis' s toboi nedarom*)'" (*AVL*, 140).[4] But his fundamental objection to Briusov's article focused on his assertion that Solov'ev's poetry was, "of course, Christian poetry." To that Konevskoi countered: "Christianity cannot *not be* a transitional, subordinate moment in the system of Vl. Solov'ev" (1:512; *ital. mine*). After dismissing the poems dealing specifically with New Testament figures and events as "lifeless and formal," Konevskoi launched enthusiastically into his own perception of the poet's syncretic vision, emphasizing the pantheistic and pagan roots of Solov'ev's poetic *Weltanschauung*.

In his 1896 essay, Konevskoi attempted to weigh six poets' grasp of that most basic philosophical topic, "the life of the *persona* in the universe"; the ultimate criterion was each poet's "position regarding personal existence in relation to death" (*AVL*, 138). Neither then nor later did Konevskoi find in Solov'ev's poetry fully satisfactory answers to those questions about death and the survival of the "I". However, as he had done before, Konevskoi found "evidence" in the poet's own words that, in Solov'ev's deepest intuitions, his and Konevskoi's views were in harmony. Konevskoi predicted that, while at present each of the competing poets had his strengths and weaknesses, the future lay with that "great man" who would meld together the virtues of each. He now saw such fusion in Solov'ev.

Crowning his arguments, Konevskoi attempted a closely reasoned explanation of Solov'ev's theology and metaphysics that might be expected to appeal to Briusov's logical mind:

His ideal of "godmanhood" is possibly meant to bring the later superstructure of Hellenic-Asiatic metaphysics into harmony with the teaching of the Teacher of Nazareth. Hellenic-Roman church organization, unity of the church — all that is in his spirit. But is that truly the ancient, fiery, and simple gospel of the Galilean fishermen? [....] Offshoots of Hellenic thinking on the religion-filled, mystery-filled soil of Egypt, Syria, among the leading movers in the building of Christianity in the late Hellenic-Roman worlds — this is the dream that went deeply into the flesh and blood of our philosopher-synthesizer. This is how he seems to me (*LN* 98:1:513).

In "Lyric Poetry…" Konevskoi laid considerable importance on an early poem that he found to be an emblem of Solov'ev's syncretic religious vision. Solov'ev wrote "Song of the Ophites (*Pesn' Ofitov*)" in Nice, in May 1876, after a year spent in the British Museum studying Indian, gnostic, and medieval texts.[5] The Ophites were a gnostic sect, named for the snake that played a central part in their ritual and belief: "[T]he snake was a medium of revelation and mouthpiece of the most sublime God."[6] In Solov'ev's encyclopedia entry on the Ophites, the serpent plays a role parallel to that of the serpent in the Garden of Eden.[7] However, the mysteries glimpsed in "Song of the Ophites" point to sublime mystical insights that emerge from the union of opposites. Some twenty years later, in his encyclopedia entry "Gnosticism," Solov'ev wrote: "At the base of this religious movement lie the seeming (*sic*) reconciliation and reunion of divinity and the world, absolute and relative being, infinite and finite".[8] Yet, despite his note of academic skepticism, gnosticism is thought to hold a significant place in Solov'ev's writings.[9]

How much Konevskoi actually knew about gnosticism is unclear, though clearly he had some acquaintance with its beliefs and imagery. The notion of opposites — heaven and earth, spirit and flesh, oneness and multiplicity, all in a state of permanent tension, — had tremendous significance for him. In 1896, he was searching for a solid basis for the assumption that underlay his own worldview: namely, that the *persona*, while sharing fully in the life of the All-One, yet maintains its own separate identity. In Solov'ev's doctoral dissertation, defended in 1880, he believed he had found it.[10]

However, in both "Lyric Poetry in Contemporary Russia" and in his letter to Briusov, it is apparent that Konevskoi's real love among Solov'ev's images is Lake Saima — specifically the mystical Saima to which Solov'ev's poems were dedicated. Indeed, as he wrote to Briusov, he saw Lake Saima as a splendid vehicle for expressing Solov'ev's precepts regarding the opposing forces that maintained the world's equilibrium. Konevskoi found there Solov'ev's "best symbols of universal turbulence and universal calm: stormy Saima and frozen Saima" (98:1:512).[11] Finland's stern, hardy, and gnarled landscape provided Konevskoi with a key to unlock Solov'ev's profound sympathy with the universe. Finnish nature also, it would seem, assisted Konevskoi in unlocking much more.

2. *Imatra*

On 1 June 1900 Konevskoi wrote to Briusov from a spot near the fabled waterfall Imatra, "I am coming to myself here on the granite slabs that I have always loved" (*LN* 98:1:502). However, in that blissful state he wrote only three poems, two of which suggest a mystical experience linked to the watery Finnish landscape. "Rushing Waters" opens with an exuberant salute to "the triumphant beast-waves, white-headed bison" in their "daring play!" (*SP 2008*, 156-157) The rest suggests his hope of things to come: initiation into the mysteries of water and forest that cleanse his senses with healing sounds and images that mute the world left behind. Major emphasis in this spirited lyric falls on sound and hearing. The first stanza opens with an exhilarating rush of onomatopoetic sound: sybillants, hushing consonants, rolling multi-syllabic words that imitate the rushing water. Stanza 2 evokes the place left behind with the roar of a crowd. The third and fourth stanzas bring the moment of crossing-over; a young messenger-god leads the poet to the place where, his ears filled with the water's roar, he is initiated into the forest's mystery.

If there is a lightness, almost playfulness, about "Rushing Waters," this second Finnish lyric is a different matter. (*SP 2008*, 157) "Murmurings," subtitled "From quiet Finnish voices," also is inspired by the sound and movement of waters. But the effect is not tumultuous. Rather it suggests a quiet sobbing or murmuring, barely audible till the last line. Like the first poem, this one follows the speaker into a wild, secluded place, where he has a moment of revelation. However, in almost every other way, they are different: imagery, narrative technique, mood, even, one might say, genre, in that fairytale elements are replaced by ruggedly realistic description.

The lexicon alone makes for difficult going at the start, creating a dense thicket of words, as it were, to match the terrain. An unbroken movement of twelve short lines with two stresses each gives the effect of labored breathing, the result of heavy slogging through wilderness, swamp, and thick brush. Then suddenly, in line 9, rhythm and meter are interrupted by an unmetrical stress: "My death!" There is no sound, no movement, only silence. His heart asks: in this desolate place, has my end come? He waits for an answer, and it comes. Jumala, Finnish god of the sky, grants mercy: somewhere water moves.

Generally, this watery northern landscape with its hushing sounds served Konevskoi admirably in all respects, physically, spiritually, and aesthetically. It may even have suggested a new way of looking at death, perhaps making it an ally in his quest to penetrate the universe's secret life.

3. *National Identity*

For Konevskoi, the power of Solov'ev's Saima poems, along with that of the lake itself and its natural surroundings, extended well beyond symbolic meanings. His interpretation of early Russian history owed something to the particular attachment to Finland that developed during his last few sojourns there, as did his personal mythology. As early as 1896-1897 a heavily romanticized piece of early history in his essay "Lyric Poetry…" related how, in the days of Novgorod's republic, "there occurred the merger of these two [Finnish and Russian] images in the figures of the Novgorod freemen, powerful, active" (*AVL,* 141).[12]

The question of nationality and national identity had held Konevskoi's attention from the time of his return to Russia after the first journey west in 1897. (See Chapter 2.) Sometime in 1899 he wrote a very short piece entitled "On the Matter of the Poet and the People," in which he berated those (possibly including Bilibin) who believed in "some kind of mysterious popular psyche" that makes itself heard in the words of great poets. (*SP 1904*, 222-225) "Of course, there can be no talk about any kind of common soul of the people. Living souls exist only in the *persona*" (224). In early June 1900, soon after the arrival of the Oreuses at Pension Rauha, a letter came from Aleksandr Bilibin. Though Bilibin's side of the correspondence is not extant, Konevskoi's reply strongly suggests that this letter was part of an ongoing debate. At any rate, he launched directly into what was presumably the main point of contention: "First of all, a few words about the fact that I absolutely cannot accept the idea of national pride and in general the notion of a 'people'. .... The one thing that unites individuals is — language [...]." (*AVL,* 182). From here, he turned to concrete illustration. "I am proud of the fact that I am, through the blood of my ancestors, in every respect international, or better, bi-national, with completely equal parts of Germanic and Slavic blood, no less than that, by language, I am completely Great Russian [...]" (183).

However, at this point in the same sentence, the topic takes an interesting turn that at first might be construed as nostalgia:

> [N]o less do I grieve over the fact that, from childhood, I have no places that I can call "native," and that there was no city, no natural landscape, that might have reared me. Therefore, I must rely on those brief summer periods in early childhood when I was able to suck in the living juices from certain noble Baltic areas and in particular from the Vyborg region in the Finnish lands, all the more since the latter was long the native soil of some of my ancestors (*AVL,* 183).

Konevskoi's interest in ancestry and historical tradition, as well as in cultural and regional roots, had noticeably intensified during the last two or three years. While steadfastly rejecting the notion of a "people" *per se*, he nonetheless never doubted the importance of actual milieu — natural and social — in the formation of the individual. "[T]he exceptional, unique characteristics of nature" surrounding the formative years influenced that formation in ways that he did not yet fully understand, but of which he felt growing certainty. (183)

A few months earlier, at the beginning of January, Konevskoi paid a visit to Moscow, along with Ivan Bilibin, Aleksandr's artist brother. In his diary Briusov noted the time they spent in ancient churches, particularly those containing well-known icons.[13] Konevskoi's attraction to Moscow as true representative of pre-Petrine Russia began in September 1896 with the memorable visit that included his introduction to the Tretiakov Gallery and his first acquaintance with the full panoply of Russian painting (Chapter 1). Two years later, after his second trip abroad, he lamented Russia's pathetic lack of proper cities, able to preserve their traditions in their architecture. "Moscow is rich in church buildings, […] but of ancient Russian architecture it has none" (SP 1904, 194).

However, north and northeast of Moscow there were other places to investigate. In May 1900, just before his departure for Finland, Konevskoi planned an excursion for later in the summer with Ivan Bilibin, whose interest in the sites of Pre-Petrine Russia paralleled his own. It was a flexible plan that might take in remote spots in the upper Vol'ga region, churches and monasteries from the early history of the Suzdal' region, and still others dating from the Muscovite era. Much was left to impulse and inspiration. (*LN* 98:1:498)

That expedition did not take place, but another did, one that may have served Konevskoi's designs and needs even better. In September he visited the estate of relatives near Ostashkov on the shores of Lake Seliger. In fact a system of bodies of water and islands lying in the Valdai uplands, Seliger formed part of the famed trading route "from the Varangians to the Greeks," from Novgorod to Constantinople. Yet Konevskoi seemed less interested in that particular feature than in what he saw there and how he saw it: "On the shores of Lake Seliger and in its environs, in those places in which are hidden the sources of the Volga, I saw the original primitive wilds of great Rus'" (*LN* 98:1:508).[14]

For some two weeks he explored on foot, seeking out the more remote and deserted parts. Once, on a bank rising above the upper Volga, he found a structure that for him amounted to a treasure: "a strange wooden place of worship, the most complete image of the most ancient wooden churches and chapels." His detailed description of the exterior of the building was matched by that of the interior. There he found an iconostasis, floor-to-ceiling, where some of the icons, faded as they were, suggested to him the color harmonies of ancient icon-painting. (98:1:508)[15]

But it was most of all the terrain that spoke to him. Writing to Briusov, he observed that "the predominant feature that gives [Russia] the unchanging wide horizon characteristic of her alone — it seems to me — is the slow measure and spacing of the waves of soil. The barely perceptible gradual rise of the slopes minimizes both plateaus and cliffs. […] Even, smooth, open — a majestic pace and harmony, breathing deeply!" (1:508) It seems to be very much the same landscape that entranced the "Varangian from beyond the blue sea." ("From Konevets")

Lake Seliger and the sources of the Volga lie closer to Novgorod than to Moscow, but in Konevskoi's personal geography they were all part of a cultural continuum, from which St. Petersburg was excluded. In the same June 1900 letter to Aleksandr Bilibin (who apparently had spoken well of St. Petersburg), Konevskoi responded: "I find it painful to think about Petersburg." He then launched into a scathing description of Petersburg's architecture and city plan in verbal images that seem to prepare the way for Andrei Belyi's novel *Petersburg* (1916):

> What do you see, when you happen on the main thoroughfares of the capital on the Neva? Killingly straight and long, with right-angled intersections and wide-yawning pavements between buildings, the monstrous vulgarity the likes of which are not to be found in any Western European or Russian city. […] While Moscow and the germanic-romanesque medieval cities wind about like a nest, and inside them you feel a living center, charming with the hidden twistings and angles of their alleys, Peter is all drafty, with its straight streets running almost from one end of the city to the other; inside it you will hardly find a center, a heart in which gather the juices of life; instead, within is yawning emptiness, lifelessness. (*AVL*, 184).

In other letters, to Bilibin and to Briusov, Konevskoi's negative feelings toward Petersburg often were associated with a physical and/or spiritual malaise from he which was suffering at the time. Nonetheless, his antipathy to St. Petersburg had a genuine base. He was forced to conclude that the city of his birth had no spiritual capital to offer, and that it lacked authenticity as a Russian city.

4. Winter 1900-1901: "The Milieu"

When Konevskoi returned to St. Petersburg in September after his summer away, the city appeared to him in an even more distressing perspective. Before long he began to cast his thoughts and feelings in a *poèma* that was to remain unfinished. He called it "The Milieu (*Sreda*)." (*SP 2008* 162-163) "Before me — the crossroads of peoples./ Sea and land all mingle here, where the waters/ flow together, to the clanging of factories." The first twenty lines are devoted to this special place where land and water mingle almost indistinguishably, where the only sign of human encroachment comes from machines, the steam of which blends with mist rising from the bogs.[16] Otherwise, this emptiness wears an air of timelessness. Transient human incursions — of Finns, Swedes, Novgorodians — came and went over the centuries, leaving little trace.

Then *he* came, the "demon of old Moscow," he who dethroned the old order and its capital, Moscow, then ravaged the watery wilderness to create a new, spiritual emptiness. Konevskoi's "Peter" (unnamed in the poem) is the Antichrist of folk imagination. Destroyer of life and sanity, he is also the ruthless defacer of Russia's noble image in the name of crass enrichment. "The Milieu" voices the conservative, anti-Petrine, Russophile position. Nearly every word pulsates with wrath, as "foreigners" stream in, corrupting Russian values and behavior, causing true Russians to flee.[17]

To Konevskoi's mind, Peter's crimes against nature and tradition were equally heinous, all part of one disastrous strike against the best of Russia, past and present. The Russian word "*narod* (people)" in its only valid sense, as he explained earlier to Aleksandr Bilibin, was a synonym for "tongue, language" in the most creative meaning, i.e., culture. (*AVL*, 182-183). In "The Milieu" this was now being overwhelmed by a mass of those he dubs "self-born," sprung from nowhere. Such was Konevskoi's vision of Petersburg's ultimate degradation.

5. Building a Mythology

Konevskoi's construction of a personal mythology was already in progress two years before the summer of 1900. The lyric "From Konevets," written in spring 1898, provided an identity and a vantage point from which future options might be surveyed: "I am a Varangian from beyond the blue sea." (See Ch. 2) The route across Lake Ladoga, with a foothold on the island Konevets, could have been followed by some of his ancestors, along with the successive waves of Swedes, Finns, and Russians who at various times occupied that island. This lyric was the first of a brief series of Varangian-*bogatyr* poems that moved through history, geography, and folklore. These poems carried with them more than a hint of mysticism.

Written at about the same time as "From Konevets," was the lyric "From Generation to Generation."(Ch. 2) It describes a brilliant wave of Varangian-*bogatyrs* that, surging over steppes aflame in the noonday sun, moves inexorably toward its fated place in legend. During that night on the steppe these warriors and their campaign take on a heroic character. Henceforward they stand forth clearly as dreamers, idealists, committed to the road without end. With this, the spiritual nature of their quest becomes increasingly apparent. The final, resounding clash takes place at noon, by evening it is over. They have gone into legend.

One of the most enthusiastic admirers of Konevskoi's Varangians was Briusov's boyhood friend Aleksandr Aleksandrovich Lang, who wrote under the pseudonym A. L. Miropol'skii. Konevskoi and Lang became acquainted during Konevskoi's visit to Briusov in September 1899. Briusov noted in his diary that Konevskoi liked many of Lang's poems. (*Dn*. 76) The reverse was certainly true. In his first letter to Konevskoi, after reading "From Konevets" and "From Generation to Generation," Lang wrote:

> As I already said to you in our conversation, your creative work goes by a completely individual path; your Varangian, indomitable lord of the northern seas, comes alive, not in ancient physical, muscular strength, but spiritualized by future ages, standing on that step of our existence when man will cease to be man and will become "half-spirit."[18]

A devoted follower of spiritualism for several years, Lang clearly was captivated by the perceived mystical aspect of Konevskoi's heroes: lifted beyond their historical and geographical parameters, freed from time and space, they entered into another, mystical dimension. Whatever interest in spiritism Konevskoi had shown so far was confined chiefly to the writings of Baron Du Prel, particularly his book *Spiritizm*, where Du Prel wrote of that other consciousness that extends beyond our bodily selves. The possibility of expanding the "inner life of our *persona*," whether by mediumistic and occult powers or by yet other means, was part of Konevskoi's constant ambition. (*AVL*, 173) The correspondence between him and Lang flourished over the next months, fed by their devotion to poetry and their common sympathies, with spiritualism perhaps chief among them.

The next Varangian-*bogatyr* poems were written a year and a half later, in fall 1900, after Konevskoi's explorations in the heart of ancient Rus'. (This theme is also linked to Konevskoi's interest in the Abramtsevo painters, Viktor Vasnetsov and especially Mikhail Vrubel', whose work he first encountered at the Nizhnii-Novgorod exhibition in 1896.[19]) "The Elder *Bogatyrs*" is a rich repository of myth and folklore. The first of the two ancients presented in "The Elder *Bogatyrs*" is Sviatogor, gigantic figure of prehistoric lore. (*SP* 2008, 159-161)[20] Konevskoi weaves together episodes that emphasize Sviatogor's weight, his strength, and, above of all, his powerful link with the earth. This last feature appears most dramatically when he is challenged by the weight of a small bag that he finds on the earth, dropped there by another *bogatyr*, Mikula Selianinovich. When Sviatogor attempts to lift it, the effort causes him to sink into the earth to his knees and to remain there permanently. To Konevskoi this is not the defeat it has appeared to some interpreters.[21] For him Sviatogor's chief appeal lies in his profound relationship with the earth. Fixed deep in that earth, he draws on its endless power and shares fully in its secret inner being. Moreover, in this condition he, the powerful one, overcomes all limitations of time and space: "You are everywhere, forever, there is no other like you."

Sviatogor's transformation into a cliff jutting from the earth has many parallels in world myth. One surely known to Konevskoi from his recent reading of the *Kalevala* was the story of Antero Vipunen and his clash with Väinämöinen.[22] Vipunen knows thousands of charms that give him power over many things in and on the earth. But Väinämöinen, using his superior powers of self-transformation and wit, vanquishes Vipunen's efforts to guard his treasure. From the charms (or curses) Vipunen pours upon his unwanted guest, clever Väinämöinen learns all he needs to know. The tale of Vipunen's duel with Väinämöinen is comic and grotesque, like the plots of many *byliny*. However, the essential point remains: "Lying grown into the earth," Vipunen is privy to the earth's secrets — like Sviatogor.

The second heroic figure, Volkh, was known in *byliny* as Volkh (or Vol'ga) Vseslavich, and identified with the magical Vseslav, prince of Polotsk, in the "Song of Igor's Campaign."[23] Konevskoi deftly blends incidents from several of these plots, while keeping his focus on features that touch the center of his vision. The image of Konevskoi's ideal that Volkh presents is far more complete than is Sviatogor's. For Volkh, time, space, bodily and mental limitations present no hindrance. According to legend, Volkh was the offspring of a princess and a serpent. In Konevskoi's view Volkh's paternal inheritance was of far greater importance, for it allowed him intimacy with every part of the natural world. After sketching broadly Volkh's prowess as warrior and leader, Konevskoi comes to the heart of the matter, addressing him as "Wondrous werewolf, wily, wise serpent!" He marvels: "You saw, with your own eyes, prophetic Volkh, how the root grew./ Within you was the grey-winged eagle, the grizzled wolf." And most significant of all, "You penetrated to life's inner structure, in bodies, to its very center./ You knew the word...."

In the *byliny* both Volkh/Vol'ga and Sviatogor are overcome by the physical strength of the plowman, Mikula Selianinovich. But in Konevskoi's presentation, Mikula's victory is belittled. Mikula breaks the soil with a golden plough. Yet what is this, compared to Volkh's exploits?

What began as youthful pride in forebears of courage and daring became elements of a personal myth. He used these tales and characters — some more, some less effectively — to help him understand where he had to go to achieve his goals, and how. The lone Varangian on Konevets was the mythical forerunner of streams of adventurers who, following their star, ultimately were transformed into legend. "The Elder *Bogatyrs*" was legend in full flower, drawn chiefly from the *byliny*. However, in Volkh's inherited ability to penetrate every particle of nature and to transform himself into that particle if he chose, Konevskoi found and encoded the basic tenets of the pantheism he had embraced.

The fourth lyric, "The Varangians," takes a different turn. For the first time, the Varangian-*bogatyrs* are placed in direct relationship to the poet himself, but the distance between them is clearly marked. No more a living force, they at last are framed in history and legend, like saints in an icon, where their descendant can contemplate them at will. In so arranging matters, that descendant, the poet, reveals a newly forged understanding of his own independent identity and, perhaps, his destiny.

The final two stanzas begin with a "prayer" that is not one of supplication, is no plea to these ancestors for protection or courage. Rather, the poet comes before them as a worthy descendant, proud of his strength and prowess, in no way dependent on his lineage. Indeed, he is of a new generation. Like Briusov's Sven, or any of the northern sea-faring heroes down to Fritjof Nansen, he can boast: "For the spirit's honor I go into battle without purpose./ But death will likely be the path to my victories; /And I shall fall before the hand of the living."

Even if only a philosophical conclusion based on the fate of the Varangians in his poem, this is a strange finale, coming from Konevskoi. Has he abandoned the struggle against death? Or is death perhaps not the end, but the means? The means to what? Fall, winter, and spring of 1900-1901 found him mulling that central question and much more.

6. *Konevskoi and Aleksandr Blok*

In 1914, ten years after publication of *Poems and Prose* (1904), the futurist poet Sergei Bobrov wrote of Konevskoi, whom he considered to be unjustly neglected: "On our poetic horizon after Tiutchev there has not been such an immense figure. Has anyone so felt ancient dark Rus', about which unclean tongues chatter now on every crossroad!"[24] Nevertheless, some poets and readers in that first decade found particular resonance in Konevskoi's portrayal of figures and events of Old Rus'. Aleksandr Blok was one of the earliest of these.

Though Blok's enthusiasm for Konevskoi's poetry began before 1904, it was the posthumous *Poems and Prose* that drew him into what Blok scholar V. Ia. Morderer described as a "dialogue." (*LN* 92:4:159.) Blok's copy of that volume, kept in the Pushkin House, contains checks and marginal notes that indicate his attentive reading of Konevskoi's poetry and prose. Morderer regards these markings, along with the occurrence of Konevskoi's name and phrases from his poetry in Blok's letters, as evidence of this "dialogue." She points to the numerous instances where the "heroic, archaicizing stratum" in Konevskoi's poetry was "probably taken in and adapted to the lyric poetry of Blok" (169). Striking examples are found in the first poem of Blok's cycle "On Kulikovo Field." "The river spread..." is saturated with reminiscences of Konevskoi's "From Generation to Generation": "quotations, motives, images, poetic meters" (92:4:170). Other such links and parallels, in his prose as well as his poetry, impressively marshaled by V. Ia. Morderer, leave no doubt of Blok's considerable debt to Konevskoi.

Blok's admiration and sympathy for Konevskoi's poetry spurred him to express it in print. Shortly before *Poems and Prose* appeared, he wrote to P. P. Pertsov, editor of *New Path*, a Petersburg literary monthly, proposing reviews of several publications, including, in particular, *Poems and Prose*: "I will wait for Konevskoi, about whom it will be necessary to write at length, but of the other books I plan to write short reviews" (Blok, 5:75).[25]

The offer apparently was not accepted: Blok had to wait till his review of A. L. Miropol'skii-Lang's *The Witch. The Spiritual Ladder (Ved'ma. Lestvitsa)*, in *The Golden Fleece (Zolotoe runo)*, No.1, January 1906.²⁶ The review's first half was devoted to Konevskoi (to whom *Lestvitsa* was dedicated). After a few introductory lines, Blok turned to his actual topic:

> In the poetry of Konevskoi and Miropol'skii there is a common feature, interesting as the illumination of that phase of Russian poetry when it has begun its transformation from "genuine decadence" to symbolism. One of the signs of that transformation was a *completely original, profound and individual feeling of connection with one's country and one's nature.*

The theoretical and historical assumptions here concerning symbolism, decadence, and Konevskoi's position in one or both are provocative. However, the most interesting underlying assumption is Blok's apparent certainty that Konevskoi's feeling for and experience of Russia were identical with his own.²⁷

One of the striking indications Morderer finds of Konevskoi's role in Blok's self-definition comes in a letter to E. P. Ivanov of 25 June 1905, where Blok used pungent phrases from "The Milieu" in order to "express hatred for the beloved city."²⁸ The "peculiar dialogue" between Blok and Konevskoi, fascinating as it is, had serious limitations. For, despite a mere three years' difference in age and a common educational and social milieu, they belonged to different cultural moments within the history of modern Russian poetry. The symbolist movement in poetry, of which Blok was a leading figure, existed primarily in the efforts of a few like Briusov to give it viable form. Moreover, Konevskoi, often mentioned as a forerunner, had set his compass in a direction quite different from that of the symbolist poets of the early 1900s, as will soon be seen.

Notes

[1] "Vl. S. Solov'ev stayed in the hotel Raukha from the end of September 1894 till May 1895" (*AVL*, 181, n.1.).

[2] Valerii Briusov, "Poeziia Vladimira Solov'eva", *Russkii arkhiv*, 1900, 8: 546-554.

[3] The poems in question were "Zemlia-vladychitsa! K tebe chelo sklonil ia", "Na palube 'Torneo'". Vladimir Solov'ev, *Stikhotvoreniia i shutochnye p'esy*. Biblioteka Poeta. Intro. Z. G. Mintz. Sovetskii pisatel'. 1974. nos. 32, 70. The exceptions Konevskoi granted were: "Tri svidaniia" (excerpts), "Imatra", "Lish' tol'ko ten' zhivykh" (with large reservations). nos. 119, 90, 94. *LN* 98:1:512.

[4] Vladimir Solov'ev, *Stikhotvoreniia i shutochnye p'esy*. no. 62, p. 92.

[5] S. M. Solov'ev, *Zhizn' i tvorcheskaia evoliutsiia Vladimira Solov'eva*. Brussels, 1977. P.113.

[6] Kurt Rudolph, *Gnosis: The Nature and History of Gnosticism*. Translation edited by Robert McLachlan Wilson. San Francisco: Harper & Row, 1983 (p.247).

[7] Z. G. Mints's notes in the 1974 edition of Solov'ev's poems mention other sources: "The cult of the serpent is related to the cult of Dionysus. The *white lily* and the *rose*, *dove* and *serpent* are images linked to the notion of the synthesis of spiritual and material (sensual love) principles and are encountered in many mystical sources" (P. 294, no.10).

[8] Solov'ev's articles "Gnosticism" and "Ophites" appeared in Brokgauz-Efron, *Entsiklopedicheskii slovar'*, vol. 22, pp. 950-952, S-Peterburg, 1893; and vol. 44, pp. 485, S.-Peterburg, 1897.

[9] A scholar of modern spiritual movements in Russia, Maria Carlson, writes her assessment: "Being a profoundly creative man, Solov'ev was creative in his appreciation of gnostic concepts [...]. Solov'ev's work contains a certain base of assumptions and uses terminology so highly evocative of the Gnostic tradition that the latter's influence cannot be lightly dismissed." "Gnostic Elements in the Cosmogony of Vladimir Soloviev." *Russian Religious Thought*. Edited by Judith Deutsch Kornblatt and Richard Gustafson. Madison, Wis.: University of Wisconsin Press, 1996. P. 50.

[10] Vladimir Sergeevich Solov'ev, «Kritika otvlechennykh nachal». (*Sobranie sochinenii*, 10 vols. St. Petersburg: Prosviashchenie, 1911. 2:323). See discussion in Ch. 1.

[11] "Saima," "Na Saime zimoi." Solov'ev (1974), nos. 82, 87.

[12] Beginning from the lyric "From Konevets," if not before, Konevskoi made clear his belief that the "Varangians" included the ancestors of all the Scandinavian peoples *and* the Finns. The Vyborg region, occupying the southern part of Karelia, had changed hands many times over the centuries, most recently between Russia and Sweden. Its population was heavily Finnish, with small numbers of Swedes, Russians, and Germans. The Oreus (or Orreus) family was a presence in the Vyborg region, at least as far back as the early seventeenth century. Konevskoi's great-grandfather Magnus (1744-1819) was governor of Vyborg; records exist of others. The tombstone of an "Orraeus" [sic] can be seen in the Vanhakirkko Park in the center of Helsinki. Ben Hellman, "On Ivan Konevskoi's Finnish Roots," *Aspekteja. Slavica Tamperensia*. V. Tampere, 1996, pp. 95-100. Eds. N. Baschmakoff, A. Rosenholm, H. Tommola. I am most grateful to Dr. Hellman for sharing his information on Konevskoi's background and for showing me the "Orraeus" gravestone in Helsinki.

[13] Briusov, *Dnevniki*, 80.

[14] Lake Seliger's shores and surrounding region, continually populated for most of their history, remained the locus of considerable boat traffic, shipping and fishing and other activity on the waterways. Konevskoi obviously was not to be distracted when he searched for signs of an earlier natural state. (*Brokgauz-Efron*, vol. 57, pp. 354-355).

[15] In his letter to Briusov Konevskoi mentioned a similar structure not far distant that was known to date from the seventeenth century. ("Church of John the Precursor, Shirkovo, Tver' *guberniia*, [1697] preserved till present day [1991]." *LN* 98:1:509, n. 5.)

[16] The gigantic industrial machinery that so awed Konevskoi on his visit to the Nizhnii Novgorod exhibition in September 1896 inspired his sonnet "Machines (Snariady)". Even then, however, his admiration was not unqualified. In the four years since, he saw and read enough for disillusion to set in. In this unquestionably he was influenced by the poems of the Belgian poet Emile Verhaeren, notably *Les villes tentaculaires*. See: Joan Delaney Grossman, "Writing the Petersburg Text: Ivan Konevskoi's 'Sreda,'" in *Perevod i sravnitel'noe izuchenie literatur. K vos'midesiatiletiiu Iu. D. Levina*. St. Petersburg: "Nauka." 2000.

17 Numerous versions of the "St. Petersburg myth," which began to form as soon as the city's foundations were laid, came into full bloom in the mid-nineteenth century. Konevskoi borrowed freely from these and added elaborations of his own to make his point.

18 A. Miropol'skii. 12 October 1899. Ed. I. G. Iampol'skii. *Pamiatniki kul'tury. Novye otkrytiia.* 1988. P. 23.

19 *SP 2008*, 159-161. See also: Joan Delaney Grossman, "Ivan Konevskoi: *Bogatyr* of Russian Symbolism." *The Silver Age in Russian Literature*. Ed. John Elsworth. New York: St. Martin's Press, 1992. Pp. 1-10.

20 "Sviatogor", V. P. (V. N. Peretts), *Entsiklopedicheskii slovar'*. Vol. 57, p. 268.

21 D. S. Merezhkovskii, "O prichinakh upadka i o novykh techeniiakh sovremennoi russkoi literatury", *Polnoe sobranie sochinenii*. Vol. XVIII: (Moscow, 1914), pp. 186-187. See also: Grossman, "*Bogatyr*...", 3, 9, n.19.

22 *Kalevala*, tr. L. P. Bel'skii. Spb: "Azbuka-klassika", 2003. Pp. 198-199 (rune 17, ll. 57-66).

23 The chief Sviatogor and Volkh/Vol'ga *byliny* are found in V. Ia. Propp, V. N. Putilov (eds.) *Byliny v dvukh tomakh* (Moscow: GIKhL, 1958). Vol. 1, "Volkh Vseslavevich," pp. 6-19; "Sviatogor," pp. 20-33. Very helpful information on the figure of Volkh is available in: Roman Jakobson and Mark Szeftel, "The Vseslav Epos," in Roman Jakobson and Ernest J. Simmons, (eds.), *Russian Epic Studies* (Philadelphia: American Folklore Society, 1949).

24 Sergei Bobrov, *Liricheskaia tema* (Moscow: "Tsentrifuga," 1914), p. 27, n.1. The first lyric of his third poetry collection, *Lyre of lyres*, "Fulfillment (*Ispolnenie*)," begins: "The prayer of Konevskoi has been fulfilled (*Ispolnena molitva Konevskogo*". *Lira lir.* Moscow: "Tsentrifuga," 1917.

25 Blok, *Sobranie sochinenii*, 5:75.

26 Blok, 5: 598-600.

27 Just as Konevskoi freely adopted and adapted the ideas and (in the case of Kol'tsov) even texts of poets with whom he felt a special kinship, so also did Blok.

28 Blok, 8:130.

Chapter 9

Abolishing Death (2)

1. Survival of the "Persona"

The lyric "Starres ich," penultimate sonnet of the cycle "Son of the Sun," gave early expression to Konevskoi's tireless effort over the next few years to conquer any possible threat to the integrity of the *persona* — the "I." (See Ch. 1.)[1] The sonnet's octet voices the young poet's horror in the face of the darkness and chaos threatening to overwhelm his innermost *self*. But in the sextet, he gathers his forces to resist that fate. And the final lines assert the tenacity of the individual human's essence — *persona* — before the universal maelstrom. Physical death occurs in nature, but, even at this early date, it is not death, but total annihilation, that Konevskoi most dreads.

"Starres ich" was dedicated to Sergei Petrovich Semenov, Konevskoi's companion during the summer of 1896 at the estate of the philosopher Ippolit Panaev. The friendship that began there, based on common interests in philosophy, psychology, and esthetics, developed into a remarkable relationship that reached its final expression in Konevskoi's last letter, dated 21 June, but unsent. It will be discussed below.

Meanwhile, the 8 July 1897 letter, giving Semenov a detailed account of his mystical experience in the Thuringian woods, opens with an interesting statement: "Dear Sergei Petrovich! Finally, on the last stage of my journey, I am fulfilling my side of the pact between us" (*AVL*, 158). While this "pact" may have been a simple agreement to keep in touch over the holiday, it may also have signaled a commitment to keep the other informed of developments in their respective searches for a spiritually coherent worldview.² Three years later, in May 1900, just before leaving for Finland, Konevskoi wrote to Semenov of the "all-consuming work" in which Semenov was engaged: "I deeply regret that I have not yet been, and I don't know when I will be, able to acquaint myself with the systematic exposition of your worldview" (*AVL*, 180). Other communications referred to discussions ongoing on various topics. Finally came their last meeting at Pavlovsk in June 1901 and the letter that followed it.³

The central narrative of Konevskoi's life has traced his progress so far in resolving the two all-important problems: ongoing survival of the *persona*, and that *persona*'s penetration into the essential life of the universe. It is a narrative with interruptions, but some markers stand out along the way. Even before entering the university, Konevskoi was fascinated by questions about the nature and extent of consciousness and the possibility of its existence in other, perhaps multiple, forms. For him, basic questions like "What is the *persona*? Is it identical with consciousness?" called for exploration. Thinkers like Karl Du Prel, author of *Die Philosophie der Mystik* and *Der Spiritismus*, offered tentative answers. "[O]ur self-awareness does not embrace all of our being," Du Prel wrote. "There is hidden within us and eluding our earthly self-consciousness, the core of our being, manifesting a totally different adaptation to the external world than that of our earthly adaptation" (*Spiritizm* 13-14).⁴

During those summers of 1897 and 1898 when he traveled the waters and remote mountain paths of foreign lands, Konevskoi moved considerably further along his path of inquiry. In certain moments of intense communion with nature, another "self" made itself known within him. However, as he was careful to stress, at those times that inner presence did not overpower his essential "I". Those moments seemed, rather, like *interpenetration* of his *persona* and that larger, mysterious self that he continued to call "the unknown 'I'."⁵

Meanwhile, questions about the *persona*, its capacity and its limitations, continued to occupy him. Long ago he had concluded that the individual *persona* cannot, must not, dissolve into the life of nature, *either before or after death*; at all times it must remain an independent whole. But neither can it exist as an isolated, self-contained monad, floating endlessly in the universe. Writing to his friend Nikolai Mikhailovich Sokolov in December 1900, he tried to order his most recent thoughts:

> No matter what it does, the *persona* cannot go outside itself. But the more one takes into oneself from outside, the fuller and richer does one's own nature become. In the encounter with the world of elements, the world outside the human, there occurs a complete exchange and balance of forces. [...] If it were not for that influx of the new, unknown, "other," the "I" would not expand, grow, manifest, express its innermost elements [...] (*AVL*, 188).

In short, he was convinced that intimate interdependence of all things is a fundamental principle governing the life of the universe. In an effort to illustrate his point, he introduced a comparison, tantalizing for its brevity, among certain writers whom he admired:

> Here, it seems to me, lies the essential difference between the sense of the universe possessed by Shelley, Tiutchev, and Fet, and the feeling for organic life, for example, of Kipling or L. Tolstoi, who experience all the instincts of plants and animals, but as [as they experience] the instincts of separate human organisms; [...] in the souls of Shelley, Tiutchev, and Fet there spreads almost that same single spirit, that single stream, which is here, and there, and now, and then, and after in every matter (*AVL*, 189).

Lev Tolstoi, the author of "Kholstomer," was no pantheist. However, the visionaries Shelley, Tiutchev, and Fet, who knew firsthand the "sensation of the abyss existing in life," somehow arrived at that enviable state where they effortlessly partook of that "single stream" that flows endlessly throughout the universe. (*SP 1904*, 201) Yet, the question remained open: how was such a state to be achieved? His December letter to Nikolai Sokolov showed an energetic attempt to move closer to an answer.

2. "You knew the word"

Konevskoi's engagement with his Nordic-Russian heritage and its rich mythology, which began in the spring of 1898, took his efforts in still another direction. The Varangian, perched on the island of Konevets, reveled in the panorama of Rus' stretched before him. But the language he mastered had also mastered him: entranced by its splendid rhythms and soaring cadence, he found himself irresistibly under its sway.

The lyric "From Konevets" provides the first outright indication in verse of Konevskoi's belief in language's power. However, the magic of the word caught and held his full attention later, through his encounter with Finland and Finnish lore in May-June 1899. Yet well before this, as a student of the oral tradition in poetry, Konevskoi was aware of the role played by privileged language in the whole range of magic, mysticism, world religions, and world folklore. Usually linked to the deity, to nature, or to gods in nature, the "word" is often coveted by humans, most frequently as a means to secret knowledge. The nameless composers of the *Kalevala*'s runes embodying folk legends may have done so for long winter nights' diversion. But while those chants preserved the ancestors' magic tales, they also preserved the deep understanding of nature and its workings that governed the lives of the tribe. It was a worldview that held attractions for Konevskoi, who was by then deeply engrossed in the question of the poet and his relationship with the word.[6]

In his short essay "The Word," written sometime in 1900, Konevskoi summed up his current thinking about the subject: "[Words] are invented by prophets, seers, and magicians."[7] The magical value of the word, then, lay in its origins. From the beginning, the "prophets," the "seers," and the "magicians" saw language as their link to the deep nature of all things, and they used it respectfully.

3. "Science and Poetry"

Konevskoi's unsent letter of late June 1901 followed closely the composition of two essays, both dating from the first half of 1901.

All three seem to form part of the ongoing dialogue between him and Sergei Semenov. "About the Life of the Bees by Maeterlinck" and "Science and Poetry" appear in that order at the end of the 1904 edition of Konevskoi's writings, but they can probably be dated more precisely.[8] "About the Life of the Bees by Maeterlinck" is identified as written in Pavlovsk, a popular summer resort close to St. Petersburg, where Konevskoi visited Semenov on several occasions. Pavlovsk served him this summer, as it had done before, as first stop on a longer journey.[9] The piece written in Pavlovsk was likely the result of spontaneous discussion of a newly published book that came into their hands. "Science and Poetry," on the other hand, though apparently an early draft, is intensely serious. Despite Briusov's assigned order (in *Poems and Prose* that essay is dated merely "1901"), it is clear from Konevskoi's letter, dated 21 June and written from Finland, where he went after leaving Pavlovsk, that "Science and Poetry" was already the subject of spirited debate between him and Semenov.

Uneven in tone, that essay's three paragraphs struggle to make their arguments clear and coherent. The long initial paragraph begins on a Gogolian note, mockingly comparing the scientific researcher to a lowly member of the civil service. However, the second paragraph, differing sharply in substance as well as tone, resumes the topic of the power of language, specifically the poet's language:

> Who is the emperor, the ruler, the wielder of power over the dead matter of the external world, and not a record-keeper of its trash? Who says to the world "Let it exist," "Be it so," who breathes "a living soul" into balls of clay, molding and shaping them according to his image and likeness? Is it not the poet, who received his name from the act of creation, and not from the act of knowing? (*SP 1904*, 231).

Here is strong confirmation of the direction Konevskoi's thought has followed since that intoxicating moment of awakening, several years ago, to the world and to his own powers. Now he goes much further: not only is the poet richly equipped in his spiritual nature, "not a *tabula rasa*, but a rich ore of inclination, taste, passion, will — ." He is a creator of new forms who can radically change the world:

> [H]e transforms every order and dimension of external things according to his image and likeness, recreates them, gives them a new nature, and thus, in every sense, resembles the creator and magician-ruler, who, by his dream, his word, enthralls and casts a spell over all that exists (232).

The key word here is "resembles." The poet strongly resembles the creator, demiurge, magician, monarch of all, transforming all reality according to his own image and likeness. We must remind ourselves here that, in Konevskoi's mind, such assertions were no mere metaphors. The lexicon of his poetry is the lexicon of his thought and of his convictions.

In the third and final paragraph of "Science and Poetry," a new notion moves abruptly to the fore and begs for definition. Traditionally, a prophet, loosely so named, has appeared in various contexts, served several functions, and possessed different powers and degrees of influence. But the genuine *prophet*, as Konevskoi intends to make clear, is marked for loftier things. Then comes the crucial step in his scheme: the *prophet*, truly inspired though unassuming, is aligned with the true *poet* — he who, overwhelmed by his own inspiration, humbly exclaims: "Ah, but that is not I myself, but someone else, great and with authority, who speaks through me." Once so empowered, the *prophet* (or poet) can assume his role as creator and wonder-worker, who, "by his dream, his word, enthralls and casts a spell on all that exists."

4. "The Prophet"

Konevskoi's letter of 21 June was obviously the latest installment of a debate with Semenov that probably began long before "Science and Poetry."

Uncertain, as well he might have been, whether his points had been made convincingly, Konevskoi wrote back to Semenov from Finland, elaborating further his central ideas. He headed the letter with four lines from the romantic poet Friedrich Hebbel's poem "An die Jünglinge."[10] The theme was a familiar one, cherished by the German romantics: the hero's initiation, a ritual common in myth, folk tradition, and religious cult. The chosen individual is called to an awesome place — "einen schaur'gen Ort" — , where, filled with sacred terror, he or she receives a new identity and mission. Once crowned with the wreath of his high calling, the poet is exhorted to use his creative power to the fullest, to speak the Genesis-Word: "Let it exist!"

Hebbel's quatrain provided an easy introduction to the thoughts that Konevskoi now laid forth. In their most recent conversation, clearly he and Semenov had disagreed about the nature and powers of traditional wonderworkers and perhaps of the poet, as well. Konevskoi's overall goal was to distinguish the genuine *prophet*, whom he identified with the "magician," from all other, presumably inferior, categories. He hoped to formulate for his friend (and probably for himself also) a satisfying definition of the *prophet*, who had now become key to the full conception of the poet for which he had been striving.

At the same time, another question had arisen from Semenov's side: what of scientific researchers' ever more amazing discoveries about the world? Do these not in some cases duplicate or even replace the revelations of traditional wonderworkers? Konevskoi's reply left no doubt: at the end of their researches, these "learned men" find that they have moved not one step toward understanding the inner life of external phenomena, but are left merely with the dead letter. On the other hand,

> in every "revelation" by a prophet, there cannot help being penetration to the innermost core, to the very bowels of the external object; once he has achieved genuine essential and intimate communication with this object, he makes contact with it in certain sensitive strings, threads, points of concentration that they have in common. So, of course, knowledge of the future is attained through deeply non-apparent (not formal), but total (organic) research of the threads and

fibers connecting events with their consequences. With his whole being the prophet travels the path between present and far distant, expected days.

Nyslott [Savonlinna]. June 21, 1901.[11]

It is worth noting that the term *prophet* in the generic sense does not occur in Konevskoi's writing before "Science and Poetry." That fact and the terms in which he tries to define the true *prophet* in this letter strongly suggest a recent discovery of considerable significance to his effort to conjure up the true likeness of the poet-mystic. The term *prophet*, which evokes biblical figures and the prophet Mohammed, as well as more obscure figures, has an obvious literary source in Pushkin's "The Prophet." Most of these sources would be known to any educated Russian. However, the last is the one most significant here.

In Konevskoi's view, "The Prophet" stood out as Pushkin's closest approach to those "worlds of supernatural, visionary inspiration, that unite the son of man with the spirits of all beings of other species" (*SP 1904*, 206). In his 1899 article "The Meaning of Poetry in the Poems of Pushkin," Vladimir Solov'ev defended Pushkin against the numerous inept interpretations forced on him during the jubilee year of 1899.[12] In the central section of his essay, which was devoted entirely to "The Prophet," he dealt forcefully and at length with those critics who, incredibly, held that "in this poem there is not a word about poetry and the calling of poet" (675). Toward the end of that section, having disposed of these wrongheaded views, he confirmed the aesthetic interpretation with his own reading of "The Prophet":

> Not being any of the Biblical prophets or, even less so, Mohammed, neither is Pushkin's "Prophet" any one of the poets, or Pushkin himself, but rather he is the pure bearer of that unconditional ideal essence of poetry that has belonged to every true poet, and above all, to Pushkin himself in the mature period of his creative work and the best moments of his inspiration (694).

Konevskoi presumably approved of Solov'ev's implied identification of "poet-prophet," as far as it went. However, he felt it essential to focus specific attention on the fearsome moment when the angel "touched my ears/ And filled them with noise and ringing: / And I heard the sky tremble.../ And the sea monsters' underwater passing."[13] In effect, "in the most penetrating and free of human powers of perception, in his hearing, the poet recognized unity with all of nature" (*SP 1904*, 207).

Pushkin's "The Prophet" clearly served at that time as a seminal text for Konevskoi, just as others — some of Tiutchev's lyrics, *Thus Spoke Zarathustra* (in parts), the *Kalevala* — had done before. "The Prophet" provided him with a matrix for the conception rapidly taking shape in his own thinking. His *prophet* is no mere messenger of gods, but rather draws on his own powers, summoned from within. The *prophet* now emerging in Konevskoi's vision is gifted with amazing access to the inner life of the universe; he is already close to embodiment in the "magic Volkh," the elder *bogatyr*.

It was imperative, then, to solidify the link of identity between this *prophet* and the poet-mystic as Konevskoi had conceived him. Six months earlier, there appeared in Konevskoi's poetry the prince-magician Volkh Vseslav'ich. Like the *prophet*, he is anchored exactly at the line separating quasi-historical and mythical time. It is notable which aspects of the Volkh narrative Konevskoi chose to portray in his poem. For Volkh, the "magic werewolf," time and space are no barriers. But even more important is his deep intimacy with nature. "You saw with your own eyes, prophetic Volkh, how the root grew[....] You penetrated to life's inner structure, in bodies, to its very center." The prince-magician and the *prophet* share the power that underlies all others: the ability to communicate with the inner heart of all being: "You knew the word."

5. Poet-Mystic and Prophet

Ivan Konevskoi's history so far has consisted of one long striving to achieve the ultimate, unrestricted freedom that would allow penetration of the inner life of the universe. Such freedom, he truly believed, must in some way be achievable through the creative power of the poet-mystic, once his nature is fully realized. This notion led him very early, as we know, to explore the realm of mystical feeling to which Tiutchev's poetry, first and foremost, introduced him. The essay "Mystical Feeling in Russian Lyric Poetry" shows the length to which Konevskoi's meditation and experience had carried him by 1900. After the splendidly succinct definition of mystical feeling near that essay's opening, he went on to add: "It is the union of personal consciousness with the being of its objects, the enlargement of the sphere of its self-awareness" (*SP 1904*, 199).

Mysticism for Konevskoi opened a major way into the depths of being that he knew surrounds us in waves — Tiutchev's "life-creating ocean." The desire to explore that realm much further had led him to constant and intense thinking about the nature of the poet-mystic and his powers. Now, with the introduction of the *prophet* into his calculations, the troubling problem of limits imposed on human freedom by time and space seemed all but conquered. The *prophet's* vision extends in all directions. From this privileged position, he has ready access to both past and future: the difference between them is effectively annihilated. The same may logically apply to space. Most significant of all, the *prophet* sees into the very core of things; he possesses that faculty that Konevskoi desired above all things and which he now believed to be essential to the poet. Any notion of death here might seem irrelevant.

The obvious link between *prophet* and poet-mystic is their command of the "word." Elaborating, through various means and examples, the power of that "word," Konevskoi believed that he was close to cementing that link. It seems quite clear that, in all this careful yet bold reasoning, he was intent, however consciously, on tailoring the notion of *prophet* to match as closely as possible that of the poet-mystic as he conceived it. The two conceptions were like two halves of a bridge under construction, moving closer and closer together.

All of this apparently was fermenting in his brain when he wrote to Sergei Semenov from Finland on 21 June 1901. Seventeen days later, on 8 July, he drowned in the river Aa, near Riga.

6. "My Death!"

From the beginning of his life as poet, Konevskoi's passionate drive for life and its obverse, terror of death, powered virtually all of his spiritual and intellectual activity. To close his eyes on the beauty and richness of the universe without knowing and possessing it was an intolerable notion that had to be negated. However, to judge from some of his later poems, as well as some prose, physical death gradually became less meaningful in his scheme of things. Ongoing survival of the individual *persona* was conceivable, he surmised, once that interpenetration described in his 1900 letter to Nikolai Sokolov was actualized: "Objects are in harness with me, I with them — the coordinates defining the location of some united being" (*AVL*, 188).

The fact that his last letter to Semenov was written from Nyslott, the Finnish Savonlinna, is, at very least, arresting. Savonlinna, situated on a neck of land in the middle of Lake Saima, marked what may have been Konevskoi's deepest penetration into "the real Finland".[14] His itinerary that summer of 1901 was and is known only sketchily; his father apparently knew merely that he planned to roam "through the regions along the Baltic."[15] This he did. But why did he return to Finland, and why did he press on into the heart of Saima? In his mystical experiences during the summers of 1897 and 1898, water in various forms played an increasingly important role. That pattern continued in the next two summers, during his stays in Finland. The poems written there in 1900 — most of all "Murmurings" — brought this role to a climax. (See Ch. 8.)

Where water is, there life is to be found — in nature. The image of water linked to life is an ancient symbol, found in nearly all religions and every culture. For Konevskoi personally that image presented itself vividly, beginning from the sonnet sequence "Son of the Sun." Thereafter it gathered meaning until, in his first long sea voyage, swept up by this totally new reality, he exclaimed: "My life is water./ All wind and water" ("At Sea," *SP 2008*, 97).

A great deal has been said throughout this account about Konevskoi's strenuous efforts to form and deepen his worldview. By now it must be

CHAPTER 9

clear also that it is, after all, his poetry and the passionate spirit that informs it that makes Ivan Konevskoi the challenging and engaging figure he is. His poetry, splendid though it be, was a means, not an end, as it was with some of the symbolists. Yet this in no way diminished in his eyes the importance of the poetic word: it must be as perfect as it can be, if it is to be an efficacious means to penetrate the secret life of all being. Konevskoi's love affair with the universe, life in nature writ large, was what drove his creative imagination.

Notes

1. "Starres ich" (*SP 2008*, 87-88). The same nighttime terror rendered here is recounted in "Lyric Poetry in Contemporary Russia," written a few months later. (*AVL*, 132-133).

2. This notion of their relationship is supported by Konevskoi's gift inscription, presumably in a copy of *Thoughts and Meditations*: "To Sergei Petrovich Semenov, my very great companion on the roads of thinking about the foundation of things[…]. I. Oreus." (*LN* 92:4:200-201, n. 11.) In the archive containing the letter (see n.3) and preceding it is a list of "correspondances" of letters and colors, and another, headed "NRAVSTVENNYE KACHESTVA I BUKVY (MORAL QUALITIES AND LETTERS)," dedicated to Semenov (l.22). Following this is a brief note by Semenov characterizing Konevskoi as he knew him. (*AVL* 84-86).

3. RGALI 259.3.21.23-24. (Copy by an unknown hand.) This letter, dated 21 June 1901, addressed to S. P. Semenov, has not been published previously. (Its full text appears in the Appendix to this book.) However, soon after Konevskoi's death it apparently reached Semenov, then circulated among close friends. Nikolai Mikhailovich Sokolov wrote to Briusov: "…from conversations with all Oreus's friends I concluded that the center of our late friend's interests was poetic creation in the widest sense of the word; this was expressed especially acutely in his letter to Semenov, written just before his death […]" (*LN* 98:1:520, n.4).

4. Writing to Aleksei Veselov in October 1898, Konevskoi invoked "that other consciousness, that with special fullness appears in the sleep of a somnambulist, and, during our time awake, independently of our will, conveys thoughts and sensations to other souls at great distances[…]. This is the inner life of our *persona* about which Du Prel speaks" (*AVL*, 173).

5. Letter to A. M. Veselov, 9 October 1898 (*AVL*, 174).

6. In his essay "Ivan Konevskoi. Poet of Thought," N. L. Stepanov claimed: "In his theoretical pronouncements, Konevskoi was perhaps the first of the Russian symbolists to formulate new principles of relationship to the poetic word" (*LN* 92:4:190). To support his assertion Stepanov quoted Konevskoi's brief essay

"The Word" in full, highlighting its complexity: "In this formulation Konevskoi, negatively regarding the 'musicality' of the word, underlined its semantic role, at the same time counting the word as 'symbol,' 'idol [image]' of 'spirit and god,' that is, assigning it 'magic' significance" (*LN* 92:4:190). Konevskoi voiced his negative view of Konstantin Bal'mont's "musical" poetry a number of times as when, in a letter to Briusov (3 May 1900), he referred to him as a "shallow and flamboyant charlatan" (*LN* 98:1:491).

7   *SP 1904*, p. 226. (See Ch. 6 for further discussion.)

8   *SP 1904*, pp. 228-230, 231-232. Maeterlinck's *La Vie des abeilles* was published in 1901 and was translated into Russian by N. M. Minskii in 1915.

9   Probably the first of these stops was in August 1896, enroute to Nizhnii Novgorod's great fair. (*RGALI* 259.1.16.25-26ob).

10 Friedrich Hebbel, "An die Jünglinge," Sämtliche Werke. 1.Abteilung: Werke, Berlin [1911 ff], S. 236-238. The lines quoted were: "Geht an einen schaur'gen Ort,/Denkt an aller Ehren Strauss,/ Sprecht dann laut das Schöpfungswort,/ Sprecht das Wort: es werde! aus."

11 *RGALI* 259.3.21.23-24.

12 *Vestnik Evropy*, Dec. 1899, pp. 660-711.

13 A. S. Pushkin, "Prorok," *Polnoe sobranie sochinenii v 10-x tomakh*. Moscow 1956-1958. Vol. 2, pp. 338-339.

14 *AVL*, 176.

15 His father, General I. I. Oreus, offered this information, along with the fact that his son sent a letter from Riga on 8 July 1901, in his unsigned biographical foreword in *Poems and Prose*, (*SP 1904*, x).

Afterword

Some fifty years after Konevskoi's death, university friend and fellow poet, and later editor of the journal *Apollon*, Sergei Makovskii, published recollections of his contemporaries that included a poetic remembrance of Ivan Konevskoi.[1] Their relationship seems to have been cordial but not intimate, though Makovskii warmly recalled student conversations about poetry during walks across the Neva. However, most vivid was his memory of encountering Konevskoi on shipboard, sailing from St. Petersburg to Helsinki in 1901, at the time of the white nights. In those magical hours they paced the deck together, while Konevskoi, trancelike, recited poems, his own and others', throughout the night.[2]

Makovskii's account of Konevskoi's death and burial follows closely the unsigned biographical foreword authored by Konevskoi's father, which appeared in the 1904 volume. However, beyond that, without further documentary sources, he turned again to memory — or was it fantasy? In his penultimate paragraph, speaking of the impact of the sad news when it reached St. Petersburg, Makovskii wrote:

> Then the rumor circulated in literary circles: Konevskoi did not drown accidentally (though the river Aa was well known for its dangerous whirlpools). No, he perished voluntarily, went from the world of the flesh (like a true romantic), swimming till he lost consciousness, to a blessed oblivion, yielding himself, beneath a dawn sky, to his beloved element.

But he added ironically: "This, of course, is a myth" (193-194).

No mention of such a rumor — or of a suicidal state of mind — appears in any of the letters or documents left by his closest friends. Nonetheless, among those who knew him less well, or not at all, Konevskoi fitted easily into the image of sacrificial victims, "those born too soon." Or as Konevskoi himself put it earlier when writing about the tragic early deaths of Nadson and Garshin: "Both were destined to fall among those counted as sacrificial victims, forever demanded by history in the fatal moments of the renewal of life" ("At Dawn," *SP 1904*, 136). Though by no means original, the sentiment lay ready to hand at the turn of the twentieth century. It was almost inevitable that it would be applied to Konevskoi.[3]

While Makovskii largely resisted this temptation, he treasured his own nostalgic image, bolstered by sympathetic and attentive reading, of the unworldly, otherworldly young poet, whose eyes seemed set always just beyond the horizon. Removed by decades from his last meeting with Konevskoi, he concluded his essay (as memoirists often do) by imagining "what might have been": "Do poets of such spiritual calibre and such religious illumination commit suicide? All the same, there is something painfully mysterious in that death by water — " (194).

Makovskii's memoir, however distant in time and space from its subject, had the advantage of poetic sensibility enriched by experience and cultural perspective. By contrast, the letters of General Oreus to Valerii Briusov after his son's death, which bore immediate testimony to the events surrounding Konevskoi's drowning, are remarkable for their simplicity and tenderness. He responded willingly and gratefully to Briusov and others who worked to gather materials for publication.

Yet, when Briusov's article "Wise Child" appeared in *World of Art* (1901, No. 8-9), the general readily admitted his incomprehension of his son's work of recent years: "You were among those few who understood and valued his work; the majority did not understand it. In that majority — I am sorry to say — was I" (*LN* 98:1:536). Presumably out of gratitude to Briusov for his determined effort to see Konevskoi's work published, General Oreus withheld any outright expression of distaste for the decadent association this implied. Nonetheless, he made one stipulation: "On one thing only I firmly insist: that you not print Vanya's real surname, but limit yourself to his pseudonym" (98:1:546-547).[4] Yet General Oreus made his own poetic contribution to the volume of his son's poetry. In the biographical introduction, which he tried to keep scrupulously "objective," he carefully enunciated the details, as far as he knew them, of his son's death and his burial near the small Livonian (now Latvian) town of Zegewol'd (now Sigulda): "The Germanic precision of the local authorities carefully gathered everything left behind by the unknown victim: clothes, belongings, papers. By these signs they discovered the identity of the anonymous corpse and reconstructed the events of that last day." Of the burial he wrote: "Konevskoi loved the forest, loved the wind: many of his inspired poems were dedicated to the forest and the wind. And they buried him in the forest and, in splendid, clear weather, a strong wind billowed. The modest grave is shaded by maple, elm, and birch" (*SP 1904*, xi).

Notes

[1] "Ivan Konevskoi (Oreus) (1877-1901)," *Na Parnase "Serebrianogo veka,"* 177-194 (Munich, 1962).

[2] The details of time and place reconstructed by Makovskii coincide with what can be conjectured of Konevskoi's movements, given his 21 June letter to Semenov. His itinerary now seems clear: St. Petersburg to Helsinki by boat, from there to Saima, and after that, presumably, to the Baltic coast and Riga.

[3] On the other hand, Makovskii could easily have heard of Dmitrii Merezhkovskii's bailful remarks about the "plague" that had come upon the decadents — Dobroliubov, Konevskoi, Erlikh! (*Dn.* 110) Dobroliubov's abandonment of his previous life as a Petersburg decadent, his wanderings in the north woods, time passed in the Solovetsky monastery, and his mysterious appearances and disappearances in Petersburg and Moscow, had made him by that time the subject of rumor and disbelief. Yakov Erlich, earlier the center of a philosophical circle frequented by Konevskoi, had since then been confined to an insane asylum.

[4] In fact, General Oreus made another request, which Briusov, fortunately for all interested parties, did not honor: after publication, "all manuscripts remaining with you I ask you to *burn.*" (*LN* 98:1:549-550, n.1).

Index

Aa (Latvian river Gauja)   117, 220, 225
Aksenov, M.S.   35
Anichkova, Elizaveta Ivanova   23
Astaf'ev, P.E.
    "The Genesis of the Moral Ideal of the Decadent"   171
Azhbè, Anton   95

Bachmann, Georg   112, 126
Bakst, Lev   157
Bal'mont, Konstantin   34, 51, 109, 111-112, 117, 124, 224
    Book of Reflections   68, 78
    "The Dead Ships"   100
    Quiet   100
Basel   82, 98, 157
Bayreuth   57, 63
Belyi, Andrei   125
    Petersburg   200
Benois, Aleksandr   83, 157, 166
Bilibin, Aleksandr   29, 68-69, 92-93, 106, 108, 123, 127-128, 133, 136, 138, 145, 149-150, 152, 158-159, 173, 198, 200-201

Bilibin, Ivan	54-55, 57-58, 70, 93, 95, 199
Blok, Aleksandr	9, 25, 207, 210
"On Kulikovo Field"	206
Bobrov, Sergei	206, 210
Böcklin, Arnold	57, 70, 82-89, 91, 95, 98-99
"The Field of Bliss"	96
"Island of the Dead"	96
"Play of the Waves"	84
'Triton und Nereide"	88
Bogomolov, N.A.	8
Russian Literature at the Beginning of the XX c...	16
Briusov, Valerii	11, 13-14, 17-20, 23, 39, 49, 68, 78, 93, 101, 108-114, 119-130, 132, 135-136, 142-151, 163, 165, 167, 174, 177-179, 182, 189-190, 193-194, 196, 199-202, 205, 207, 209, 215, 223-224, 228
"On Russian Versification"	115, 124, 139, 141
Tertia Vigilia	116-117, 126
"To the Tsar' of the North Pole"	118-119, 126, 145
"Wise Child"	9-10, 12, 16, 226
Browning, Robert	32, 77, 100
Burne-Jones, Edward	32, 55
Buslaev, F.I.	165
"Epic Poetry"	152
Chebotarevskaia, Aleksandra	84, 88
Cologne	89
Cosmopolis	172, 188

Darwin, Charles	34, 62
Descartes, René	
Discours de la Method	37
Diakonov, Nikolai Grigorievich	150
Dobroliubov, Aleksandr	40-41, 50, 109, 113-117, 119, 124-125, 141-143, 228
Collected Poetry	114, 139
Dostoevskii, Fedor	25, 35, 39, 65, 122, 187
Du Prel, Baron Karl	43, 50, 76, 91, 122, 190, 223
Die Philosophie der Mystik	33, 35, 73, 212
"Dream as Physician"	73
Der Spiritismus	35-36, 46, 90, 203, 212
Erlikh, Iakov	70-71, 86, 114, 116, 124, 143, 187, 228
Evers, Franz	110
Fechner, Gustav	73, 85
Fet, Afanasy	26, 30, 45, 49, 58-59, 159, 178, 180, 190, 213
Fofanov, Konstantin	40-44, 113
Gallén-Kallela, Akseli	157
"Lemminkainen's Mother"	156, 158, 166
Garshin, Vsevolod	39, 70, 226
Gippius, Anna Nikolaevna	11, 77, 101-103, 105-107, 121-122, 127, 149-150, 164
Gippius, Vladimir	50, 99, 116, 124, 142, 144, 187

Gippius, Zinaida	101
"Criticism of Love: Decadent Poets"	115
Grot, Nikolai	170, 187
"The Journal's Tasks"	171
"The Moral Ideals of Our Time"	171
Gudzii, N.K.	48
Hamsun, Knut	50
Hebbel, Friedrich	
"An die Jünglinge"	217, 224
Hegel, Georg	71, 86
Helmholtz, H.L.F	50, 73
Hugo, Victor	110
Ibsen, Henrik	32, 136
Imatra (Finnish waterfall)	196
Ivanov, Viacheslav	9-10, 18, 84
James, William	50-51, 98
Principles of Psychology	72, 79
Psychology	43, 73
Jules-Bois, Henri Antoine	55
Kant, Immanuel	27, 37, 50, 70, 72, 79, 86-87
Critique of Pure Reason	71
Keats, John	22
Kierkegard, Soren	22
Kiev	64, 77, 89, 92

INDEX

Kol'tsov, Aleksei	77, 178-180, 182, 186, 190, 210
"God's World"	184
"The Poet"	185
"The Question"	183, 185, 191
Konevskoi, Ivan. Works	
"About the *Life of the Bees* by Maeterlinck"	215
"Agreement"	106
"All Clear"	164, 167
"Amid the Waves"	29
"Autumn Voices"	163
"Beauty in Motion" ("Beauty in Action")	37
"Böcklin's Paintings (A Lyrical Characterization)"	70, 83
"Contemporary French Lyric Poetry"	70
"Contempt"	133
"The Cornerstones of My Worldview"	71, 81, 162
"At Daybreak"	39
"Declaration to Truth"	110, 135
"Dedication to Da Vinci's 'Gioconda'"	129
Dreams and Meditations	11-14, 23, 26, 68, 76-77, 83, 103, 116-117, 120, 124-125, 128-129, 131, 135, 139, 143-145, 149-150, 161, 193
"A Dream of Battle"	132
"Drought"	92
"Echoes"	132
"The Elder Bogatyrs"	160, 203, 205
"Elements of Two Peoples"	64, 67
"The Exile's Song"	151, 154-156, 158, 165, 167
"In Flight"	28
"Fragment"	21-23, 26, 45, 71
"From Afar"	93-95, 133
"From 'Eternal Vaults'"	129, 144

INDEX

"From Generation to Generation"	69, 94, 119, 131, 202, 206
"From Konevets"	67-68, 92, 119, 128, 131, 200, 202, 209, 214
"From Sun to Sun"	29, 45
"Genius"	76, 134
"Gratitude"	164, 167
"Growth and Delight"	28-29
"Holiday Cantata"	102
"Infinity"	74
"On a Lightsome Night"	151
"Long Ago and Now"	103-105
"Lyric Poetry in Contemporary Russia"	24, 30, 38, 41, 65, 126, 160, 194, 196, 223
"Machines"	29, 209
"The Magic Word"	151, 153, 159-160
"On the Matter of the Poet and the People"	198
"Memories of a Meeting"	102-103, 105
"The Milieu"	78, 128, 201-202, 207
"Murmurings"	196-197, 221
"Nature"	26, 45, 48
"A New Spiritual Frontier"	60
"A Page from Summer Impressions"	70
"Pale Spring"	105-106
"In Passing"	128, 130-131
"Personifications of Forces"	86-87
Poems and Prose	9-11, 13, 17-18, 23, 76, 78, 206, 215, 224
"The Quarrel"	134
"Renunciation"	108, 164
"Resurrection"	23, 26, 45, 82, 130, 178
"Rushing Waters"	196
"Science and Poetry"	215-216, 218
"At Sea"	81-82, 90, 96, 221
"The Sea of Life"	95, 131

"Shame Before Earth's Mother"	60, 63, 76
"Signs"	103, 105
"A Solemn Vow"	131
"Son of the Sun"	28-30, 44, 109, 130, 145, 211, 221
"Stanzas on the *Persona*"	162, 167
"Starres Ich"	28-30, 44, 211, 223
"Stirrings"	103, 105
"The Sultry Hour"	63
"A Summons"	130
"Surges"	161-162, 167
"Toward the Study of the *Persona* of Aleksandr Droboliubov"	115, 124, 139
"Visions of Travels"	130
"A Wild Place"	65-66, 77, 131-132
"Winter Night"	133
"With Cold Freedom"	133

Krylov, I.A.
    "The Grasshopper and the Ant"   29, 48

Krymski, S.   17-18

Kuusi, Matti   155

Laforgue, Jules   78
    Poésies complètes   70

Lago Maggiore   82

Lang, A.A.   112, 145, 202-203

Lavrov, A.V.   8, 10, 14, 18-19, 27, 47-48, 116, 120, 123, 125

Leibniz, Gottfried   71, 85-86

"Literary-Intellectual Circle"   35, 50, 70

Lönnrot, Elias
    Kalevala   119, 151-156, 158, 160, 165-166, 204, 214, 219

Lopatin, L.M.
   "'Morbid Sincerity': Notes on V. P.
      Preobrazhenskii's Article 'FN'"   171
Luter, Fedor Aleksandrovich   39, 50-51, 144

Maeterlinck, Maurice   15, 34, 56, 136, 159, 224
   Serres Chaudes   32
   Le Trésor des Humbles   33
Makovskii, Sergei   225-226, 228
Mallarmé, Stephane   110, 123
Mandel'stam, Osip   10
Maupassant, Guy   22
Mediumism (See also Spiritualism)   16, 34, 49, 76, 122
Mendel, Gregor   86
Mendeleev, Dmitrii   34, 49
Menzhinskii, V.R.   187
   "About Nietzsche"   172
Merezhkovskii, Dmitri   43, 45, 51, 117, 228
   "Leda"   44
   "On the Causes of Decline
      and New, etc."   40
Michelangelo
   Pieta   157
Mikhailovskii, Nikolai   22
Mikhailovskoe   27-28, 31-32, 59
Millet, Jean-Francois   32
Minskii, Nikolai   40-42, 117, 224
Mirsky, D.S.   11
   "The Symbolists"   10
Morderer, V.Ia.   19, 78, 206-207
Morris, William   32

Müller, Max	152, 165
Munich	18, 54-55, 57, 70, 82-83, 86, 88-89, 95, 99, 157
Mystic	15, 17, 31-33, 41, 43, 45-46, 50, 56, 58-59, 84, 91, 115, 159-160, 164, 169, 177-178, 186, 193, 218-220
Mysticism	15, 19, 32-35, 56, 64, 73, 77, 84, 115, 119, 131, 159, 178, 180-181, 202, 214, 220
Nadson, Semen	39, 70, 226
Necheporuk, E.I.	13
Nietzsche, Friedrich	102, 135-137, 146, 162, 167, 169-178, 186-190
Beyond Good and Evil	176-177, 189
"The Drunken Song"	138, 146, 174-175
Die Geburt der Tragödie	138, 173
"Noon"	138, 146, 174-175
"Our Virtues"	176
Also Sprach Zarathustra	102, 122, 137-139, 146, 173-176, 187-189, 219
"We Scholars"	176
"What is Noble"	176-177
Nizhnii Novgorod	29, 92-93, 158, 203, 209, 224
Nol'de, Boris	92
Nuremberg	58
Occultism	16-17, 32, 35-36, 203
Oreus Sr., Ivan Ivanovich	12, 21, 23, 25-26, 93, 99, 123, 128, 136, 150-152, 165, 176, 189, 198, 209, 224, 226, 228

Panaev, Ippolit Aleksandrovich	27, 28, 48, 211
The Light of Life	27
Seekers of Truth	27
Panaev, I.I.	27
Pantheism	30, 45-46, 48, 56, 71, 85-86, 91, 136, 160, 181, 205
Panpsychism	85-86, 89
Paulsen, Friedrich	71, 98
Einleitung in die Philosophie	79, 86
Pension Lang	127, 149
Pension Rauha	193, 198
Pertsov, P.P.	206
Philosophical Currents in Russian Poetry	30-31, 49
Poe, Edgar Allen	
"Ulalume"	104-105
Preobrazhenskii, V.P.	187
"Criticism of the Morality of Altruism"	169
Problems of Philosophy and Psychology	34, 102, 169, 171
Psychic Phenomena	32, 35, 73
Psychic Research	15, 33, 190
Pushkin, Aleksandr	78, 128, 144, 178, 180-181, 190, 206
"The Prophet"	218-219
Rebus	34-36, 49
Régnier, Henri de	20, 70, 123, 129, 135
Repin, Ilya	95
Rhine	82

Robertson, John G.	173
"The Literary Movement in Germany. Friedrich Nietzsche and His Influence"	172, 188
Rossetti, Dante Gabriel	32, 42, 135, 143, 159
"Memorial Thresholds"	54
Russian Thought	84
Rzewuski, Stanislas	188
"La Philosophie de Nietzsche"	172-173
Saima	149, 193, 196, 221, 228
Salzburg	53-54, 57, 89
Schacht, Richard	175, 188
Schelling, Friedrich	71, 86, 185
Schopenhauer, Arthur	37, 77, 188
Schwind, Moritz von	55-56
Scorpio	9-10, 13, 19, 114, 124, 139, 142-143, 145, 147, 167, 180, 189
Segevold	11
Semenov, Sergei Petrovich	27, 30, 35, 50, 55, 57-59, 70, 90, 93, 99, 158, 179, 193, 211-212, 215-217, 220-221, 223, 228
Shakespeare, William	34
Shelley, Percy Bysshe	15, 48, 56, 213
Shesterkina, Anna Aleksandrovna	117, 120, 125
Siikala, Anna-Leena	155, 166
Sokolov, Nikolai Mikhailovich	12, 19, 176, 179, 189-190, 213, 221, 223
Sologub, Fedor	40-41, 84, 108, 113, 124

Solov'ev, Vladimir	15, 19, 31, 38, 40, 45, 50, 71, 76, 86, 134, 193-197, 208, 219
"The Meaning of Poetry in the Poems of Pushkin"	218
"Mysticism"	33
"The Poetry of F.I. Tiutchev"	30
"Song of the Ophites"	195
"We came together not by chance"	194
Spinoza, Baruch	37, 71, 85-86, 98
Spiritualism (*see also* Mediumism)	34-35, 49, 160
St. Petersburg	11, 43, 53-54, 64, 68, 77, 95, 101, 109, 113, 125, 127, 144, 150, 157-158, 165, 172, 200-201, 210, 215, 225, 228
St. Petersburg University	11, 37, 79, 95, 116
Stepanov, N.L.	19, 22, 71, 107, 116, 140-141, 171, 223
Swinburne, Algernon Charles	32, 135-136, 143, 167, 173
"Anactoria"	138
"Genesis"	138, 162
"Hertha"	137, 146, 162
Thuringia	57-58, 60, 62-63, 65-66, 74, 85, 90, 103, 131, 211
Tiutchev, F.I.	15, 26, 30-31, 45, 48-49, 58-59, 103, 130, 159, 178, 180-182, 190-191, 206, 213, 219-220
Tolstoi, Aleksei	32, 39, 178-180, 190
Toorop, Jan	55

INDEX

Vasnetsov, Victor — 94, 203
   "After Igor' Sviatoslavich's Battle with the Polovetskians" — 93
Vengerova, Zinaida — 84-85
Verhaeren, Emile — 20, 78, 120, 123, 135, 142, 167, 209
   "Mon coeur, où le héros?" — 69
   Poèmes — 70
Veselov, Aleksei — 22, 28, 36-38, 77, 82, 89, 91-92, 98, 103, 223
Viélé-Griffin, Francis — 20, 70, 123, 135, 143, 167
Vienna — 53, 172
Volynskii, A.L.
   "Literary Comments about *Philosophical Currents in Russian Poetry* and about Tiutchev" — 31
Vvedenskii, Aleksandr — 37, 71

Wagner, Richard — 63
   Parsifal — 57
Warsaw — 53
Wordsworth, William
   "For the power of the hills is on thee…" — 130-131
Wundt, Wilhelm — 49, 73

Zhdanov, I.N. — 165, 179

APPENDIX

Selected Poems in Russian
(page references are to *SP 2008*)

Illustrations

1.

Воскресение

Небо, земля... что за чудные звуки!
Пестрая ткань этой жизни людской!
Радостно к вам простираю я руки:
Я пробужден от спячки глухой.

Чувства свежи, обаятельны снова,
Крепок и стоек мой ум.
Властно замкну я в жемчужины слова
Смутные шорохи дум.

Сон летаргический, душный и мрачный,
О, неужель тебя я стряхнул?
Глаз мой прозревший, глаз мой прозрачный,
Ясно на Божий мир ты взглянул!

Раньше смотрел он сквозь дымку тумана —
Нынче он празднует свет.
Ах, только б не было в этом обмана,
Бледного отблеска солнечных лет...

В сторону — чахлые мысли такие!
Страстно я в новую жизнь окунусь.
Хлещут кругом меня волны мирские
И увлекают в просторы морские:
В пристань век не вернусь!..

(19 февраля, 1895 г., 75)

2.

Рост и отрада

В полуязыческой он рос семье
И с детства свято чтил устав природы.
Не принял веры в ранние он годы:
К нам выплыл он пытателем в ладье.
И вот однажды, лежа в забытье
Под деревом, в беспечный миг свободы,
Постиг он жизни детской хороводы
И стрекозы благое бытие.

«Ты, стрекоза, — гласил он, — век свой пела.
Смеяться, петь всю жизнь — да, это — дело
И подвиг даже... после ж — вечный сон».
А солнце между тем ему палило
Венец кудрей, суровый свет свой лило
В отважный ум — и наслаждался он.

(20 августа [1896 г]. Михайловское. 86.)

3.

Средь волн

И плавал он в сверкающих волнах,
И говорил: вода — моя стихия!
Ныряя в зыби, в хляби те глухие,
Как тешился он в мутных глубинах!
Там он в неистовых терялся снах.
Потом, стряхнув их волшебства лихие,
Опять всплывал, как божества морские,
В сознаньи ясном, в солнечных странах.

С собой он брызги вынес из пучины.
Мы брызгаться пустились, как дельфины,
И ослепительный поднялся плеск.
Я ослеплен и одурен метался.
Его же прояснял тот водный блеск:
Дух в лучезарных взрывах разрастался.
(87.)

4.

Starres Ich

С. П. Семенову

Проснулся я средь ночи. Что за мрак!
Со всех сторон гнетущая та цельность,
В которой тонет образов раздельность:
Всё — хаоса единовластный зрак.
Пошел бродить по горницам я: так...
В себе чтоб чуять воли нераздельность,
Чтоб не влекла потемок беспредельность,
Смешаться с нею в беспросветный брак.

Нет, не ликуй, коварная пучина!
Я — человек, ты — бытия причина,
Но мне святыня — цельный мой состав.
Пусть мир сулит безличия пустыня —
Стоит и в смерти стойкая твердыня,
Мой лик, стихии той себя не сдав.

(87-88)

5.

В море

посв. П. П. Конради

С душой, насыщенной веками размышлений,
С чужими образами, красками в уме,
Которыми я жил в стенах в домашнем плене,
И брезжил бледный свет в привычной полутьме;

Тебя почуял я и обнял взором, море!
Ты обдало меня, взяло и унесло.
И легок я, как луч, как искра в метеоре.
И жизнь моя — вода; в ней сумрачно светло.

Все ветер да вода... И ясно все, и сумно.
Где умозрений ткань? Молчит, но явен мир.
И вьются помыслы, так резво и безумно,
Туда, за даль, где мысли — вечный мир.

Май. (Балтика)

(97)

6.

С Коневца

Я — варяг из-за синего моря,
Но усвоил протяжный язык,
Что, степному раздолию вторя,
Разметавшейся негой велик.

И велик тот язык, и обилен:
Что ни слово — увалов размах,
А за слогом, что в слове усилен,
Вьются всплески и в смежных слогах.

Легкокрыло той речи паренье,
И ясна ее смелая ширь,
А беспутное с Богом боренье
В ней смиряет простой монастырь.

Но над этою ширию ровной
Примощусь на уступе скалы,
Уцепившися с яростью кровной
За корявые сосен стволы.

Чудо-озеро, хмуро-седое,
Пусть у ног ее бьется, шумит,
А за ним бытие молодое
Русь в беспечные дали стремит.

И не дамся я тихой истоме,
Только очи вперю я в простор.
Все, что есть в необъятном объеме, —
Все впитает мой впившийся взор.

И в луче я все солнце постигну,
А в просветах берез — неба зрак.
На уступе устой свой воздвигну,
Я, из-за моря хмурый варяг.

(Весна 1898 г.)

(94-95)

7.

В роды и роды: 1

Где вы, колена с соколиным оком,
Которым проницалась даль небес, —
Те, что носились в пламени глубоком
    Степей, как бес?

Махал над ними смуглыми крылами
Он, бес лихой полуденной поры.
Раскидывал над тягостными днями
    Их он шатры.

И ночь сходила, лунная, нагая.
А всё кругом — куда ни взглянешь — даль.
И свалятся в пески, изнемогая…
    Луна — как сталь!

Хоть не было конца пути степному.
Порой им зрелась в воздухе мета.
И стлалась ширь, и к мареву цветному
    Влеклась мечта.

С коней срываясь, приникали ухом
Они к земле, дрожавшей под конем.
И внятен был им, как подземным духам,
    Рок день за днем.

Им слышалось нашествие незримых
Дружин за гранью глади голубой.
Так снова в стремена! Необоримых
  Зовем на бой!

Сходились в полдень призрачные рати.
Далече разносился бранный гром.
А к вечеру уж нет безумных братий:
  Уж — за бугром!

Яснее дня был взор их соколиный,
И не напрасно воля их звала.
Примчалися ли буйною былиной
  Во град из злата и стекла?

April 1898 г. Spb. (96-97)

8.

Призыв

Валерию Я. Брюсову

Давно ли в пущах безответных,
И в недрах гор, и в лоне рек
Витал народ существ заветных.
Кому смешон был человек!

Сей человек, столь закоснелый
В своей коре, в своих корнях —
Он чужд и мертв природе целой,
Вращаясь в безысходных днях.

О племя оборотней чудных,
Всему чужих, всему родных,
Как часто, средь мгновений скудных,
Я бредил о житьях иных —

О днях таинственной свободы
И в горних, там, и под землей,
И к вам, прельстители природы,
Стремился дух ничтожный мой.

(3 мая 1899 г. 74)

9.

Издалека

Ивану Билибину

Были великие, славные брани...
Брошен я в диких полях,
Здесь, под кустарником... рана на ране.
Ветер шуршит в ковылях.
За мной дымятся дальние Карпаты,
И корни дубов въелись в грудь земли.
Где вы, друзья? беритесь за лопаты,
Курган насыпьте, кости чтоб легли.
В дали степей еще сеча гуляет.
Люди иль пыль — не видать.
В небе уж ястребы вольно ширяют:
С ними ли вам совладать?
Забылся я под тению ракиты...
И всё мне снились темные глаза,
Что́ в плоть мою вклевались, ядовиты —
И смолкла вдруг побоища гроза.
Снова и день... и ногой мне не двинуть,
Ну же, взметайте курган!
Братцы, о дайте под землю мне сгинуть:
Пусть веселится каган.
Здравствуй, ночь слепая и глухая!
Рыхло, сыро сыпется песок...
Любо жить под ним мне, издыхая.
О курган мой, гордо ты высок!

(114-115)

10.

Море житейское

Откуда, откуда — из темной пучины
И смутных, и светлых годов
Мелькнули подводного мира картины
С забытых и детских листов?

Всё — синие хляби, открыты, пустынны...
Строй раковин, строго-немой.
Кораллы плетутся семьею старинной
Полипов, семьей вековой.

И звезды морские, и звезды морские...
Зеркально и влажно вокруг.
И снятся чертоги, чертоги такие,
Что весь занимается дух.

Читал одинокую мудрость я в книге,
Где ум по пределам плывет —
И вот мне припомнились мертвые бриги
Глубоко, под пологом вод.

Я ваш, океаны земных полушарий!
Ах, снова я отрок в пути.
Я — в плаваньи дальнем в страну араукарий,
Я полюс мечтаю найти.

И смотрят киты из волнистого лона
Тем взором немым на меня,
С которым встречался преступный Иона,
Что в чреве томился три дня.

Я ваш, я ваш родич, священные гады!
Влеком на неведомый юг,
Вперяю я взор в водяные громады
И вижу морской полукруг.

О, правьте же путь в земли гипербореев,
В мир смерти блаженной, морской...
За мною, о томные чада Нереев —
Вкушать вожделенный покой!..

(111-112)

11.

Зимняя ночь

Александру Билибину

Я слышу — на осях бегут шары,
Светящиеся точки небосвода.
И вот уж член я мерной той игры,
И снова мне дарована свобода.

Над теменем вращаются миры,
Звездятся с легким шипом год от года.
Встают снегов печальные пары...
Я — член живой ночного хоровода.

Всё — шум колес, всё — твердый бег игры,
А где же грань победного похода?
Неизъясним размер ночной поры.
Я сам кружусь по воле кислорода.

(117)

12.

Памяти встречи

Она стояла прямо, ясно,
Она была из юных стран,
И жизнью светлой, жизнью страстной
Жил так же лик ее, как стан.

Улыбка зыбилась немая
На бледных и густых устах,
Простую доброту скрывая
За горечью, внушавшей страх.

Пред этой бледной, свежей силой
Зеленых, как вода, очей
Я трепетал, как пред могилой
Моих решений и речей.

Но вскоре я собрался с духом,
Собрал весь пыл безумных дум
И знал, что овладею слухом
Той, чей приветный взор угрюм;

Что сфинкс откликнется на пенье
И странный бред мечты моей,
Почуяв в нем и те виденья,
Что над реками льнули к ней.

Я не любил, но как стремился
Любить: мой дух кипел, творя,
И ждал, чтоб деве он явился,
Как налетевшая заря.

Но снова носится бесцельно
Она по пустошам земли,
Не вняв тому, что так смертельно
К ней мчится из моей дали.
   (20 September [1898.] 120-121)

13.

К ней

Когда-нибудь,
В иные дни
Мы встретимся опять.
Дни — всё вперед,
И не кляни,
Что не уйти им вспять.

Их песнь гласит,
Вещает нам
Про изобилье сил.
Нам час грозит
И даст нам сам
Чего вовек не приносил.

(128)

14.

Отречение

Посвящено А. Н. Г.

Да, всё бегут часы, но уж не так, как прежде.
И светы радуют, и волны дум растут;
Но места нет в душе единственной надежде:
    Восторги первой страсти не взойдут.

Ты там же всё вдали, о легкая, как пламя,
И мощная, как плоть густых, сырых дубрав.
С тобой расстались мы широкими словами,
    И мысли зов и воли суд мой прав.

Я не создатель, нет — я только страстный голос.
Могу я жаром обаятельным дохнуть.
Но жизнь моя, увы! на части раскололась,
    И иногда не дышит грудь ничуть.

5 ноябрь 1899 г. (150)

15.

Слово заклятия

Кругом стеснились камней громады.
Под нами мутный проток урчит.
Сырые своды, в дворах — засады,
Но дух — властитель мой — не молчит.
    И против злого
    Я знаю слово.

Куда ни взглянешь — нагие степи
И стаи хищные карих птиц.
От наших сил лишь клочки отрепий,
И перед небом мы пали ниц.
Что делать, девушка, чтоб не сгинуть
Иль смолкнуть пред ведьмой, злой судьбой?
Нет, погоди! вот я наземь кинусь.
Шепну ей слово, мой зов на бой:
    Твой род я знаю
    И проклинаю!

В глуши лесов, по тропе безвестной
С тобой идем мы, и сумрак нем.
Но всюду души в тайге окрестной —
Ужель безответны и чужды всем?
    Дохни лишь слово:
    Им нет покрова.

О слово вещее, слово — сила,
О мысли членораздельный звук!
Ты всю вселенную допросило.
Познанье — мощь наших слабых рук.
  Из тьмы былого
  Спасло нас слово.

(124-125)

16.

Взрывы вод

Ликующие волны-звери,
Белоголовые зубры,
Хвала стремящей вашей вере,
Надежде дерзостной игры!

В пустынях гама несвободных,
Где с пыли высохла гортань,
Толпе скитальцев сумасбродных,
Тоске, унынью нес я дань.

И в бор пушистый, в бор корнистый
Меня привел младенец-бог.
И там распелся голосистый
Широкопенистый порог.

Я был спокойный и согбенный,
И обуял меня испуг.
Я окроплен святою пеной,
И гулом захлебнулся дух.
(30 May [1900 г.] Imatra. 156-157)

17.

Всхлипывания

Из финских голосов

По тропам и по омутам,
По лядинам я брел.
Пробирался я к дрому там —
Ничего не обрел.
Ничего... ни дыхания,
Ни струи не плеснет.
Лишь ольхи издыхание
К тихой тине все льнет.
Смерть мне! — сердце подумало, —
Здесь, где камни и хлябь...
Смилосердился Юмала:
Где-то тронулась рябь...

8 June 1900 г. Pellisenranta (157).

18.

Песнь изгнанника

на мотив из Калевалы

Из той унылой Сариолы,
Земли изгнания больной,
Я вновь пришел в крутые долы,
Перевалив за кряж лесной.

Преданья предков вспоминая,
Вхожу под сумрачный намет.
Так — мать на мо́лодца родная
Пролила неба вечный мед.

Давно спустил я сети, шалый,
На дно чернеющей реки,
За мрачной щукою Маналы,
В пучины те земной тоски.

Все — похвальба была пустая:
Не удалец я, не герой,
И самого река густая
Сманила в топь глуби сырой.

Нечистые впилися силы
И в грудь, и в плечи мне, и в лик
И истерзали жизни жилы,
И вещий окоснел язык.

Но плоти мерзостную груду
На дне трясины роковой
Открыла мать. Сбылося чудо.
Бессмертен дар пчелы живой.

Обретен мед благоуханный,
Что ломти трупа вновь целит.
А мать снесла на брег желанный,
Который сердце веселит.

И жилы ветхие стянулись
От влаги сладостной небес.
И мысли мертвые очнулись,
Когда узнал я отчий лес.

(18 июля 1899 г. 144)

19.

Text of Konevskoi's last letter to Sergei Semenov.
See Ch. 9.

В тех же стихах перед тем встречаются и другие еще слова, так же близко прикасающиеся к моему ходу мыслей:
> Geht an einen schaur'gen Ort,
> Denkt an aller Ehren Strauß,
> Sprecht dann laut das Schöpfungswort,
> Sprecht das Wort: es werde! aus.[1]

В последней беседе с вами я поэтому, конечно, и сделал к концу указание на тип заклинателей — врачебных ли, ремесленных ли, ратных, или мечтательных, все это древле действовало в великих людях воедино, — чтобы особенно явственно и ярко оттенить против вашего примера тайновидцев, объявляющихся носителями и посланниками чужой воли, чужого духа, таких лиц, которые с особенной сознательностью выступали в качестве борцов со всякими чужими судьбами и влияниями, во всеоружии своего воображения и замысла этих предметов. Но, повторяю, и большую часть пророков считаю, конечно, такими же творцами, которые только вследствие особенного побуждения вынесли из себя вон центр тяжести своего действия.

Наконец мне остается прибавить, что в силу этого же внутреннего недоразумения пророков и действительной тождественности их с волхвами, самые результаты их видений, восприятий или мечт [sic! — JG], творческих образов, все равно — бывают существенно иного свойства, нежели выводы научного восприятия (на что я в тот же раз точно так же вам указывал).

«Открытия» пытателей и наблюдателей не дают ничего кроме, в лучшем случае, голого остова разных процессов математического счета, неизбежных для мыслительного аппарата (математика, физика, отчасти — химия), в худшем случае — аналогии самого плоского и скудного такого воображения, которое заимствуется все же из сферы человеческих влечений (биологические науки) и тем самым, у конца этих исследований человек сознает, что он не подвинулся ни на шаг в самую внутреннюю жизнь внешних явлений. Иначе и не может быть, раз «ученый» воспринимает внешние вещи в пустые клетки своего познания, и так они и остаются для него мертвой буквой. — Напротив того, во всяком «откровении» пророка не может не быть проникновения в самую внутреннюю сердцевину, в самые недра внешнего предмета, раз у него идет истинное кровное и задушевное сообщение с этим предметом, он соприкасается с ним в некоторых общих чутких струнах, нитях, средоточиях. Так, познание грядущего совершается, конечно, через глубоко не кажущееся (не формальное), а всецелое (органическое) исследование нитей и волокон, связующих дела с их последствиями. Всем существом своим пророк проходит путь между нынешними и далекими, ожидающими днями.

Nyslott [Savonlinna]. 21 Юн. 1901 г.[1]

---

[1] From "An die Jünglinge." Friedrich Hebbel, *Sämtliche Werke*. Hamburg; 1865-1867.

[2] *RGALI* 259.3.21.23-24.

Leut.-General Ivan Ivanovich Oreus,
father of Ivan Konevskoi

Ivan Konevskoi
mid-1890s. St. Petersburg
St. Pbg Historical Archive

Ivan (Oreus) Konevskoi (l.r.),
Aleksandr Bilibin, A. F. Kal', Ivan Bilibin,
students of St. Petersburg University. Dec. 1899

ILLUSTRATIONS

**Valerii Briusov,
symbolist poet. 1873-1924**
Source: Institute of World Literature,
Russian Academy of Sciences archive

Arnold Böcklin. Im Spiel der Wellen. 1883
Neue Pinokothek, Munich

ILLUSTRATIONS

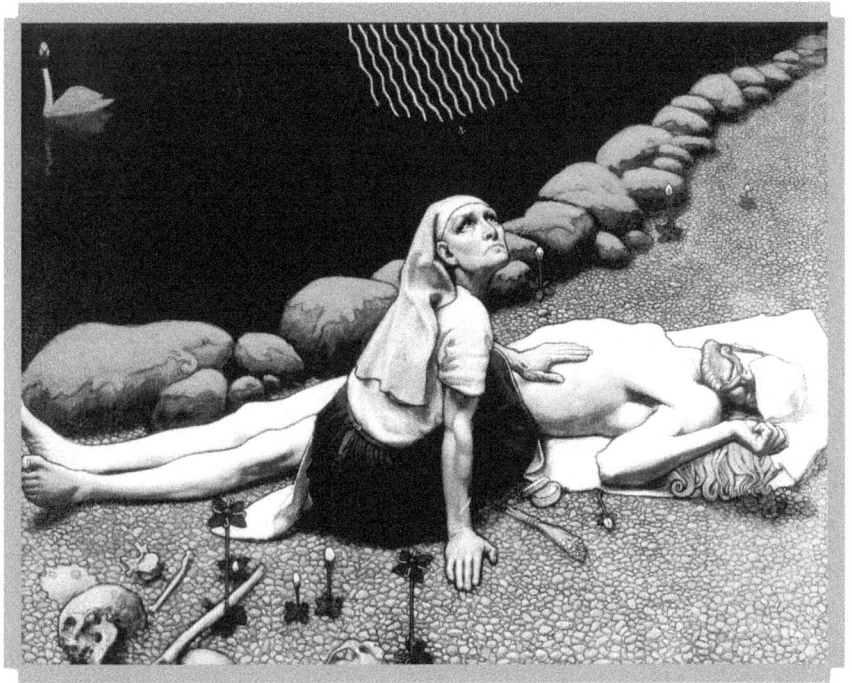

Akseli Gallen-Kallela. Lemminkäinen's Mother. 1897
Helsinki, Ateneum

www.ingramcontent.com/pod-product-compliance
Ingram Content Group UK Ltd.
Pitfield, Milton Keynes, MK11 3LW, UK
UKHW021847140426
5217IPUK00022B/1646